Strobel & Miller, Women's Hist.-Vol. II

Selected Reading Lists and Course
Outlines from American Colleges
and Universities

Women's History

Second updated and enlarged edition, 1988

edited by Peg Strobel and Marion Miller
University of Illinois, Chicago

 Markus Wiener Publishing, Inc.

Library of Congress Cataloging-in-Publication Data
(Revised for vol. 2)

Women's history.

    (Selected reading lists and course outlines from
American colleges and universities)
    Vol. 2 edited by Margaret Strobel and Marion Miller.
    Includes bibliographies.
    Contents: [v. 1. Without special title] -- v. 2
European and Third World history.
    1. Women--United States--History--Outlines, syllabi,
etc. 2. Women--Europe--History--Outlines, syllabi, etc.
3. Women--Developing countries--History--Outlines,
syllabi, etc. I. Baxter, Annette Kar. II. Stevenson,
Louise L. III. Series.
HQ1410.W683 1987   305.4'07'1173   87-8286

ISBN 0-910129-78-9 (pbk. : v. 1)
ISBN 1-55876-000-8 (pbk. : v. 2)

Printed in America

PREFACE

This volume is the second edition of a project begun by the late Professor Annette K. Baxter and has been expanded beyond the original plan of course materials on the history of European women to include those from the developing historical field of women in Africa, Asia, Latin America, and the Middle East.

In the solicitation of course outlines for the first edition, we discovered that most scholars in women's history were not offering specialized courses in their specific research fields but rather were engaged in teaching general European or Third World surveys of varying periodical, topical, or methodological approaches. Perhaps this new edition illustrates some modifications of this approach. Again, we have tried to present as broad a representation as possible by way of surveys as well as topical and interdisciplinary conceptualizations of the field. The reader will see that we include syllabi at various undergraduate or graduate levels taught in diverse forums from the lecture to the seminar format. Our inclusion of an enlarged Third World section juxtaposed to the European, it is hoped, will not only stimulate a wider definition of the field of women's history but also provide a larger basis for comparative approaches. We trust that the selections in this volume will again do more than whet the reader's curiosity about how others approach the teaching of women's history and will encourage further innovation in the field. May these course outlines also continue to illustrate ways in which certain topics relating to the role of women may be integrated into courses not specifically on the history of women.

This new edition is again a cooperative effort generated by the contributors. Their prompt responses to our requests for new and up-dated course outlines we most gratefully acknowledge.

Marion Miller
Margaret Strobel
April 1988

Table of Contents

Preface.. i

I. EUROPEAN WOMEN'S HISTORY

A. Surveys

1. WILLIAM E. MONTER, Northwestern University
   Women in European Civilization.. 1

2. JUDITH WALKOWITZ, Rutgers University
   Roles of Women in History.. 3

3. DEBORAH HERTZ, State University of New York, Binghamton
   The Rise of Public Women... 8

4. ROBERT MOELLER, Columbia University
   Women in Industrial Europe, 1750-Present.. 12

5. ROBERT MOELLER, Columbia University
   Women in Industrial Societies: Comparative Perspectives on England and Germany,
   1870-1945.. 17

6. MERRY WIESNER, University of Wisconsin-Madison
   Women in the Modern World: The European Experience.................................. 24

7. JANE SLAUGHTER, University of New Mexico
   History of Women... 20

B. Periods

8. SUSAN COLE, University of Illinois at Chicago
   Women in Antiquity... 30

9. PENELOPE D. JOHNSON, New York University
   Colloquium on Women in the Middle Ages... 36

10. NATALIE ZEMON DAVIS, Princeton University
    Society and the Sexes in Early Modern Europe.. 43

11. MIRIAM SLATER, Hampshire College, and
    HAROLD GARRETT-GOODYEAR, Mount Holyoke College
    Women and the Shaping of Early Modern Europe... 47

12. SUSAN M. STUARD, Haverford College
    Women in Pre-Industrial Europe.. 53

13. MARY NOLAN, New York University
    Women in Modern European Society and Politics.. 55

14. THERESA M. MCBRIDE, College of the Holy Cross
    Women's History Seminar.. 59

15. ATINA GROSSMAN, Columbia University
    Women in Modern Europe, 1750-1950.. 61

16. JANE SLAUGHTER, University of New Mexico
    Seminar in Women's History... 66

C. Topics

17. DEBORAH HERTZ, State University of New York, Binghamton
    Women's History Colloquium... 72

18. DOROTHY HELLY, Hunter College, CUNY
    Women and Society in Victorian England... 76

19. MARTHA VICINUS, University of Michigan
    Victorian Women... 81

20. SUSAN GROAG BELL and KAREN OFFEN, Stanford University
    The Woman Question in Western Thought in Europe and America, 1750-1950............... 86

21. KAREN OFFEN, Stanford University
    The Woman Question in Western Thought, 1750-1950.................................... 88

22. ZIVA GALILI Y GARCIA, Rutgers University
    Women, Family, and Education in the Soviet Union.. 93

23. PENNY GOLD, Knox College, and WARREN ROSENBERG, Wabash College
    Love, Marriage, and the Family.. 98

24. ATINA GROSSMAN, Columbia University
    The New Woman in Interwar Years... 101

25. JUDITH WALKOWITZ, Rutgers University
    History of Sexuality.. 107

26. JANE SLAUGHTER, University of New Mexico
    History of Sexuality.. 109

27. PENELOPE D. JOHNSON, New York University
    Seminar on Witchcraft in Pre-Modern Europe... 111

28. HELEN LEMAY, State University of New York, Stony Brook
    The Healer and the Witch in History... 113

29. ROBERT MOELLER, Columbia University
    Case Studies in Women's Collective Action in Modern Europe, 1750-1945............... 124

30. PENNY GOLD, Knox College
    History of Feminism.. 130

31. MARION S. MILLER, University of Illinois at Chicago
    Mediterranean Women.. 133

32. MARY GIBSON, John Jay College of Criminal Justice, CUNY
    The Female Offender in Western Society... 135

II. WOMEN IN AFRICA, ASIA, LATIN AMERICA, AND THE MIDDLE EAST

A. General Courses

33. SUSAN GEIGER, University of California
    Women and World Culture... 141

34. SONDRA HALE, California State College, Long Beach
    Women in Cross-Cultural Perspective.. 145

35. NORMA CHINCILLA, California State College, Long Beach
    Women in Cross-Cultural Perspective.. 149

36. MARYSA NAVARRO and LEO SPITZER, Dartmouth College
    Women and Social Change in the Third World.. 153

37. ELIZABETH SCHMIDT, Macalester College
    Women and Social Change in the Third World.. 157

38. IRIS BERGER, State University of New York, Albany
    Women in the Modern Economy.. 165

39. CLAIRE C. ROBERTSON, Ohio State University
    Women, Class, and Colonialism.. 167

40. JEANNE PENVENNE, Tufts University
    Women, Patriarchy, and Capitalism... 172

41. SUSAN GEIGER, University of Minnesota
    Women, Colonialism and Problems of Underdevelopment................................ 178

42. SUSAN GEIGER, University of Minnesota
    Women in Liberation Struggle: China, Cuba, Mozambique and Guinea Bissau.................. 182

43. SONDRA HALE, University of California, Los Angeles
    Women and Social Movements.. 188

44. KATHY STAUDT, Scripps College
    Women in International Development.. 195

45. CHERYL JOHNSON-ODIM, Loyola University of Chicago
    Third World Women in Development: Africa and the Caribbean......................... 202

B. Women's History by World Regions

46. EDWARD A. ALPERS, University of California, Los Angeles
    African Women's History.. 209

47. IRIS BERGER, State University of New York, Albany
    Women in African History... 211

48. SUSAN GEIGER, University of Minnesota
    Social History of African Women, 1850 to the Present....................................... 214

49. DAVID NEWBURY, University of North Carolina, Chapel Hill
    Women in African History... 218

50. KATHLEEN O'MARA, State University of New York, Oneonta
    Women in Africa and the Middle East.. 223

51. CLAIRE C. ROBERTSON, Ohio State University
    African Women... 227

52. MARGARET STROBEL, University of Illinois at Chicago
    South African Women.. 233

53. GUITY NASHAT, University of Illinois at Chicago
    Women in the Middle East: Past and Present.. 236

54. JUDITH TUCKER, Georgetown University
    Women in Europe and the Middle East.. 238

55. JUDITH TUCKER, Georgetown University
    Women in the Middle East.. 242

56. BARBARA N. RAMUSACK, University of Cincinnati
    Women in Asia: India, China, Japan.. 247

57. SHARON SIEVERS, California State University, Long Beach
    Asian Women.. 257

58. SILVIA M. ARROM, Indiana University
    Latin American Women: Historical Perspectives.. 260

The universities and colleges listed are those at which the courses were taught.
The documents were reproduced from the originals as submitted.

History B-40-1   E. W. Monter
Women in European Civilization   Fall 1986

SYLLABUS

You will be expected to purchase the following paperbacks:

Keenz and Bridenthal, eds., Becoming Visible (Houghton, Mifflin)
Emily Putnam, The Lady (Phoenix)
Sarah Pomeroy, Godesses, Whores, Wives, Slaves (Shocken)
M. Barnard, tr., Sappho: A New Translation (California)
Eileen Power, Medieval Women (Cambridge)
Meg Begin, The Women Troubadors (Norton)
Mary Wollstonecraft, A Vindication of the Rights of Women (Norton)

Two anthologies, recommended but not required, are available at
Great Expectations: Berenice Carroll, ed., Liberating Women's
History (Illinois), is a collection of scholarly articles, while
O'Faeolian and Martines, eds., Not in God's Image (Harper) is a
collection of primary sources in translation. Each is the best
of its kind; both are frequently techinical and sometimes difficult
reading for students without a good background in history.

****

TOPICS AND ASSIGNMENTS:

I. (Sept. 23-25) INTRODUCTORY.
     Read Becoming Visible, pp. 1-59.

II. (Sept. 30-Oct. 2 GREEK WOMEN.
      Read Pomeroy, pp. 1-119; Sappho (entire).

III. (Oct. 7-9) ROMAN WOMEN.

        Read Pomeroy, pp. 120-230; Putnam, Lady, pp. 39-68; Becoming
        Visible, pp. 60-89; and Juvenal, Satires, 6th Satire (in Core:
        871/J77/ 1F40).

 IV. (Oct. 14-16) IMPACT of CHRISTIANITY.
        Read Putnam, pp. 69-105; Becoming Visible, pp. 90-109; and
        St. Paul's obiter dicta in I Corinthians 7 (any Bible you
        prefer).

  V. (Oct. 21-23) MEDIEVAL WOMEN.
        Read Power (entire).

 VI. (Oct. 28-30) INVENTION of CHIVALRY
        Read Putnam, pp. 106-157; Becoming Visible, pp. 119-128; and
        Begin, The Women Troubadors (entire).

VII. (Nov. 4-6) WOMEN in RENAISSANCE and REFORMATION.

        Read Putnam, pp. 158-210; Becoming Visible, pp. 128-191.

1

VIII.   (Nov. 11-13) AGE of the SALON.
         Read Putnam, pp. 211-246; Becoming Visible, pp. 217-235.

  IX.   (Nov. 18-20) WOMEN and REVOLUTION.
         Read Becoming Visible, pp. 236-254; Wollstonecraft, Vindi-
         cation, pp. 5-36, chaps. 2-6, 9, 12.

   X.   (Nov. 25) EUROPEAN MARRIAGE PATTERN.
         Read Becoming Visible, pp. 192-216.

  XI.   (Dec. 12) READING PERIOD.
         No assignment, but an optional review session is planned
         for the usual class hour on Tuesday.

                            ****

     There will be a mid-term examination on Tuesday, Oct. 28; students
who would prefer to do an 8-10 page term paper instead (or who do not
want their exam grade to count towards their final grade) should have
their topics approved by the instructor by Friday, November 9.

ROLES OF WOMEN IN HISTORY   J. Walkowitz
210:250   Spring 1985
                                             Tues(Hickman 205)-
                                             Th.(Hick 210) 3rd period
                                             Office Hours:
                                                 Weds. Van Dyck 219B
                                                        2-3 P.M.
                                                 Thursday Hickman
                                                 409/410

Requirements:
     There will be one hourly exam (Feb 21) , one essay
assignment based on the readings (due April 4, assignment sheet
to follow), and a final exam. Students are required to attend
lectures and discussions and to have read the assigned readings
by class meetings. Attendance will be taken, and only three
unexcused absences are permitted.

Readings (available at Douglass Bookstore):
          Mary Kinnear, Daughters of Time
          S.G. Bell, Women from the Greeks to the French
Revolution
          E.Gaskell, Mary Barton
          V. Woolf, A Room of One's Own
          Linda Kerber and Jane Mathews, Women's America

Plus there is a packet of articles and documents to be bought at
Kinko's (next to Rutgers Bookstore in that shopping area).

SYLLABUS

Jan 22,24
               Introduction

               The Christian Tradition: The Possibilities of
Christianity for Women
                    Readings: Kinnear, intro., chapters 5 and 6
                              Bell, pp.70-90.
                              Readings from the Bible in packet.

     What do these excerpts from the Old and New Testament say
about women's spiritual nature and status and their relationship
to men and the church?

Jan.29,31 The Early Middle Ages

     Feudal Society

     The Medieval Church

          Readings: Kinnear, ch.6
                    Bell, pp. 96-118, 118-38
                    McNamara and Wemple, "Sanctity and Power" in
                    packet

3

Feb. 5,7 Collapse of Feudalism
        Commercial Revolution and the Rise of the State

        Medieval Working Women, Disorderly Women and the Life
of the Cities

                Readings: Kinnear, ch.7
                          Bell, 138-81
                          Davis, "Women on Top," (packet)

We are reading Chaucer's "Wife of Bath" in Bell. What does her
story tell us about the sources of power for medieval women and
the hostility generated against powerful women like the Wife?

Feb. 12,14 Renaissance and Reformation

        Courtly Love, Humanism, and Renaissance Queens
            Reading: Kinnear , chapter 7
                     Bell, 81-106,214-218
                     Kelly-Gadol, "Did Women have a Renaissance?"
                                (packet)

        Reformation
            Reading: Bell,212-214, 220-231
                      Koehler, "The Case of the American
                      Jezebels:Anne Hutchinson" in Kerber,36-50

            What new opportunities did Protestantism offer
women;what institutional supports were lost?

Feb.19,21 Early Modern Society: New Possibilities and Defeats

        Feb. 19: Review

        HOURLY EXAM; FEB.21

Feb.26, 28, March 5,7   Early Modern Society, Witchcraft,
Science, and the Age of Exploration
        Feb. 26, Goodwives
        Reading:Ulrich, "A Friendly Neighbor" in
packet
                        Kerber, 428-431

        Feb.28, Witchcraft
        Readings: "Witches" and Thomas, "The Making of a Witch"in
                packet

        March 5 Science
        REading: Scholten, "On the Importance of the Obstetrik
                Art"in Kerber, 51-64
                    Ortner, "Is Female to Male as Nature is to
Culture,"in packet, 71-81

        March 7 Impact of European Colonization on Women
        Reading: Young, "Women , Civilization and the Indian

4

Question," in Kerber

March 12,14 Women in the AGe of Reason and Revolution

    March 12 The Enlightenment and American Revolution
            Reading: Kinnear, ch.8
                     Kerber, "Daughters of Columbia," in Kerber
                     Bell, pp. 232-51

    March 14 The French Revolution : Guest Speaker Martha Howell
            Reading: Kinnear, ch. 9
                     Bell, 262-79
                     Kerber, pp.80,81

March 19,21 VACATION
        read Mary Barton

March 26,28 The Industrial Revolution
    March 26 Slide Show: Who are the People of the Industrial
REvolution
            Reading: Kinnear, ch.10,11
                     keep reading Mary BArton
                     Stansell, "The Making of the Sweatshop," in
packet, 89-100

    March 28 Separate Spheres
            Reading: documents on women's sphere in packet,
126-134
                     Carroll Smith -Rosenberg, "Female World of
Love and Ritual," in Kerber

April 2,4,9 The Other Side of Ladyhood: Exploitation

    April 2 Working Women and Sexual Danger
        Reading: Walkowitz, " The Making of an Outcast Group," in
packet, 112-126
                 "Black-Eyed Susan," in packet, 102-112

    April 4 Mary Barton
        paper due

    April 9 Black Women and Slavery
        Reading: Kerber, pp.99-113
                 Genovese, "Life in the Big House," in packet, 138-
142

April 11 Politics of Sexuality
      REading: Kinnear, ch.12
               Mohr,"Abortion in America,"in Kerber, 179-189
               Sanger, "My Fight for Birth Control," 310-319

April 16,18, 23   Economic and Social Changes in the Twentieth
Century

April 16 Sex and Consumerism: "Our Dancing Mothers"
          Reading:
          Cowan, "The Industrial Revolution in the Home," in
Kerber, 324-3375

     April 18, New Developments
          Reading:
          Benson, "The Customer Ain't God," in packet, 157-
170

          Garrison, "Tender Technicians" in packet 171 -181
          Ehrenreich,"Women in the Global Factory," 182-193

     April 23 Immigrant Women and Urban Networks
          Reading:
          Ross. "Domestic Networks," in packet, 196-202
          Hyman, "Immigrant Women and the Kosher Meat
Strike," 142-149
          "Isolation," in packet, 150-156

April 25,30,May 2 Feminism

     April 25 A Room of One's Own

     April 30, The First Wave of Feminism
          readings to be determined

     May 2   The Second Wave: Feminism since the 1960s
          Readings to be determined

WRITING ASSIGNMENT:

During the industrial revolution, domestic melodrama emerged
as popular theater for the working classes. In the packet is
included the most popular melodrama of the nineteenth cnetury, Black-Eyed
Susan , first produced in 1829. Look closely at the relationship
between the upper-class villain, the working class hero, and the
victimized working-class heroine. What do the plot and action
say about the working class family, male-female relations, and
class and sexual oppression?

In Mary Barton, Elizabeth Gaskell has written a
middle-class woman's version of a melodrama, complete with an
erotic triangle of upper-class villain, working-class hero, and
working-class heroine. However, she has complicated the story
significantly and changed its meaning by giving some more agency
to the heroine.

I want you to compare and contrast Gaskell's melodramatic
story to Black Eyed Susan. Does her story carry the same message
about the working-class family, male-female relations, and class
and sexual oppression?

Due April 4.
Length : 5 typed pages.

HISTORY 196H and Women's Studies 195
THE RISE OF   PUBLIC WOMAN
Fall, 1981

Tu & Th 11:40-1:05
L.H. 9

Deborah Hertz
L.T. 715; 798-2503
Office Hours:
  Tu. 1:30-2:30;
  Wed. 4:30-5:30;
  Thur. 10:30-11:30

Deborah Symonds
WD 3G

Course Description: In this course we chart the entry of European women into new activities between 1750 and 1945. These new and public activities included participation in public education, socialist, liberal and feminist parties, political revolutions and professional careers. At the same time we trace the changing nature of female participation in the public world of paid manual labor by study of women in cottage industries, in factories and in domestic service. We also explore the history of private woman in the family by examination of love, sex, birth control and fertility in past time. Throughout, our intention will be to learn how the division between public and private spheres has effected the lives of women over time.

Format: Class will meet twice weekly for lecture and class discussion. The only required student work will be in-class midterm and final examinations.*
No incompletes will be given, except in the case of documented medical emergencies.

Texts:

    Richard Sennett, The Fall of Public Man
    J. Scott and L. Tilly, Women, Work and Family (S and T)
    R. Bridenthal and C. Koonz, ed., Becoming Visible (B and K)
    Richard Evans, The Feminists
    E. Riemer and J. Fout, eds., European Women (R and F)
    M. Boxer and J. Quataert, Socialist Women (B and Q)

Recommended:

    E. Shorter, The Making of the Modern Family
    L. Rupp, Mobilizing Women for War

All texts have been placed on reserve.

Class Schedule:

September 1   Introduction: Females and Public Space
                  Read: Sennett, 1-44

                  WOMEN IN OLD REGIME EUROPE, 1500-1800

September 3   Elite Women as Queens and Salonieres
                  Read: Sennett, 45-122

September 8   The Domestic Economy and Female Reproductive Labor
                  Read: B and K, Ch. 8, and S and T, 9-60.

* Lists of possible exam questions will be distributed one week before the
  examination.

September 10	Courtship, Love, and Sex for Rich and Poor Women
	Recommended Reading: Shorter, 120-167
September 15	Women for the Philosophes and in the French Revolution
	Read: B and K, ch. 9 and 10, and Evans, 13-23

INDUSTRIALIZING EUROPE, 1800-1850

September 17	Why Industrialization? How Industrialization?
	Read: Sennett, 123-149
September 22	Single Women's Manual Work
	Read: B and K, Ch. 11 and S and T, 61-88
September 24	Married Women's Manual Work
	Read: S and T, 89-146, and B and K, Ch. 12
September 29	NO CLASS-- RELIGIOUS HOLIDAY
October 1	The Creation of Private Woman; the Mother
	Read: Sennett, 150-194;
	Recommended Reading: Shorter, 168-204
October 6	Illegitimacy, Contraception, and Abortion
	Read: R and F, 202-216;
	Recommended, Shorter, 80-98
October 8	NO CLASS-- RELIGIOUS HOLIDAY
October 13	The Tyranny of Fashion
	Read: Sennett, 195-218

THE ERA OF RAPID INDUSTRIALIZATION, 1850-1914

October 15	Women Workers and Efforts to Aid Them
	Read: R and F, 1-56
October 20	Defining Feminism and A Survey of the Suffrage Movement
	Read: Evans, 23-38 and 63-137, and F and R, 87-98
October 22	The Struggle For Education
	Read: R and F, 115-131, and 163-175
October 27	Wives of Middle-Class Males: Leisure, Charity, and Servants
	Read: B and K, Ch. 13, and R and F, 141-156
October 29	IN-CLASS MIDTERM EXAMINATION

Sept. 23   6: Popular Action in the French Revolution
                Read: M & D, 32-43

Sept. 25   7: From Estates to Classes
                Read: Laslett, 23-54; M & D, 84-97

INDUSTRIALIZING EUROPE, 1800-1870

Sept. 30   8: The Standard of Living Debate
                Read: Laslett, 113-134; M & D, 44-53, 68-83; Taylor, 6-42;
                      Lieberman, 159-236

Oct. 2   9: The Political Making of the European Working Class
                Read: Laslett, 159-212; Taylor, 63-84

Oct. 7   10: Deviance, Crime, and Punishment

Oct. 9   11: Food, Drink, and Fashion

Oct. 14   12: Romantic Love and Motherhood: On the Rise?
                Recommended: E. Shorter, Making, 168-254

Oct. 16   13: Guest Lecture by Ms. N. Grey Osterud, Brown University
                Domestic Manufacture in Town and Country

Oct. 21   14: Single Women's Work and Ties to Families
                Read: T & S, 61-88, 104-146

Oct. 23   MIDTERM EXAMINATION

Oct. 28   15: Birth Control, Abortion, and the Decline of Fertility
                Read: T & S, 63-88; Lieberman, 277-290

Oct. 30   16: Literacy, Students, and University Life
                Read: M & D, 187-194

Nov. 4   17: Why Industrialization? England, France, German and
                Russia Compared
                Read: M & D, 128-144, 156-169; Taylor, 1-5, 101-110;
                      Lieberman, 9-42, 425-473

MATURE INDUSTRIAL ECONOMIES, 1870-1945

Nov. 6   18: Sex and Labor in the Victorian Household
                Recommended: Clio's Consciousness Raised, 38-53

Nov. 11   19: The Political Economy of Prostitution
                Recommended: Walkowitz essay, Clio's Consciousness Raised

Nov. 13   20: European Imperialism in Theory and Practice

November 3   Female Socialists: Feminists?
                      Read: Evans, 144-159, and B and Q, 1-18

November 5   Female Socialists in Germany and Austria
                      Read: Evans, 159-170, and B and Q, 112-145 and 215-248

November 10   Female Socialists in France, Italy, and England
                      Read: Evans, 170-177, and B and Q, 19-50, 75-111, 146-181

November 12   The Suffrage Victory
                      Read: B and K, Ch. 14; Evans, 189-228

November 17   Nevertheless, The Decline of Feminism
                      Read: Evans, 232-245

November 19   Females in Russa; Nihilists, Terorists, Revolutionaries
                      Read: B and K, Ch. 15; B and Q, 51-74, 182-214; Evans, 177-183

November 24   Interwar Women at Work
                      Read: B and Q, Ch. 18

November 26   NO CLASS -- THANKSGIVING RECESS

December 1   Women Endorse, Yet Suffer Under Fascism: The Case
                          of Nazi Germany
                      Read: B and K, Ch. 19; R and F, 104-114

December 3   Female Labor in World War Two: A Decisive Factor?
                      Recommended Reading: Leila Rupp, <u>Mobilizing Women for War</u>

December 8   Assigned to the Consumer Role: Women in Postwar Economies
                      Read: S and T, 147-226

Robert Moeller
Fall 1984

WOMEN IN INDUSTRIAL EUROPE, 1750-PRESENT

This course is intended as an introduction to the literature and
methodologies in European women's history from the Industrial
Revolution to the present. Readings concentrate primarily on
Britain, France and Germany. They have been selected both to
offer an outline of the history of women in modern western Europe
and, in addition, to illuminate the varieites of women's history,
the problems of greatest interest to women's historians, and the
methods and sources which historians of women employ to approach
their topic, not to provide a complete account of the history of
women in any one country. A general knowledge of the history of
modern Europe is an essential prerequisite for the course, and a
wide-ranging survey of this type cannot be successful unless
students come equipped with this general background. The course
focuses on areas which have been of particular concern to
historians of women in recent years: the family, motherhood,
women's work, sexuality, the role of ideology in defining gender
and "separate spheres," and the variety of feminist political
responses. The course thus takes a thematic approach within a
straightfoward chronological framework. Course requirements will
include one brief paper by mid-term (a 6-8 page review of a
monograph relevant to our concerns), an oral presentation
outlining a framework for class discussion of one week's
readings, and a term paper which will examine in greater detail
one of the problems raised in our review of the literature.

All readings will be on reserve in the college library. In
addition, the following are availabe in the bookstore:

John Gillis, The Development of European Society 1770-1870

Barbara Taylor, Eve and the New Jerusalem

Joan Scott and Louise Tilly, Women, Work and the Family

Zillah Eisenstein, The Radical Future of Liberal Feminism

Janet Sayers, Biological Politics: Feminist and Anti-Feminist
Perspectives

Jeffrey Weeks, Sex, Politics and Society: The Regulation of
Sexuality Since 1800

Margaret Llewelyn Davies, Maternity

Margery Spring Rice, Working-Class Wives

Week I - General Introduction

Week II - Women, Work and Family Structures in Early Industrial Europe

- John Gillis, The Development of European Society 1770-1870, Ch. 1-3, 7-9
- Joan Scott and Louise Tilly, Women, Work and the Family, Parts I and II

Week III - Women in the Age of Light

- Gillis, Chapter 4
- Abby R. Kleinbaum, "Women in the Age of Light," in R. Bridenthal and C. Koonz, Becoming Visible, 217-36
- Zillah R. Eisenstein, The Radical Future of Liberal Feminism (New York, 1981), pp. 31-144
- Jane Abray, "Feminism in the French Revolution," American Historical Review 80 (1975): 43-62
- Barbara Taylor, Eve and the New Jerusalem. Socialism and Feminism in the Nineteenth Century, Introduction and Chapter 1

Week IV - Working Women and Early Forms of Socialist Feminism

- Gillis, Chapter 6, 10, 11
- Taylor, Eve and the New Jerusalem (complete)

Week V - Relocating Difference: The Tyranny of Science

- Jeffrey Weeks, Sex, Politics and Society: The Regulation of Sexuality Since 1800, Ch. 2, 3, 5, 8
- Janet Sayers, Biological Politics: Feminist and Anti-Feminist Perspectives Chapters 1, 2, 3, 8
- Elizabeth Fee, "The Sexual Politics of Victorian Anthropology," in Mary Hartman and Lois W. Banner, Clio's Consciousness Raised, 86-102
- Lorna Duffin, "The Conspicuous Consumptive: Woman as Invalid," in Sara Delamont and Lorna Duffin, The Nineteenth Century Woman, 26-56

Week VI - Institutionalizing Difference: The State and Ideology

- Rachel Harrison and Frank Mort, "Patriarchal Aspects of 19th Century State Formation: Property Relations,

Marriage, Divorce and Sexuality," in P. Corrigan, ed., _Capitalism, State Formation and Marxist Theory_ (London, 1980)

- Bonnie G. Smith, "Religion and the Rise of Domesticity: Ladies of the Nord in the Nineteenth Century," _Marxist Perspectives_ 6 (Summer 1979): 56-82
- Pat Thane, "Women and the Poor Law in Victorian and Edwardian England," _History Workshop_ Nr. 6 (1978): 29-51
- Carol Dyhouse, "Towards a 'Feminine' Curriculum for English Schoolgirls: The Demands of Ideology 1870-1963," _Women's Studies International Forum (WSIF)_ 1 (1978): 297-312
- Judith Walkowitz, "Jack the Ripper and the Myth of Male Violence," _Feminist Studies_ 8 (1982): 543-74
- Iris Minor, "Working-Class Women and Matrimonial Law Reform, 1890-1914," in D. Martin and D. Rubinstein, eds., _Ideology and the Labour Movement_, pp. 103-24

Week VII - The Changing Nature of "Women's Work"

- Robyn Dasey, "Women's Work and the Family: Women Garment Workers in Berlin and Hamburg Before the First World War," in Richard Evans, ed., _The German Family_, 221-55
- Leonore Davidoff, "The Separation of Home and Work? Landladies and Lodgers in Nineteenth and Twentieth-Century England," in Sandra Burman, ed., _Fit Work for Women_ (New York, 1979) pp. 64-97
- Leonore Davidoff, "Mastered for Life: Servant and Wife in Victorian and Edwardian England," _Journal of Social History_ (Summer 1974): 406-28
- Ellen Ross, "Women's Neighborhood Sharing in London Before World War I," _History Workshop_ Nr. 15 (1983): 4-27
- Louise A. Tilly, "The Family Wage Economy of a French Textile City: Roubaix 1872-1906," _Journal of Family History_ 4 (1979): 381-94

Week VIII - The Joys of Motherhood?

- Angus McLaren, "Women's Work and the Regulation of Family Size," _History Workshop_ Nr. 7 (1977): 70-81
- Cissie Fairchilds, "Female Sexual Attitudes and the Rise of Illegitimacy: A Case Study," _Journal of Interdisciplinary History_ 8 (1978): 627-67
- Patricia Knight, "Women and Abortion in Victorian England," _History Workshop_ Nr. 4 (1977): 57-69
- Carol Dyhouse, "Working-Class Mothers and Infant Mortality," _Journal of Social History_ 12 (Winter 1978): 248-67
- Margaret Llewelyn Davies, ed., _Maternity_

Week IX - Forms of Women's Collective Action - The Middle Classes

- Richard Evans, "Liberalism and Society: The Feminist Movement and Social Change," in Richard Evans, ed., Society and Politics in Wilhelmine Germany, pp. 186-214
- Barbara Caine, "Feminism, Suffrage and the Nineteenth-Century English Women's Movement," WSIF 5 (1982): 527-50
- Marilyn J. Boxer, "'First Wave' Feminism in Nineteenth-Century France: Class, Family and Religion," WSIF 5 (1982): 551-59
- Sheila Jeffreys, "'Free From All Uninvited Touch of Man': Women's Campaigns around Sexuality, 1880-1914," WSIF 5 (1982): 629-45
- Christl Wickert, Brititte Hamburger and Marie Lienau, "Helene Stöcker and the Bund für Mutterschutz (The Society for the Protection of Motherhood)," Women's Studies International Forum 5 (1982): 611-18
- Judith Walkowitz, "Male Vice and Feminist Virtue: Feminism and the Politics of Prostitution in Nineteenth-Century Britain," History Workshop Nr. 13 (1982): 77-93

Week X - Forms of Women's Collective Action - Women of the Laboring Classes

- Louise A. Tilly, "Women's Collective Action and Feminism in France, 1870-1914," in Louise A. Tilly and Charles Tilly, eds., Class Conflict and Collective Action (London and Beverly Hills, 1981), 207-33
- Louise Tilly, "Paths of Proletarianization: Organization of Production, Sexual Division of Labor and Women's Collective Action," Signs 7 (1981): 400-17
- Temma Kaplan, "Other Scenarios: Women and Spanish Anarchists," in Becoming Visible, pp. 400-21
- Temma Kaplan, "Female Consciousness and Collective Action: The Case of Barcelona," Signs 7 (1982): 545-66
- Jill Liddington, "Women Cotton Workers and the Suffrage Campaign: The Radical Suffragists in Lancashire, 1893-1914," in Fit Work for Women, 98-111
- Jean Quataert, "Feminist Tactics in German Social Democracy: A Dilemma," International Wissenschaftliche Korrespondenz zur Geschichte der deutschen Arbeiterbewegung 13 (1977): 48-65

Week XI - The Changing Nature of Work in the Twentieth Century

- Scott and Tilly, Women, Work and the Family, Part III
- Renate Bridenthal, "Something Old, Something New: Women Between the Two World Wars," in Bridenthal and Koonz, Becoming Visible, 422-44

- Margery Spring Rice, _Working-Class Wives_ (Virago)

Week XII - Presentation of Oral Reports on Term Papers

Week XIII - The Rationalization of Sex?

- Weeks, _Sex, Politics and Society_, Ch. 10-11
- Atina Grossmann, "The New Woman and the Rationalization of Sexuality in Weimar Germany," in A. Snitow, C. Stansell, S. Thompson, eds., _Powers of Desire_ (New York, 1983), pp. 153-71
- Jane Lewis, "The Ideology and Politics of Birth Control in Inter-War England," _Women's Studies International Forum_ 2 (1979): 33-48
- Gisela Bock, "Racism and Sexism in Nazi Germany: Motherhood, Compulsory Sterilization and the State," _Signs_ 8 (1983): 400-21

Week XIV - Feminist Politics in the Interwar Period

- Virginia Woolf, _Three Guineas_
- Ray Strachey, _The Cause_ (selections)
- Helen L. Boak, "Women in Weimar Germany: The 'Frauenfrage' and the Female Vote," in R. Bessel and E.J. Feuchtwanger, eds., _Social Change and Political Development in Weimar Germany_, pp. 155-73
- Claudia Koonz, "Conflicting Alliances: Political Ideology and Women Legislators in Weimar Germany," _Signs_ 1 (1975/76): 663-83
- Claudia Koonz, "Mothers in the Fatherland: Women in Nazi Germany," in _Becoming Visible_

Robert Moeller
Spring 1984

Women in Industrial Societies: Comparative Perspectives

on England and Germany, 1070-1945

This course is intended as an introduction to the study of women
in advanced industrial socities. The course focuses on a
national comparison of Germany and England. The seminar will
concentrate on such crucial topics as the role of ideology in
shaping popular notions of the "separation of spheres" and the
sexual division of labor, the nature of women's work, women's
role in the family and community life, forms of women's
collective action and the varieties of feminist politics, the
impact of the welfare state on women's lives, the organization of
women under National Socialism and the mobilization of women
workers for wartime employment. Not all topics can be treated
with equal care for each of the two national cases, but where
possible, comparisons are suggested. The restriction of readings
to two national cases is intended to allow us more effectively to
see national differences and similarities. To what extent is it
possible to identify a female experience which transcends
national borders? What elements in national economic development
explain differences in the structure of women's work? How should
we interpret the importance of a national "political culture" for
defining forms of collective action and a language of feminist
politics? These concerns are central to our work in this
seminar, and by the end of the semester, we should be able to
offer some answers to these important questions.

Class participation is essential to the success of this seminar.
Come prepared to offer your questions, observations and insights.
In addition, students will be expected to prepare:

   1. a framework for the discussion of one week's readings.
      This should not be a recapitulation of the readings
      but rather should identify key points of controversy
      or interest for our discussion. The presentation
      should last no longer than 10 minutes and will serve
      to get our discussion started.

   2. a brief paper (6-8 pages) which offers a discussion of
      a book which addresses an important element of
      historical context in the course, but which does not
      specifically discuss women. You will be asked to
      summarize the information of relevance for our
      discussion and also to suggest the points at which
      women and feminist concerns might be integrated into
      such a text.

3. a brief paper (6-8) pages which discusses the usefulness of a memoir or a contemporary eyewitness account as a historical source.

4. a brief paper (6-8) providing a critical evaluation of a monograph relevant to our concerns in the course.

Additional information on these assignments along with due dates will be provided early in the semester. No term paper will be required in the course.

Most of the readings are taken from journal articles, all of which should be on reserve in the college library. Request edited collections under the _editor's_ _name_, not the author of the specific article assigned. In addition, we will read substantial portions of the following texts which have been ordered in the university bookstore:

- Patricia Hollis, ed., _Women_ _in_ _Public,_ _The_ _Women's_ _Movement_ _1850-1900_ (George Allen & Unwin)

- Margaret Llewelyn Davies, _Maternity,_ _Letters_ _from_ _Working_ _Women_ (Norton)

- Maud Pember Reeves, _Round_ _About_ _a_ _Pound_ _a_ _Week_ (Virago)

- Margery Spring Rice, _Working-Class_ _Wives_ (Virago)

Week I General Introduction

Week II Ways of Seeing Women in History

- Heidi Hartmann, "Capitalism, Patriarchy and Job Segregation by Sex," in Zillah Eisenstein, ed., _Capitalist_ _Patriarchy_ _and_ _the_ _Case_ _for_ _Socialist_ _Feminism_, 206-47

- Joan Scott and Louise Tilly, "Women's Work and the Family in Nineteenth Century Europe," _Comparative_ _Studies_ _in_ _Society_ _and_ _History_, 17, 1975, 36-64

- Patricia Hilden, "Family History v. Women in History: A Critique of Tilly and Scott," and reply by Scott, _International_ _Labor_ _and_ _Working_ _Class_ _History_, No. 16 (1979), 1-27

- Heidi Hartmann, "The Unhappy Marriage of Marxism and Feminism: Towards a More Progressive Union," in Lydia Sargent, ed., _Women_ _and_ _Revolution_, Boston, 1981, 1-42

Week III Forms and Use of Ideology - Men Defining Women's Place

- Karin Hausen, "Family and Role-division: The Polarisation of Sexual Stereotypes in the Nineteenth Century - an Aspect of the Dissociation of Work and Family Life," in Evans, ed.,The German Family, 51-84

- Lorna Duffin, "Prisoners of Progress: Women and Evolution," in Delamont and Duffin, eds., The Nineteenth Century Woman, 57-91

- Alice Kessler-Harris, Women Have Always Worked, 62-70

- Judith Walkowitz, "Jack the Ripper and the Myth of Male Violence," Feminist Studies, 8, 3, 1982, 543-74

- Gary D. Stark, "Pornography, Society and the Law in Imperial Germany," Central European History, 14, 1981, 200-29

- Hollis, 15-30, 142-47

Week IV Varieties of Women's Work

- Jennie Kitteringham, "Country Work for Girls," in Raphael Samuel, ed., Village Life and Labour, 760138

- Robyn Dasey, "Women's Work and the Family: Women Garment Workers in Berlin and Hamburg Before the First World War," in Evans, ed., The German Family, 221-55

- Leonore Davidoff, "The Separation of Home and Work? Landladies and Lodgers in Nineteenth and Twentieth-Century England," in Sandra Burman, ed., Fit Work for Women, New York, 1979, 64-97

- Katharina Schlegel, "Mistress and Servant in Nineteenth Century Hamburg," History Workshop Journal, Nr. 15 (1983), 60-77

- Edward Higgs, "Domestic Servants and Households in Victorian England," Social History, 8, 2 (1983), 201-10

- Hollis, 53, 57-89

Week V Biology as Destiny?

- Carol Dyhouse, "Working-Class Mothers and Infant Mortality," JSH, 12 (Winter 1978), 248-67

- Stefan Bajohr, "Illegitimacy and the Working Class: Illegitimate Mothers in Brunswick, 1900-1933," in Evans, ed., The German Working Class, 142-73

- Anna Davin, "Imperialism and Motherhood," History Workshop Journal, 5

- Margaret Llewelyn Davies, ed., Maternity

Week VI Family Life and Community
Ellen Ross, "Women's Neighbourhood Sharing in London Before World War I," History Workshop, Spring 1983, 4-27
- Ellen Ross, "'Fierce Questions and Taunts': Married Life in Working-Class London 1870-1914," Feminist Studies, 8, 1982, 575-602

- Nancy Tomes, "A 'Torrent of Abuse': Crimes of Violence Between Working-Class Men and Women in London, 1840-1875," JSH, 11 (1978), 328-45

- Maud Pember Reeves, Round About a Pound a Week

Week VII "We Are not Beasts of the Field"

- Richard Evans, "Prostitution, State and Society in Imperial Germany," Past and Present, Nr. 70 (1976), 106-29

- Marion Kaplan, "Prostitution, Morality Crusades and Feminism: German-Jewish Feminists and the Campaign Against White Slavery," Women's Studies International Quarterly, 5, 6 (1982): 619-27

- Judith Walkowitz, "The Making of an Outcast Group: Prostitutes and Working Women in Nineteenth Century Plymouth and Southampton," in Martha Vicinus, ed., Widening Sphere, 72-93

- Judith Walkowitz, "Male Vice and Feminist Virtue: Feminism and the Politics of Prostitution in Nineteenth-Century Britain," History Workshop Journal, Nr. 13 (1982), 77-93

Week VIII Defining a Feminist Political Response (I) - England

- Ray Strachey, The Cause, Ch. IV, XIV-XIX

- Jill Liddington, "Women Cotton Workers and the Suffrage Campaign: The Radical Suffragists in Lancashire, 1893-1914," in Sandra Burman, ed., Fit Work for Women, 98-111

- Hollis, sections 9.2-9.5.2, 10.1-10.2

Week IX Defining a Feminist Political Response (II) - Germany

- Amy Hackett, "The German Women's Movement and Suffrage, 1890-1914: A Study of National Feminism," in Robert Bezucha, Modern European Social History, 354-86

- Richard J. Evans, "Bourgeois Feminists and Women Socialists in Germany 1894-1914: Lost Opportunity or Inevitable Conflict?" Women's Studies International Quarterly, 3, 4 (1980): 355-76

- Jean Quataert, "Feminist Tactics in German Social Democracy: A Dilemma," Internationale wissenschaftliche Korrespondenz zur Geschichte der deutschen Arbeiterbewegung, 13, 1977, 48-65

- Karen Honeycutt, "Clara Zetkin: A Socialist Feminist Approach to the Problem of Woman's Oppression," Feminist Studies, 3, 3/4, 1975/76, 141-41

- Richad Evans, "Politics and the Family: Social Democracy and the Working Class Family in Theory and Practice Before 1914," in Evans, ed., The German Family, 256-88

Week X War and the Changing Nature of Women's Work

- Janet McCalman, "The Impact of the Great War on Female Employment in England," Labour History (November 1971)

- Harold Smith, "The issue of 'equal pay for equal work' in Great Britain, 1914-1919," Societas, VIII, 1, Winter 1978

- Renate Bridenthal, "Beyond Kinder, Küche, Kirche: Weimar Women at Work," Central European History, 6, 1973, 148-66

- Rosina Whyatt, "Munitions-Factory Worker," in John Burnett, ed., Annals of Labour

- Vera Britten, Testament of Youth, III-V, VIII

Week XI Sexual Reform Movements in the Interwar Period

- Jane Lewis, The Politics of Motherhood, pp. 165-226

- Ellen M. Holtzman, "The Pursuit of Married Love: Women's Attitudes Toward Sexuality and Marriage in

Great Britain, 1918-1939," <u>Journal of Social History</u>,
16, 2 (1982), 39-51

- Atina Grossmann, "The New Woman and the Rationalization
of Sexuality in Weimar Germany," in A. Snitow,
C. Stansell, S. Thompson, eds., <u>Powers of Desire. The
Politics of Sexuality</u>, New York, 1983, 153-71

- Atina Grossman, "'Staisfaction is Domestic Happiness'"
Mass Working-Class Sex Reform Organizations in the
Weimar Republic," in M. Dobkowski and I. Williman,
eds., <u>Towards the Holocaust: The Social and Economic
Collapse of the Weimar Republic</u>, Westport, Ct.,
Greenwood Press, 1983, 243-64

- Atina Grossman, "Abortion and Economic Crisis: The
1931 Campaign Against 218 in Germany," <u>New German
Critique</u>, #14 (Spring 1978), 119-37

Week XII Women and the Welfare State

- Elizabeth Wilson, <u>Women and the Welfare State</u>, Ch. 1-3,
6-7

- Margery Spring Rice, <u>Working-Class Wives</u> (Virago)

Week XIII German Women and National Socialism

- Renate Bridenthal, "Class Struggle around the Hearth:
Women and Domestic Service in the Weimar Republic," in
Dobkowski and Walliman, eds., <u>Towards the Holocaust</u>,
243-64

- Tim Mason, "Women in Nazi Germany," <u>History Workshop
Journal</u>, Nr. 1-2

- Claudia Koonz, "Mothers in the Fatherland: Women in
Nazi Germany," in Bridenthal and Koonz, <u>Becoming
Visible</u>, 445-73

- Gisela Bock, "Racism and Sexism in Nazi Germany:
Motherhood, Compulsory Sterilization and the State,"
<u>Signs</u>, 8, 3 (1983), 400-21

- Eleanor Riemer and John Fout, eds., <u>European Women. A
Documentary History</u>, 104-14

Week XIV Mobilizing Women for War

- Leila Rupp, "I Don't Call that Volksgemeinschaft," in
C.R. Berkin and C.M. Lovett, <u>Women. War and</u>

Revolution, pp. 37-54

- Rupp, Mobilizing Women for War, 115-36

- Penny Summer, "Women Workers in Britain in the Second
  World War," Capital and Class, 1

- Denise Riley, "The Free Mothers: Pronatalism and
  Working Mothers in Industry at the End of the Last War
  in Britain," History Workshop Journal, Nr. 11

History 242   Women in the Modern World: The European Experience
Fall, 86-87   M. Wiesner
Freshman/Sophomore Level   University of Wisconsin-Milwaukee

Required readings:

   Mary Kinnear: Daughters of Time: Women in the Western Tradition
                       (DT)
   Bridenthal/Koonz: Becoming Visible: Women in European History
                       (BV)
   Riemer/Fout: European Women: A Documentary History (EW)

Course requirements:

   Book review; research or reaction paper; optional midterm; final.

Lecture topics and reading assignments:

   Week One: Introduction and Ancient World
                   BV: Introduction (Suggested readings: Ch. 1-3)
                   DT: Ch. 1-4
                   EW: Introduction

   Week Two: Christianity and Medieval Europe
                   DT: Ch. 5-6
                   BV: Suggested readings: Ch. 4

   Week Three: The Renaissance
                   DT: pp. 78-82
                   BV: Ch. 6

   Week Four: Reformation and Witchcraft
                   DT: pp. 82-90
                   BV: Ch. 5 and 7

   Week Five: Capitalism and Women's Work
                   DT: Ch. 10
                   BV: Ch. 8
                   EW: No. 1

   Week Six: Courts and the Enlightenment
                   DT: Ch. 8
                   BV: Ch. 9

   Week Seven: The French Revolution
                   DT: Ch. 9
                   BV: Ch. 10
                   EW: No. 16

Week Eight: The Industrial Revolution
                 DT: Ch. 11
                 BV: Ch. 11, 12
                 EW: Nos. 2-4; Sec. II; No. 15

Week Nine: Victorian Sexuality and Family Life
                 DT: Ch. 12
                 EW: Part Three and Sec. XIV

Week Ten: Nineteenth Century Reform Movements
                 DT: pp. 141-150
                 BV: Ch. 13
                 EW: pp. 157-62; nos. 13, 14, 17, 18

Week Eleven: The Suffrage Movement
                 DT: pp. 150-155
                 BV: Ch. 14
                 EW: Nos. 20-22

Week Twelve: Women in Socialism
                 DT: Ch. 14
                 BV: Ch. 15 and 16
                 EW: Sec. VI; No. 41, 50

Week Thirteen: The 1920s and 1930s
                 BV: Ch. 17, 18
                 EW: No. 37; Sec. XII, Sec. XIII

Week Fourteen: Women in Fascism
                 DT: Ch. 15
                 BV: Ch. 19
                 EW: Sec. VII

Week Fifteen: Post World War II
                 DT: Ch. 16
                 BV: Ch. 20

MW/pjg

25

History of Women — 315

Fall 1986   Prof. Jane Slaughter
                                        Office: 2081 Mesa Vista

I. REQUIRED READINGS

   A. Books: (These are available at Full Circle Books,
                 2305 Silver SE, near corner of Yale and Silver)

       Jo Ann McNamara, A New Song: Celibate Women in the First
          Three Christian Centuries (Haworth, 1983).
       Shulamith Shahar, The Fourth Estate: A History of Women in
          the Middle Ages (Methuen, 1983).
       Angus McLaren, Reproductive Rituals: The Perception of
          Fertility in England from the 16th to the 19th Century
          (Methuen, 1984).
       Mary Beth Norton, Liberty's Daughters: The Revolutionary
          Experience of American Women, 1750-1800 (Little Brown,
          1980).

   B. Articles: (A packet of five articles has been re-printed
       and is available for purchase at Alpha Graphics, located
       on Lomas one block west of Yale) On the course outline
       these materials appear as Article, followed by author's
       name.

   Readings will provide the basis for discussion on assigned dates,
   and examinations will include material from the readings. Attendance at discussions is required.

II.   EXAMINATIONS

   There will be three hour exams, each of equal weight, and each
   constituting 25% of your grade.

            First Exam   September 29
            Second Exam   November 3
            Third Exam   As scheduled during Finals Week

III. Each student will write a research paper: it will consist of a
   series of diary entries written by a fictional woman whom you
   create on the basis of fact.   You will be presenting the daily
   life experiences of this woman, and the experiences must reflect
   accurately a geographic area and conditions of an historic
   epoch. (They must be limited to the Mediterranean or European
   world, or the Western Hemisphere, and can be set in any time
   period before 1800.)
   There should be approximately eight diary entries; paper should
   be 10 typed, double-spaced pages;   PAPERS ARE DUE November 26;
   late papers drop 1/2 letter grade for each class day late.
   The paper will be fully documented and include a bibliography.
   More detailed instructions will be forthcoming.

Readings

Marcia Guttentag, "Women's Roles in Classical Athens and
    Sparta" (from _Too Many Women: The Sex Ration Question)_

Sarah B. Pomeroy, "Women of the Roman Lower Classes" (from
    Goddesses, Whores, Wives and Slaves)

Judith Hauptman, "Images of Women in the Talmud," (from Rose-
    mary Ruether, ed., _Religion and Sexism_)

Judith C. Brown, "Lesbian Sexuality in Reniassance Italy," (from
    Signs 9:4 Summer 1984)

Ruth Bloch, "Untangling the Roots of Modern Sex Roles," (from
    Signs 4:2 Winter 1978)

Fall 1986		Topics	Assignments
Aug.	25	Introduction	
	27	Patterns and Questions	
	29	The Family, State and Patriarchy	
Sept.	3	"	
	5	"	
	8	Goddess Worship and Defeat of the Goddess	
	10	The Judaic Heritage	Article, Hauptman
	12	Women and the Greek Ideal	
	15	"	Article, Guttentag
	17	"	
	19	Rome: Republican Matron to	
	22	Imperial Rebel	Article, Pomeroy
	24	"	
	26	"	
	29	EXAMINATION	
Oct.	1	Women and Early Christianity	
		Discussion	McNamara (all)
	3	"	
	6	Importance of Women in the Celtic and Germanic Traditions	
	8	Changing Status of Women in Feudalism	
	10	"	
	13	Discussion	Shahar, 1-21, 65-173 220-50
	15	Medieval Church Doctrine and the Second Sex	
	17	"	Shahar, 22-64
	20	Varieties of Life in the Later Middle Ages	
	22	Discussion	Shahar, 174-219
	24	Renaissance Ladies	
	27	Heretics, Revolutionaries and	Shahar, 251-80 and
	29	Witches	Article, Brown
		(vacation)	
Nov.	3	EXAMINATION	
	5	Comparative Status of Women in the	
	7	Societies of the Western Hemisphere	
	10	Roots of Modern Sex Roles	
		Discussion	Article, Bloch
	12	Capitalism, Protestantism and	
	14	Patriarchy	
	17	The 17th Century: Salon or	
	19	Revolution?	
	21	U.S. Colonial Life and Experience	Norton, Pt. I, 3-150
	24	"	
	26	Second Race and Third Sex	PAPERS DUE
		(vacation)	

Dec.   1   Science and Reproduction
              Discussion   McLaren (all)
       3   Proper and Fitting in the
              18th Century
       5   Feminism and the Enlightenment
       8   The Revolutionary Era
       10   Discussion   Norton, Pt. II, 155-
                                                      299
       12   Conclusions

WOMEN IN ANTIQUITY: SYLLABUS

History 210, Classics 251, Women's Studies 251;

Susan Cole

Books:

- Pomeroy, *Goddesses, Whores, Wives and Slaves* (=Pomeroy)

- Lefkowitz and Fant, *Women's Life in Greece and Rome* (=L & F)

- Sappho, *A New Translation* (trans. M. Barnard)

- Euripides, *The Bacchae and Other Plays*

- Aristophanes, *Lysistrata*

- Thompson, *The Athenian Agora: An Ancient Shopping Center*

1. *TUESDAY, 1 APRIL*

    Introduction. Assignment: Handout

2. *WEDNESDAY, 2 APRIL*

    Slides: Women from the Past.

3. *FRIDAY, 4 APRIL*

    Gods and Goddesses. Assignment: Pomeroy, 1-31

4. *TUESDAY, 8 APRIL*

    Praise and Blame. Assignment: Pomeroy, 48-52; L & F, nos. 21-49

5. *WEDNESDAY, 9 APRIL*

    The Spartan Alternative and the Law Code of Gortyn. Assignment: Pomeroy, 32-48; L & F, nos. 64, 89-90

6. *FRIDAY, 11 APRIL*

    Sappho and Poetry by Women. Assignment: Sappho, poems; Pomeroy, 52-56; L & F, nos. 1-20.

7. *TUESDAY, 15 APRIL*

    Women in Classical Athens. Assignment: Pomeroy, 57-70, 79-84; L & F, no. 105

8. *WEDNESDAY, 16 APRIL*

Women and War: Euripides. Assignment: Euripides, *Trojan Women*

9. *FRIDAY, 18 APRIL*

Women and War: Aristophanes. Assignment: Aristophanes, *Lysistrata*

10. *TUESDAY, 22 APRIL*

A Woman's Work... Assignment: Pomeroy, 71-74; L & F, nos. 50-63, 106; Agora pamphlet

11. *WEDNESDAY, 23 APRIL*

Women and Literacy. Assignment: On reserve: Cole, "Could Greek Women Read and Write?" in *Reflections of Women in Antiquity*, ed. Foley.

12. *FRIDAY, 25 APRIL*

Sex and the Law. Assignment: Pomeroy, 86-88; L & F, nos. 65-76

13. *TUESDAY, 19 APRIL*

Women and Citizenship: Biography of a Courtesan. Assignment: Pomeroy, 88-92; L & F, no. 77

14. *WEDNESDAY, 30 APRIL*

Women in Myth. Assignment: Euripides, *Bacchae*

15. *FRIDAY, 2 MAY*

Greek Religion and Women's Festivals. Assignment: Pomeroy, 75-78; L & F, nos. 113-131

16. *TUESDAY, 6 MAY*

Homosexuality and Heterosexuality. Assignment: L & F, nos. 104, 107-109

17. *WEDNESDAY, 7 MAY*

Gynaecology: Theories of Procreation and Medical Knowledge of the Female Body. Assignment: Pomeroy, 84-86; L & F, nos, 91-103

18. *FRIDAY, 9 MAY*

Pregnancy and Birth: Abortion and Exposure, Strategies for Family Planning. Assignment: L & F, no. 112; Handout

19. *TUESDAY, 13 MAY*

    The Greek Philosophers. Assignment: L & F, nos. 86-88; Pomeroy, 115-119

20. *WEDNESDAY, 14 MAY*

    The Hellenistic Period And New Opportunities for Women. Assignment: Pomeroy, 120-48; L & F, nos. 78-85, 110-111

21. *FRIDAY, 16 MAY*

    Praiseworthy Women of Roman Legend and History. Assignment: L & F, nos. 134-54, 158-69, 203-210

22. *TUESDAY, 20 MAY*

    Women and Roman Law. Assignment: L & F, nos. 187-202

23. *WEDNESDAY, 21 MAY*

    The Roman Matron and Roman Marriage. Assignment: Pomeroy, 151-89; L & F, nos. 220-41

24. *FRIDAY, 23 MAY*

    Slaves and Freedwomen. Assignment: Pomeroy, 190-204

25. *TUESDAY,27 MAY*

    Women in Roman Religion. Assignment: Pomeroy, 205-230; L & F, nos. 242-69

26. *WEDNESDAY 29 MAY*

    Women's Work in Roman Times. Assignment: L & F, nos. 170-86

27. *FRIDAY, 30 MAY*

    Anti-Feminism in Roman Literature. Assignment: L & F, nos. 155-57

28. *TUESDAY 3 JUNE*

    Roman Medical Practice. Assignment: L & F, nos. 211-219

29. *WEDNESDAY, 4 JUNE*

    Review and Discussion.

Books on Reserve in Library:

- Cameron and Kurt (eds.), *Images of Women in Antiquity*

- Cantarella, *Pandora's Daughters: The Role and Status of Women in Greek and Roman Antiquity*

- Foley (ed.), *Reflections of Women in Antiquity*

- Humphreys, *The Family, Women and Death*

- Lefkowitz and Fant, *Women's Life in Greece and Rome*

- Lloyd, *Science, Folklore and Ideology*

- Peradotto and Sullivan (eds.), *Women in the Ancient World: The Arethusa Papers*

- Pomeroy, *Goddeses, Whores, Wives and Slaves*

- Skinner (ed.), *Rescuing Creusa: New Methodological Approaches to Women in Antiquity (Helios 13.2 [1987]).*

- *Women's Studies 7/8 (1980/81)*

- Zinserling, *Women in Greece and Rome*

Written Assignments: There will be 3 short papers on assigned topics and a take home final exam.

WOMEN IN ANTIQUITY: PAPER TOPICS

Paper due Wednesday, June 4

Assignment:

Choose a project from either part 1 or part 2; write a paper about five pages in length on your chosen project. Please type your paper.

1.   Read a book from the following list and write a critical review of the book. Relate your discussion to issues and topics covered in class. Evaluate the author's use of sources, and describe how the book contributes to our knowledge about women in antiquity.

    a.   W.K.Lacey, *The Family in Classical Greece.*

    b.   K.J.Dover, *Greek Homosexuality.*

    c.   J.P.Hallett, *Fathers and Daughters in Roman Society.*

    d.   D.Schaps, *Economic Rights of Women in Ancient Greece.*

    e.   G.E.R. Lloyd, *Science, Folklore, and Ideology.*

    f.   Sarah Pomeroy, *Women in Hellenistic Egypt.*

    g.   Grace Macurdy, *Hellenistic Queens.*

    h.   J.P.V.D.Balsdon, *Roman Women: Their History and Habits.*

    i.   J.Crook, *Law and Life of Rome.*

    j.   Susan Okin, *Women in Western Political Thought.*

    k.   Amy Richlin, *The Garden of Priapus: Sexuality and Aggression in Roman Humor.*

    l.   Robert Sutton, *The Interaction between Men and Women Portrayed on Attic Red-Figure Pottery.*

2.   Choose one of the following problems related to specific works of literature. Read carefully the work you choose and read any analytical articles suggested. When your write your paper, take into account the issues discussed in the analytical articles, make references to your chosen literary work or works, and relate your own discussion to the issues and subjects discussed in class.

    a.   Read Plato's *Republic,* Book 5, selections from the *Laws* (ask for handout), and at least two of the following articles: J. Annas, "The Function of Equal Education in Plato's *Republic* and *Laws,*" *Philosophy* 51 (1976) 307-21; A.Dickason, "Anatomy and Destiny: the Role of Biology in Plato's View of Women," *Philosophical Forum* 5 (1974) 3-15; M. Osborne, "Plato's Unchanging View of Women: a Denial that Anatomy Spells Destiny," *Philosophical Forum* 6 (1975) 447-52. What is Plato's attitude toward women in each of these works, and how did that attitude seem to change between the time he wrote the *Republic* and the time he wrote the *Laws?*

b. Read Aristophanes' *Ecclesiazusae*, and Plato's *Republic*, Book 5. Aristotle says that Plato was the first to propose a community of wives and children (*Politics* 1266a34), but Aristophanes' play was probably written at least 20 years before Plato's *Republic*. What ideas in Aristophanes are similar to ideas in Plato? Do you think the two authors could have been influenced by a common source? What conditions in Athens might have provoked these discussions? At what targets is Aristophanes' humor directed? You may find helpful Foley's article, "The Female Intruder Reconsidered: Women in Aristophanes' *Lysistrata* and *Ecclesiazusae*," in *Reflections of Women in Antiquity* (on reserve).

c. Read Aristophanes' *Thesmophoriazusae*. What criticisms do the women of the play believe Euripides leveled against them in his plays? Choose three of Euripides' tragic heroines and show how they do or do not reflect the criticisms alleged by the women in the *Thesmophoriazusae*. Suggested plays of Euripides: *Alcestis, Medea, Hipolytos, Helen*. Read as well F.Zeitlin, "Travesties of Gender and Genre in Aristophanes' *Thesmophoriazusae*," in *Reflections of Women in Antiquity*.

d. Read the Homeric Hymn to Demeter (available in the library in several translations of *The Homeric Hymns*). Read as well M. Arthur, "Politics and Pomegranates," *Arethusa* 10 (1977) 7-48 and M.L.Lord, "Withdrawal and Return: and Epic Story Pattern in the Homeric Hymn to Demeter," *Classical Journal* 62 (1966) 241-48. What are the central themes of the hymn? How does it relate the lives of women to the agricultural cycle, and what does it tell us about the relation between mother and daughter? You may find helpful: J. Redfield, "Notes on the Greek Wedding," *Arethusa* 15 (1982) 181-202.

e. Describe the arrangement of the typical Greek house in the classical period. Compare this description with the relevant literary sources that we have studied (e.g., Lysias and Xenophon, especially), and show how they supplement the archaeological evidence. What does the arrangement of the conventional Greek house imply about the lives of women who lived there? Sources: David Robinson, *The Hellenic House*; Rider, *The Greek House*; Wycherley, *How the Greeks Built Cities*; Susan Walker, "Women and Housing in Classical Greece: The Archaeological Evidence," in *Images of Women in Antiquity* (on reserve).

Penny Johnson   Office hrs: M 3-5
Monday 6:10   Rm: 513 19 Univ. Pl.
fall, 1986   598-3322/3

This course examines women's experience in and contributions to
medieval Europe as well as the context and factors which shaped women's
lives. The colloquium can be taken on either of two tracks.

Track A: This is for the new-comer to the history of women in
pre-modern European history. The student will read and prepare to discuss
all of the assigned reading for each meeting. (Weekly reading is quite
short: 186 pp. average, but often the primary sources are demanding.) In
addition, the student will hand in a weekly journal of responses to that
reading. Class participation will be an important component of the
student's input, and the grade will reflect the quality of both the
journal and class participation.

Track B: This is for the student already familiar with the literature
of the history of women in pre-modern European history. This student will
be expected to be conversant with all the reading and to be prepared to
discuss it each week in class. Early in the term the student will define
(in consultation with the instructor) either a reading or a research paper
topic. A summary of the findings will be presented informally in class in
a brief oral report at one of the final two class meetings, and a paper of
between 12-20 pages will be due at the end of exam period. The grade for
Track B will be based primarily on the paper.

N.B.: To choose which of these tracks is appropriate for your level,
look at the assigned reading; if you have already read better than half of
it, you belong on Track B.

CLASS MEETINGS

Mon. Sept. 22   Introduction

Sept. 29   The Shaping of Attitudes (88pp.)
    The Bible   Genesis 1-3
            Leviticus 12, 15:19-32; 20:10-21.
            1 Corinthians 5-7; 11:1-15; 14:34-6.
            Galatians 3:26-29.
            1 Timothy 2:9-15; 5:3-16.
    *Aristotle, Politics, Bk. 1, Ch. 12-13.
    *Jerome, Letter 22 to Eustochium. Select Letters of St. Jerome, tr.
            F. A. Wright, (Cambridge, Eng.:1933).
    *Rosemary Ruether, "Misogynism and Virginal Feminism in the Fathers of
            the Church," Religion and Sexism ed. R. Ruether (1974), 150-183.
    *Vern Bullough,"Medieval Medical and Scientific Views of Women,"
            Viator 4 (1973), 484-501.

Oct. 6 The Early Middle Ages (235 pp.)
    Medieval Women Visionary Literature, ed. Elizabeth Petroff
        (Oxford:1986) Perpetua, "The Passion of Ss. Perpetua and
        Felicitas." pp. 70-77.
    Elaine Pagels, The Gnostic Gospels (N.Y.:1981) intro., ch. 1-3.
    Rosemary Rader, Breaking Boundaries: Male/Female Friendship in Early
        Christian Communities (N.Y.:1983).

Oct. 13 Yom Kippur no class

Oct. 20 The Barbarian Period (205 pp.)
    St. Leoba, "The Life of St. Leoba." pp. 106-114 in Petroff.
    Suzanne Wemple, Women in Frankish Society (Philadelphia:1981).

Oct. 27 Life, Death, and Influence (99 pp.)
    *David Herlihy, "Life Expectancies for Women in Medieval
        Society," in The Role of Woman in the Middle Ages
        ed. Rosmarie Morewedge (Albany:1975), 1-22.
    *_____, "Land, Family, and Women," Traditio
        18 (1962), 89-120 and in Women in Medieval Society, ed. Susan
        Stuard (Philadelphia:1976), 13-45.
    *Vern Bullough, "Female Longevity and Diet," Speculum
        55 (1980).
    Emily Coleman, "Infanticide in the Early Middle Ages", in
        Stuard 47-70.
    *Jo Ann McNamara and Suzanne Wemple, "The Power of Women
        through the Family in Medieval Europe: 500-1000,"
        Feminist Studies 1 (1973), 126-141 and in Clio's Consciousness
        Raised, ed. Mary Hartmann and Lois Banner (N.Y.:1976), 103-118.

Nov. 3 Women and the Family (187 pp.)
    Christina of Markyate pp. 144-150 in Petroff.
    David Herlihy, Medieval Households (Cambridge:1985).
    *Robert Hajdu, "Family and Feudal Ties in Poitou, 110-1300,"
        J.I.H. 8 (1977), 117-139.
    Barbara Hanawalt, "Childrearing Among the Lower Classes of Late
        Medieval England," JIH 8 (1977), 1-22.

Nov. 10 Marriage (383 pp.)
    *The Marriage Ceremony from the Old Sarum Missal, (my translation)
    Georges Duby, The Knight, The Lady and The Priest tr. Barabara
        Bray (N.Y.:1983).
    *Emily Coleman, "Medieval Marriage Characteristics: A Neglected Factor
        in the History of Medieval Serfdom,"J.I.H. 2 (1971), 205-219.
    *John Noonan, "Power to Choose," Viator 4 (1973), 419-434.
    *Michael Sheehan, "The Influence of Canon Law on the Property Rights
        of Married Women in England," Medieval Studies 25 (1963),
        109-124.
    *_____, "The Formation and Stability of Marriage in
        Fourteenth Century England: Evidence of an Ely Register,"
        Medieval Studies 33 (1971), 228-263.
    Judith Bennett, "The Tie that Binds: Peasant Marriages and Families in
        Late Medieval England," JIH 15 (1984), 111-129.

Nov. 17   The Cloister: The Alternate for Women (162 pp.)
    Medieval Women Writers, ed. Katharina Wilson (Athens, Ga.:1984),
        Heloise in pp. 90-108.
    Hrotsvit of Gandersheim pp. 114-135, Hildegard of Bingen and
        Elisabeth of Schonau, pp. 151-170, Clare of Assisi, pp. 242-5 in
        Petroff.
    Brenda Bolton, "Mulieres Sanctae" in Stuard, 141-158.
    *Penelope D. Johnson, "The Stereotype of the Naughty Nun: Sexual
        Scandal in Thirteenth-century Norman Monastic Communities."

Nov. 24   Courtly Love and Social Reality (96 pp.)
    Marie de France, pp. 64-89 in Katharina Wilson.
    Castelloza, pp. 131-152 in Katharina Wilson.
    Christine de Pizan, pp. 340-346 in Petroff.
    *John Benton, "Clio and Venus," in The Meaning of Courtly Love,
        ed. Francis Newman (Albany:1968), 19-42.
    *Herbert Moller, "The Social Causation of the Courtly Love Complex,"
        Comparative Studies in Society and History, 1 (1959), 137-63.

Dec. 1   The Mystical Route (261 pp.)
    Catherine of Siena, pp. 263-275 and Julian of Norwich, pp. 308-314 in
        Petroff.
    *Caroline Bynum, "Fast, Feast, and Flesh: The Religious Significance
        of Food to Medieval Women," Representations 11 (1985), 1-25.
    *Mary Mason, "The Other Voice: Autobiography of Women Writers," Auto-
        biography: Essays Theoretical and Critical ed. James Olney
        (Princeton:1980), 207-235.
    Rudolf Bell, Holy Anorexia (Chicago:1985).

Dec. 8   Women Active in Society (262 pp.)
    Christine de Pizan, The Book of the City of Ladies tr. Jeffrey
        Richards (N.Y.:1982).
    *"The Case of a Woman Doctor in Paris," The Portable Medieval Reader
        ed. James B. Ross and Mary McLaughlin (Harmondsworth:1977),
        635-40.

Dec. 15   The Constriction of the Late Middle Ages (76 pp.)
    Marie d"Oignies, Christina Mirabilis, Hadewijch pp. 179-200 and Na
        Prous Boneta pp. 284-290 and Marguerite Porete, pp. 294-8 in
        Petroff.
    *Diane Owen Hughes, "Earrings for Circumcision: Distinction and
        Purification in the Italian Renaissance City," Persons in Groups
        ed. Richard C. Trexler (Binghamton:1985), 155-177.
    *Leah Otis, "Prostitution and Repentance in Late Medieval
        Perpignan," Women of the Medieval World, ed. J. Kirshner & S.
        Wemple (1985), 137-160.

Winter vacation

Jan. 5   oral reports by Track B students

Jan. 12   oral reports by Track B students

SUPPLEMENTARY READING FOR THE COLLOQUIUM

I have added a supplemental reading list that is extremely idiosyncratic. It can be added to infinitely by looking through the bibliographies mentioned here as well as by using the bibliographies and footnotes from the works we are reading. The purpose of appending this list is to bring readily to your hand either very recent titles which may not yet appear in other lists or what are to my mind the best of the older studies which are truly deserving of note.

Important bibliographic tools:

*Dietrich, Sheila C., "An Introduction to Women in Anglo-Saxon Society (c. 600-1066)", in The Women of England, Interpretive Bibliographical Essays ed. Barbara Kanner (Hamden, Ct:1979), 32-56.
*Erickson, Carolly and Kathleen Casey. "Women in the Middle Ages: a Working Bibliography." Medieval Studies 37 (1975).
Frey, Linda, Marsha Frey, and Joanne Schneider. Women in Western Europe and History: A Select Chronological, Geographical, and Topical Bibliography from Antiquity to the French Revolution. Westport, CT: 1982.
*Kelly, Joan, et. at. Bibliography in the History of European Women. 5th ed. A Sarah Lawrence College Women's Studies Publication: 1982.
*Krueger, Roberta L., and E. Jane Burns. A Selective Bibliography of Criticism: Women in Medieval French Literature. Romance Notes 26 (1985), 375-390.

Bibliographic and Historiographic Essays:

Davis, Natalie. "Women's History in Transition: The European Case." Feminist Studies 3 (1976), 83-103.
Hartman, Mary and Lois Banner, ed. Clio's Consciousness Raised: New Perspectives on the History of Women. N.Y.: 1974.
Kelly, Joan. Women, History and Theory: The Essays of Joan Kelly. Chicago: 1984.

NOTE:

*All citations marked with an asterix are available in xerox both on reserve in Bobst and in the department. You may check out the departmental copies for a few hours only.
Be considerate of your fellow class members.
   All of the books on the reading list have been requested for reserve so that, for instance, you can get Jerome by looking under my name for a xerox of the letter, or by requesting the Select Letters in which the letter appears and which is also on reserve. Library books on reserve are usually under the author's or editor's name (but occasionally under the title). Be creative and persistent; the reading should be there somewhere. If you would rather not use the xeroxes, articles can be read in the original journals often bound and in the stacks, or in the edited collections.

General Bibliography:

Atkingon, Clarissa. Mystic and Pilgrim: The Book and the World of
     Margery Kempe. Ithaca: 1983.
Barstow, Anne. Married Priests and the Reforming Papacy: The
     Eleventh-century Debates. N.Y.: 1982.
Boyd, Catherine. A Cistercian Nunnery in Mediaeval Italy: The
     Story of Rifreddo in Saluzzo, 1220-1300. Cambridge: 1943.
Brooke, Christopher. "Marriage and Society in the Central Middle
     Ages" Marriage and Society: Studies in the Social History of
     Marriage. Ed. R. B. Outhwaite. London: 1981.
Bynum, Caroline. Jesus as Mother: Studies in the Spirituality of
     the High Middle Ages. Berkeley: 1982.
_____. Holy Feast and Holy Fast: The Religious
     Significance of Food to Medieval Women (Berkeley: 1987).
Dronke, Peter. Women Writers of the Middle Ages: A Critical Study
     of texts from Perpetua (+203) to Marguerite Porete (+1310).
     Cambridge, Eng.: 1984.
*Eckenstein, Lina. Women under Monasticism. Cambridge, Eng.:
     1896, reissued 1963.
Farmer, Sharon. "Persuasive Voices: Clerical Images of Medieval
     Wives," Speculum 61 (1986), 517-543.
Fell, Christine. Women in Anglo-Saxon England. Bloomington, Ind.:
     1984.
Flandrin, Jean-Louis. "Contraception, Marriage, and Sexual
     Relations in the Christian West." Biology of Man in History,
     ed. Robert Forster and Orest Ranum.
Glasser, Marc. "Marriage in Medieval Hagiography," Studies in
     Medieval and Renaissance History 4 (1981), 3-34.
Gazeau, R. "La clôture des moniales au XIIe siècle en France."
     Revue Mabillon 58 (1974).
Gold, Penny. The Lady and the Virgin: Image and Attitude, and
     Experience in 12th-Century France. Chicago: 1985.
Goodrich, Michael. "The Contours of Female Piety in Later Medieval
     Hagiography." Church History 50 (1981), 20-32.
Hanawalt, Barbara A. The Ties that Bound: Peasant Families in
     Medieval England. Oxford: 1986.
_____. ed. Women and Work in Preindustrial Europe
     (Bloomington: 1986).
Herlihy, David. Women in Medieval Society. Houston, TX: 1971.
_____. Medieval Households. Cambridge, MA.: 1985.
Howell, Martha C. Women, Production, and Patriarchy in Late
     Medieval Cities. Chicago: 1986.
Hughes, Diane. "Urban Growth and Family Structure in Medieval
     Genoa." Past and Present 66 (1975).
Hughes, Muriel. Women Healers in Medieval Life and Literature.
     Reissued Freeport, N.Y.: 1968.
Jordan, William. "Jews on Top: Women and the Availability of
     Consumption Loans in Northern France in the Mid-Thirteenth
     Century." Journal of Jewish Studies 29-30 (1978-9).
Klinck, Anne. "Anglo-Saxon Women and the Law." Journal of
     Medieval History 8 (1982).
Kraus, Henry. "Eve and Mary: Conflicting Images of Medieval
     Women." in The Living Theatre of Medieval Art. Bloomington:
     1967.

Labalme, Patricia A. Ed. Beyond Their Sex: Learned Women of the
    European Past (N.Y.: 1980).
Leclercq, Jean. "Medieval Feminine Monasticism: Reality versus
    Romantic Images." Benedictus: Studies in Honor of St. Benedict
    of Nursia. Ed. Rozanne Elder (1981).
Lucas, Angela. Women in the Middle Ages: Religion, Marriage and
    Letters. N.Y.: 1983.
McDonnell, Ernest. The Beguines and Beghards in Medieval Culture.
    New Brunswick, NJ: 1954.
McNamara, Jo Ann. A New Song: Celibate Women in the First Three
    Christian Centuries. N.Y.: 1983.
Macfarlane, Alan. Marriage and Love in England: Modes of
    Reproduction 1300-1840. London:
Milsom, S. F. C. "Inheritance by Women in the Twelfth and Early
    Thirteenth Centuries." On the Laws and Customs of England:
    Essays in Honor of Samuel E. Thorne. Chapel Hill: 1981.
Mitterauer, Michael & Reinhard Sieder. The European Family:
    Patriarchy to Partnership from the Middle Ages to the
    Present. Chicago: 1977.
Moller, Herbert. "The Meaning of Courtly Love," Journal of
    American Folklore 73 (1960), 39-52.
Moore, John "'Courtly Love': A Problem of Terminology," Journal of
    the History of Ideas 40 (1979), 621-632.
Newman, Barbara. Sister of Wisdom: St. Hildegard's Theology of
    the Feminine (Berkeley: 1987).
Nicholas, David. The Domestic Life of a Medieval City: Women,
    Children, and the Family in Fourteenth-Century Ghent. Lincoln,
    NE.: 1985.
Nichols, John and Lillian Shank, eds. Distant Echoes: Medieval
    Religious Women. Kalamazoo, MI: 1984.
Otis, Leah. Prostitution in Medieval Society: History of an Urban
    Institution in Languedoc. Chicago: 1985.
Parisse, Michel. Les nonnes au Moyen âge. LePuy: 1983.
_____ ed. Les religieuses en France au XIIIe siècle.
    Nancy: 1985.
Pernoud, Regine. Blanche of Castile. N.Y.: 1972.
_____. La femme au temps des cathédrales. Paris: 1980.
Petroff, Elizabeth. Consolation of the Blessed. N.Y.: 1979.
Plummer, John F. ed. Vox Feminae: Studies in Medieval Woman's Songs
    Kalamazoo, MI: 1981.
Power, Eileen. "The Position of Women." The Legacy of the Middle
    Ages. Ed. C. G. Crump and E. F. Jacob. Oxford: 1926.
    _____. Medieval English Nunneries 1275-1535. Cambridge, Eng.:
    1922.
Reilly, Bernard. The Kingdom of Leon-Castilla under Queen Urraca,
    1109-1126. Princeton: 1982.
Rose, Mary Beth ed. Women in the Middle Ages and the Renaissance:
    Literary and Historical Perspectives. Syracuse: 1986.
Searle, Eleanor. "Seigneurial Control of Women's Marriage: The
    Antecedents and Function of Merchet in England." Past and
    Present 82 (1979).
Shahar, Shulamith. The Fourth Estate: A History of Women in the
    Middle Ages. Tr. Chaya Galai. London: 1983.
Walker, Sue Sheridan. "Free Consent and Marriage of Feudal Wards
    in Medieval England." Journal of Medieval History 8 (1982).

Ward, Benedicta. "The Image of the Prostitute in the Middle Ages," _Monastic Studies_ 16 (1985).

Warner, Marina. _Joan of Arc: The Image of Female Heroism_. N.Y.: 1982.

_____. _Alone of all her Sex: The Myth and Cult of the Virgin Mary_. N.Y.: 1976.

Warren, Ann K. _Anchorites and their Patrons in Medieval England_. Berkeley: 1985.

Wilson-Kastner, Patricia et. al. eds. _A Lost Tradition: Women Writers of the Early Church._ Washington, D.C.: 1981.

Wood, Charles T. "Queens, Queans, and Kingship: An Inquiry into Theories of Royal Legitimacy in Late Medieval England and France." _Order and Innovation in the Middle Ages_. Ed. William C. Jordan, Bruce McNab, Teofilo F. Ruiz. Princeton: 1976.

PRINCETON UNIVERSITY

Department of History

Fall, 1983   N. Z. Davis
                                                           Preceptor: Laurie
                                                                       Nussdorfer

   History 348: Society and the Sexes in Early Modern Europe

Books and Readings

     The following books are available at the PUS:

          The Memoirs of Glückel of Hameln, tr. M. Lowenthal

          Alan Macfarlane, The Family Life of Ralph Josselin

          Alice Clark, Working Life of Women in the Seventeenth Century

          Mary Wollstonecraft, A Vindication of the Rights of Women

     In addition, the following book is recommended (course assignment will be
about 80 pages): Lillian Federman, Surpassing the Love of Men. All five of
these books will also be on reserve in Firestone in at least one copy.

     Beside these books, various other primary and secondary sources will be
used in the following forms:

          - Mimeographed readings, to be handed out in class

          - a Packet of Readings in two volumes, on reserve for our course
            in four copies   Call number: X HIST 348 PAC

          - a few individual books or photocopied readings on reserve in
            two or three copies. Call numbers given within

Papers and Exams: A paper no more than three pages at length analysing an
          assigned reading is due on Friday, Sept. 23 at 4 p.m. in the Davis In
          box in the History office. A second paper no more than five pages in
          length comparing two major readings is due on Friday, Oct. 21 at 4 p.m.
          in the Davis In box in the History Office. The specific assignments for
          these papers will be handed out well in advance. The final examination
          will be drawn primarily from Study Questions given out in class. It's
          possible that we'll decide to make part of the exam a position paper
          arguing for one of the historical stances toward women studied in the
          course.
Grading: Students will be assessed on their critical mastery of material
          presented at lecture and in readings and on their participation in
          the course. The grade will be apportioned roughly as follows: papers
          for first half of term, 40%; precepts, 20%; final, 40%.

Abbreviations used in the syllabus

     min -- mimeographed reading distributed in class

     Pack -- in Packet of Readings on reserve. Call number: X HIST 348 PAC
             Volume I or II

43

Fall, 1983   - 2 -   N. Z. Davis
History 348   Preceptor: Laurie
                                                     Nussdorfer

I. IMAGES OF MEN AND WOMEN: ASSUMPTIONS ABOUT SEXUAL TEMPERAMENT (weeks 1-2)

Medical sources on sexual temperament

Excerpts from Laurent Joubert, Aretaeus of Cappadox,
    "Trotula of Salerno", Louise Bourgeois and   mim
    Thomas Sydenham

Theological and literary sources on the nature of men and women

Excerpts from Thomas Aquinas, Jean Calvin, Christine de   mim
    Pisan and François Poullain de La Barre
Excerpt from J. Sprenger and H. Kramer, Malleus Maleficarum   Pack I
Excerpt from Maimonides, "The Menstruant"   mim

Patricia Crawford, "Attitudes to Menstruation in 17th-   X HIST 348 CRA
    Century England"   res

[Optional: If you wish to read further from Christine de Pisan,
           her City of Ladies is on reserve, PQ 1575 L 56 E5.
           Further on images of the sexes in Judaism, Judith
           Hauptman, "Images of Women in the Talmud," pack I.]

II. DEMOGRAPHY, SEX, LOVE, FAMILY, MARRIAGE, FRIENDSHIP, CHILDREARING
     (weeks 3-6)

Lawrence Stone, "The Rise of the Nuclear Family in Early Modern
    England". This article is also available in The Family in   Pack I
    History, on reserve, HQ 503.F318

N. Z. Davis, "Ghosts, Kin and Progeny: Some Features of Family   Pack I
    Life in Early Modern France"

Elizabeth Clinton, The Countess of Lincoln's Nursery   Pack I

Lucy Hutchinson, Memoirs of the Life of Colonel Hutchinson,
    read her Autobiographical fragment, description and
    character of her husband, pp. 1-53   res 1444.488.48 1885
                                                 vol. I
                                      1444.488.48.12
                                             vol. I

Jeanne du Laurens, The Genealogy of Messieurs du Laurens   mim

[Optional: If you wish to read a remarkable critique of the
           legal status of English wives, see [Anon.], The
           Hardships of the English Laws in relation to Wives
           (1735) in Packet I]

Jacques Du Val, excerpt from Treatise on Hermaphrodites   mim

Glückel of Hameln, The Memoirs of Glückel of Hameln (background   res
    on the Jews in early modern Europe can be found in Jacob   1580.165.428
    Katz, Tradition and Crisis, chs. 2, 6, 14, DS 112.K373.1971
    and in the article by Judith Hauptman in Pack I)

Fall 1983   N. Z. Davis
History 348   - 3 -   Preceptor: Laurie
                                                        Nussdorfer

II. Demography, sex, love, family, marriage, friendship, childrearing (cont.)

    Alan Macfarlane, The Family Life of Ralph Josselin, chs.   res 5515.4994
        2, 5-9, appendices A and B

    Solomon Maimon, An Autobiography, chs. 1-16, 22   res
        (read all if you can)   B3068.A32 1967

    Lillian Faderman, Surpassing the Love of Men, pp. 65-143 res
                                            HQ 75.5F331981b

    Eleanor Butler, excerpts from her diary describing her
        life with Sarah Ponsonby, from The Hamwood Papers
        of the Ladies of Llangollen(a study of the Ladies
        of Llangollen by Elizabeth Mavor is on reserve, if
        you wish to read further, 1446.23.625).

    Alan Bray, Homosexuality in Renaissance England, ch. 4   res
                                            HQ 76.3.G7B72
                                          and X HIST 348 BRA

III. "WOMEN'S WORK", PAID AND UNPAID (weeks 7-8)

    N. Z. Davis, "Women in the Crafts in 16th-Century Lyon," res - Davis
                                            Writings on Women
                                          X HIST 348 DAV

    Alice Clark, The Working Life of Women in the Seventeenth res
        Century   H D6137C59 1968

    Olwen Hufton, "Women and the Family Economy in Eighteenth Pack II
        Century France."

    Louise Bourgeois, excerpt from her Observations diverses   mim

    Joyce Irwin, "Anna Maria Van Schurman: From Feminism to   Pack II
        Pietism"

    Mary Astell, A Serious Proposal to the Ladies, pp. 1-43   res
                                          HQ 1 201.A8 1970
                                    and X HIST 348 AST
    François Fénélon, Fénélon on Education, pp. 1-14, 65-96   Pack II

IV. WOMEN IN RELIGIOUS MOVEMENTS (weeks 9-10)

    N. Z. Davis, "City Women and Religious Change," also   Pack II
        available as ch. 3 in Davis, Society and Culture
        in Early Modern France, 1512.286

    Witchcraft in Europe, ed. A. C. Kors and E. Peters, pp.   Pack II
        229-35, 266-71

    Marie Guyart, also known as Marie de L'Incarnation,   mim
        selected letters from Québec

IV. Women in Religious Movements (cont.)

    Keith Thomas, "Women in the Civil War Sects"   Pack II

    Margaret Fell Fox, Women's Speaking Justified   Pack II

    Hannah More, "On the Importance of Religion to the   Pack II
        Female Character"

V. WOMEN IN POLITICAL MOVEMENTS: THE BEGINNING OF POLITICAL
    FEMINISM (weeks 11-12)

    N. Z. Davis, "Men, Women and Violence"   res Davis,
                                                Writings on Women
                                              X HIST 348 DAV

    Request of Women for their Admission to the Estates   mim
        General

    Olympe de Gouges, Les Droits de Femme, translated excerpt mim

    Condorcet, "Condorcet's Plea for the Citizenship of   Pack II
        Women"

    Jane Abray, "Feminism in the French Revolution"   Pack II

    Darlene Levy, Women in Revolutionary Paris, pp. 158-71,   res. Levy
        205-12, 267-70   HQ1616.W65

    Mary Wollstonecraft, A Vindication of the Rights of Women res
                                              HQ1596W61 1975

Women and the Shaping of Early Modern Europe
Spring, 1980

Miriam Slater   Harold Garrett-Goodyear
Franklin Paterson Hall G6,   Library 637, MHC
   Hampshire College   538-2451 and, to leave
549 4600 x366 and, to leave   538-2377
   messages, x409   Wed. 1:15 - 4:15
Wed. 9:30 - 11:30

     "An inquiry into the place of women in families and
communities of Europe, 1300-1700, and into the institutions,
practices and ideas which determined or changed that place during
centuries of "Renaissance," "Reformation," "Expansion," and
"Centralization." Among the critical questions that we shall ask:
Are labels such as "Renaissance" appropriate to the experience of
women, or whould we reconsider the use of such categories in light
of how women lived and though during those centuries? What were
women expected to be and do in the aristocratic courts, peasant
households, and urban communities of western Europe, and what did
they do? How critical is the relationship between women and men
for an understanding of other relationships.-- between governors
and subjects, lords and tenants, priests and parishioners, or
employers and laborers -- during those centuries?"

     Books for Purchase from the College Bookstore, MHC

     Richard DeMolen, ed., The Meaning of the Renaissance and
          Reformation
     Renate Bridenthal and Claudia Koonz, eds., Becoming Visible,
          Women in European History
     Jack Goody et al., Family and Inheritance. Rural Society in
          Western Europe

     In addition to these books, packets of multilithed materials
will also be available for purchase through the History Department
Office, Library 205, MHC. Three packets will contain the articles
and selections identified by an asterisk in the schedule of
readings.

47

Schedule of Classes and Reading Assignments

Please note that class discussions and readings follow a
roughly chronological order: 14th and 15th centuries, Feb.11-
Mar. 31; and 17th century, Apr. 7-Apr.21. The first four classes
after the introductory meeting, however, are also intended as an
introduction to three major issues raised by the study of women's
experience in early modern Europe: political change,
centralizaiton of power and authority, and state-building;
Christian spirituality, the Protestant Reformation, and
secularization; and work, property, and the development of a
capitalist economy.

Feb. 4.   An introduction to participants in the course and issues
          to be discussed during it. Discussion of the case,
          "Everard c. Benyt" (1376) and a film by John Berger,
          "Ways of Seeing: Women."

Feb. 11. Power and authority in Late Medieval Europe

                  Background: Essays by Martines and De Lamar Jensen
                      DeMolen, The Meaning of the Renaissance and
                      Reformation

                  *David Herlihy, "Women in Medieval Society"
                  Joan Kelly-Gadol, "Did Women Have a Renaissance?"
                      in Bridenthal, Becoming Visible
                  *"Joan of Arc by Herself and Witnesses"

Feb.18.   Christian Spirituality and Morality

                  Background: Essay by Aston in DeMolen, Renaissance
                      and Reformation

                  *Elizabeth Petroff, "Aggression and Eroticism in the
                      Visions of Medieval Women Saints" Saints" and
                      "Paradox of Sanctity"
                  *Eleanor McLaughlin, "Women, Power and the Pursuit
                      of Holiness in Medieval Christianity"
                  *Selections from The Book of Margery Kempe
                  *Selections from Letters of Saint Catherine of Siena
                  *Christine de Pisan, The Book of the Duke of True
                      Lovers
                  *Saint Jerome on the evils of women (from Chaucer:
                      Sources and Backgrounds)

                  Suggested: JoAnn McNamara and Suzanne Wemple,
                      "Sanctity and Power: The Dual Pursuit of
                      Medieval Women" in Becoming Visible;
                      E. McLaughlin in Sexism and Religion (Library
                      Reserve); *"Form of Solemnization of Matrimony"
                      and "Scriptural Authorities" (Chaucer: Sources
                      and Backgrounds)

Feb.25.   Work, Property and the Family in Rural Europe

*Heidi Hartmann, "Capitalism and Patriarchy"
*F.D.H. DuBoulav, An Age of Ambition, chaps. on
    family and marriage
 Essays by Goody and Howell in Goody, Family and
    Inheritance
 *The Paston Correspondence, esp. letters 52-63,
    2-12, and 83-86, but read any of the letters
    to or from Agnes and Margaret Paston

 Suggested: "R.H. Hilton, "Women in the Village"

Mar. 3.   Work, Property and the Family in Urban Communities
          *Diane Owen Hughes, "Urban Growth and Family
              Structure in Medieval Genoa"
          *Frances and Joseph Gies, "A City Working Woman"
              and "Wargherita and Datini"
          *Selections from Alberti, The Fmily In Renaissance
              Florence
          *Selections from Francesco Barbaro, On Wifely
              Duties

Mar.10.   Religious Change and the Protestant Reformation in the
          16th Century.
          Background: Essays by Headley and Slavin in Demolen,
          Renissance and Reformation

          *Jane Douglass, "Women and the Continental
          Reformation"
          *Natalie Davis, "City Women and Religious Change"
          *Anne Askew, Examination
          *John Foxe, "History of Queen Catherine Parr"

          Suggested: Sharrin Wynties,"Women in the Reformation
          Era" in Becoming Visible; Chrisman, "Women and the
          Reformation in Strasberg" and Roelker "The Role of
          Noblemen in the French Reformation" in Archiv fur
          Reformationsgischite, 63 (1972), 143-195 (Literary
          Reserve)

Mar.24.   Rulers and Governance in 16th century Europe
          *Natalie Davis, "Women on Top"
          *Lawrence Stone, The Family, Sex and Marriage in
          England, selections from chaps.1,2,3, and 5.
          *Elizabeth I, Speeches of 1566, 1588, and 1601
          *Thomas Smith, De Republica Anglorum (excerpt at
          end of Elizabeth's speeches)
          *Catherine de Medici, Letter to Charles IX (1569)

          Suggested: Lawrence Stone, Crisis of the Aristocracy
          chap on, "Marriage"; Robert Harding, Anatomy of a
          Power Flite, chaps. 5 and 10 (both on Library
          Reserve)

Mar.31.   Law, Property, and the Family in the 16th century
          Essays by Le Roy Ladurie, Spufford, and Cooper in

Goody, Family and Inheritance
*Keith Thomas, "The Double Standard".
*A Gentlewoman's Diary (Lady Mildmay)
*Law Reports (Custom amd adultory, A Wife's Contract
and A Wife's abduction)
Thomas Wentworth to Christopher Danby, 1617
Suggested: *Darrel-Hungerford divorce Proceedings

Apr.7. Witches, Saints, and Religious Mobements of late 16th and
        early 17th century Europe.
        Background: Essay by Olin in DeMolen, Renaissance
        and Reformation.
        *Monter,"The Pedestal and the State: Courtly Love
        and Witchcraft" in Becoming Visible
        * Keith Thomas, "Women and the Civil War Sects"
        *Excerpt from Malleus Malafficarum
        *"Confessions of the Chelmsford Witches, 1566"
        *"Trial of Suzanne Gawdry"
        *Proceedings against Anne Hutchison
        *Bastardy Inquest, 1613

        Suggested: * Ben Barker-Benfield, "Anne Hutchison
        and the Puritan Attitude toward Women"

Apr.14. Women's Duties towards God and Family in the 17th century
        *L Stone, Family, Sex and Marriage, selections
        from chap 6
        *Jean-Louis Flandrin, Families in Former Times
        chap 3
        *Richard Vann, "Toward a New Lifestyle: Women in
        Preindustrial Capatalism" in Becoming Visible
        *Miriam Slater, "The Weightiest Business: Marriage
        in an upper-Gentry Family in Seventeenth-Century
        England"
        *Autobiography of Mrs Alice Thornton (Selection)

Apr.28. Discussions of independent Investigations, Reflections
        and (Tentative)n Generalizations.

                    Written Assignments

     Please regard all of your written work this semester as
contributions to the dialogue or conversation among participants
in this course. Write two short essays or memoranda (3pp or so)
in which you discuss, analytically and critically,either a
document or article assigned for one of our classes or an issue or
problem discussed during an earlier class. Use ditto masters to
prepare enough copies of each essay or memorandum for all members
·of the course. The first may be submitted during any class
meeting between 4 Feb, and 3Mar. The second, during any meeting
between Mar,10 and Apr,21.

     In addition to the common reading that we shall discuss in
class, you should explore other material on one of the several
topics or themes·pertinent to an understanding of the experience

                           50

of Women in late Medieval and early modern Europe, or to an
understanding of relationships between women and men in the
context of major social, religious, and political changes. Choose
one of the following topics for your investigation, or propose a
topic of your own devising.

> Marriage and the Family
> Custom. Law and State-Building
> Christian Spirituality, Religious Dissent, and
>   Reform Movements in the Church
> Humanist Studies and Educational Practices and
>   Institutions
> Medicine and Childbirth Practices
> Work (both Rural and Urban)
> Property and Inheritance
> Sexuality
> Women as Artists and Writers, and Women in Art and
>   Literature
> Debates over the Nature of Women

These topics are not mutually exclusive, and they are not very
precise in their present form. They may, however, suggest a
direction and give shape to your independent inquiry into "Women
and the Shaping of Early Modern Europe." By "independent" we do
not mean that you need to work in isolation; on the contrary, you
should think seriously about working with some of your colleagues
on a topic or a group of related topics, and you and your
colleagues may well wish to present results of your investigation
as a collective project. As a result of your inquiry, you may
decide to write an essay on your topic or some aspect of it, but
you may choose an alternative format for presenting the results of
your reading and thinking. Consider, for example, drawing up a
research proposal, in which you would set out goals for a
sustained and systematic investigation of the topic, identify and
discuss critically the sources that you might use and the existing
literature on the topic, and sketch out a tentative thesis. If
you should decide to work with other members of the class, you and
they might well prepare a study or research guide to your topics.
Such a guide might include an introductory essay that surveys
themes, issues, and problems relating to your topics, a selection
of original sources pertinent to the topics with explanatory
headnotes, and a bibliographical essay or annotated bibliography
that reviews critically the scholarly literature available to
students working on subject.

    You may find the following bibliographical or methodological
works useful for your investigations:

> Barbara Kanner, ed., The Women of England from Anglo-Saxon
>   Times to the Present. Interpretative Bibliographical
>   Essays.
> Berenice Carroll, ed., Liberating Women's History
> Joan Kelly-Gadol, "The Social Relation of the Sexes:
>   Methodological Implications of Women's History,"
>   Signs, Summer 1976, 809-823.

Carolyn C. Lougee, "Modern European History. Review
    Essay," _Signs_, Spring 1977, 628-650
Joan Kelly-Gadol, ed., _Bibliography in the History of_
    European Women
Natalie Davis, "'Women's History' in Transition: The
    European Case," _Feminist Studies_ 3, nos. 3-4 (1976),
    83-103

    Please note that Anne Edmonds, The Librarian of MHC, has
agreed to assist us in this course, and we can count on her for
guidance and advice in research. A copy of the bibliographical
projects completed by students in this course last spring will be
available on Library Reserve, if you wish to consult tham for
ideas about your own approach to this enterprise. We shall also
have the benefits of aid and counsel from Augusta Pipkin, who took
this course last spring and who will assist in directing it this
semester. Your research projects, whatever the form you give your
results, must be completed by _Monday, April 28_, in order that we
may discuss your discoveries (and frustrations in the project of
discovery) during our final class meetings.

    Students who took this course last spring, when it was
offered for the first time, were warned at the outset not to
expect a neat package of information or ideas and conclusions.
Women's experiences, activities and choices in history have not
been incorporated into textbooks or general syntheses of the early
modern world, and the objectives and methods of "women's history"
remain controversial and imprecise. Although the efforts of
students last year helped to refine and strengthen the course to
your advantage now, you should also regard your work and play in
this class as a step towards creating a course and, indeed,
towards creating a field of scholarship. Your final assignment,
due by the end of the exam period (may 15), will be a revised
syllabus for a course of this kind, in which you tell us what
changes in content, organization and objectives should be made,
and why they should be made.

Women in Pre-industrial Europe

History 219b   W & F 12:30-2:00
S. M. Stuard, Hall 107   X. 1068

This course will ask the question whether women's history follows the same course as men's over the long term in Western Civilization, paying particular attention to the 12th through the 17th centuries. There will be four text books:

Joan Kelly, Women, History and Theory
Hilda Smith, Reason's Disciples
Becoming Visible, ed. Bridenthal/Koonz/Stuard, 1987.
Ian MacLean, Renaissance Notion of Woman (optional)
Christina Larner, Religion and Witchcraft
Natalie Davis, The Return of Martin Guerre (optional)

Two suggested books, of which Haverford Bookstore has copies:

Margaret Bacon, Mothers of Feminism
Barbara Harawalt, Women and Work in Pre-industrial Europe.

There will be three written assignments:
    1st due before spring break. A critique of an assigned article.
    2nd due April 9th--to be assigned.
    3rd due exam week. A "found" woman. Question: may an age be
    understood through a woman's life as well as a man's?

W & F Jan 20 & 22 Introduction
    John Noonan, Contraception, Chap. I, xerox on reserve.
    Venerable Bede," Gregory the Great's Answer to the English Church,"
        xerox on reserve.
    Becoming Visible, Chaps. 2, 3, and 4.

W & F Jan. 27 & 29 Medieval heritage--likeness and difference
    S. Stuard, Women in Medieval Society, Introduction and David Herlihy
        "Land, Family and Women in The Middle Ages." Xerox.
    Elaine Pagels, The Gnostic Gospels, Chap. III, "God The Father/God The
        Mother," xerox on reserve.

W & F Feb 3 & 5--Change in the 12th and 13th century--gender
    Thomas Aquinas, Question 92 from the Summa Theologica.
    S. Stuard, "Dominion of Gender," Becoming Visible, 1987 ed. Chap. 6
    Betty Bandel, "English Chronicler's Attitude Toward Women,"   __.

W & F Feb. 10 & 12--Renaissance: The South, Ian MacLean, The Renaissance
        Notion of Woman, p. 1-46.
    Christian Klapische Zuber, "Childhood in Tuscany at the Beginning of
        the 15th C. pp. 94-116 in Women, Family and Ritual in Renaissance
        Italy.

53

W & F Feb. 17 & 19--Renaissance: The South, Ian MacLean, <u>The Renaissance</u>
    <u>Notion of Woman</u>, pp. 47-92.
Diane Owen Hughes, "Sumptuary Law and Social Relations in Renaissance
    Italy."
Joan Kelly, "Did Women Have a Renaissance?" Chap. 7 in <u>Becoming</u>
    <u>Visible</u>, 1987.

W & F Feb. 24 & 26--Renaissance: The North
Natalie Z. Davis, "Women on Top" in <u>Society and Culture in Early</u>
    <u>Modern France</u>, xerox on reserve.

W & F Mar 2 & 4--Women's Work in the Early Modern Economy
B. Hanawalt, <u>Women and Work in Pre-industrial Europe</u>, articles by
    Bennett, Howell, and Kowaleski.

W & F Mar. 16 & 18--Reformation
William Monter, "Protestant Wives, Catholic Saints and the Devil's
    Handmaid" Chap. 8 in <u>Becoming Visible</u>, 1987
Merry Wiesner, "Spinning Out Capital," Chap. 9 in <u>Becoming Visible</u>,
    Chap. 9.

W & F Mar. 23 & 25--Catholic Reformation
Joseph Grisar, "Many Ward, 1585-1645," xerox on reserve
Christine Larner, <u>Religion and Witchcraft</u>.

W & F Mar. 30 & Apr. 1--Witchcraft
Christina Larner, <u>Religion and Witchcraft</u>.
Febvre, Lucien, "Witchcraft: Nonsense or a Mental Revolution?
    xerox on reserve.

W & F Apr. 6 & 8--Infanticide
Deborah Symonds, "Infanticide and the Transformation of Scottish
    Agriculture," xerox on reserve.
"Eppie Morrie" hand-out in class.

W & F Apr. 13 & 15--17th Century Voices. Quakers and others.
Margaret Bacon, <u>Mothers of Feminism</u>, chap. 1-3, pp. 1-54 on the
    Quaker, Margaret Fell and her circle of women.
Olwen Hufton, "Women in History: Early Modern Period," <u>Past and</u>
    <u>Present</u> 101 (1983) xerox on reserve.
Hilda Smith, <u>Reason's Disciples</u>, Chaps. 1 and 2.

W & F Apr. 20 & 22--17th Century Voices--Midwives and others.
Hilda Smith, <u>Reason's Disciples</u>, Chap. 3, pp. 75-114.
Merry Weisner, "Wet Nurses" in B. Hanawalt, <u>Women and Work in</u>
    <u>Pre-industrial Europe</u>.

W & F Apr. 27 & 29--Conclusions
Elizabeth-Fox Genovese, "Women of the Enlightenment," Chap. 10
    <u>Becoming Visible</u>, 1987.
Hilda Smith, <u>Reason's Disciples</u> (remainder of book)

Women in Modern European Society and Politics

This course will explore the economic, social, cultural and political position of women in Britain, France and Germany from the late eighteenth century to the present. The course will explore the interaction of class and gender in different periods and national cultures. It will focus on women's work; sexuality, marriage and motherhood; and women's political activity.

The course meets Wednesday, 4:20-6:00. You are expected to do the reading before each class and to participate actively in class discussions. You will write either two 8-10 page analytic essays or one 18-20 page research paper.

All books are on reserve in Bobst. All articles are on reserve in Bobst and one copy is available in a box in the History Department 19 University Place, Rm. 400. (The material in the History Department may be taken out briefly   . Otherwise it is to be read only in the History Department.)

The following books have been ordered at the NYU Book Center:

Tilly, L. and Scott, J. Women, Work and Family

Taylor, Barbara. Eve and the New Jerusalem (Pantheon)

Davies, M. L. ed. Life As We Have Known It (Norton)

Weeks, Jeffrey. Sex, Politics and Society (Longman)

Walkowitz, Judith. Prostitution and Victorian Society (Cambridge)

Davies, M. L. ed. Maternity (Norton)

Smith, Bonnie. Ladies of the Leisure Class (Princeton)

Gissing, George. The Odd Women (Norton)

Fairbairns, Zoë. Benefits (Avon)

The Smith and Gissing books will not be in the bookstore until later in the term.

My office hours are Wednesday, 1:30 to 4:00 and by appointment. My office is 19 University Place, Rm. 409. 598-2447.

I. Jan. 25: Introduction

Part I: Women, Work and Family

II. Feb. 1: Women, Work and Industrial Capitalism

Tilly, L. and Scott, J. Women, Work and Family. entire.

Graves and White, "An Army of Redressers," International Labor and Working Class History, 1980.

III. Feb. 8: The Peculiarities of Women's Work and the Working-class Family

Davies, ed. Life As We Have Known It

Alexander, Sally, "Introduction" to Marianne Herzog, From Hand to Mouth

Davidoff, Leonore. "Mastered for Life: Servant and Wife in Victorian and Edwardian England," Journal of Social History, 7:4, Summer 1974.

Schlegel, Katharina, "Mistress and Servant in Nineteenth Century Hamburg," History Workshop Journal, Issue 15, Spring 1983, pp. 60-77.

Gamarnikow, Eva, "Sexual Division of Labour: the case of Nursing," in Kuhn, A. and Wolpe, A. Feminism and Materialism.

Bridenthal, Renata, "Beyond Kinder, Küche, Kirche: Weimar Women at Work," Central European History, 6, 1973, 148-66.

Part II: Women and Revolutionary Movements in the 19th Century

IV. Feb. 15 Women and Utopian Socialism

Taylor, Barbara. Eve and the New Jerusalem. entire.

V. Feb. 22 Women and French Revolutions

Hufton, Olwen, "Women in Revolution, 1789-96," Past and Present, 53, 1971.

Thomas, Edith. The Women Incendaries, Chapters 1, 2, 4, 5, 7, 3, 10-12, and pp. 223-30. (The library has two copies on reserve and there will be 2-3 copies in the department.)

Part III: Sexuality, Marriage and Motherhood

VI. Feb. 29: Toward a History of Sexuality

Weeks, Jeffrey, Sex, Politics and Society. entire.

VII. Mar. 7: The Politics of Prostitution

Walkowitz, Judith. Prostitution and Victorian Society. entire.

March 14 Spring Vacation.

VIII. Mar. 21: Marriage and Motherhood in the English Working Class

Davies, ed. Maternity.

Davin, Anna. "Imperialism and Motherhood," History Workshop Journal, Issue 5, Spring 1978, pp. 9-88.

Ross, Ellen, "'Fierce Questions and TAunts': Married Life in Working-class London, 1870-1914," Feminist Studies, 8, nr. 3, Fall 1982, pp. 575-602.

McLaren, Angus, "Women's Work and the Regulation of Family Size," History Workshop Journal, Issue 7, 1977, pp. 70-81.

Part IV: Bourgeois Women

IX. Mar. 28: The Dilemmas of Single Women
     Gissing, George. <u>The Odd Women</u>. entire.

X. Apr. 4: The Ambiguities of Domesticity

     Smith, Bonnie. <u>Ladies of the Leisure Class</u>. entire.

Part V: Women and Twentieth Century Politics

XI. Apr. 11: Women and Socialism

     Hartmann, Heidi. "The Unhappy Marriage of Marxism and Feminism:
Towards a More Progressive Union," in Lydia Sargent, ed. <u>Women and
Revolution</u>, pp. 1-42.

     Liddington, Jill and Norris, Jill. <u>One Hand Tied Behind Us.</u> excerpts
to be selected.

     Quartaert, Jean, "Feminist Tactics in German Social Democracy: A
Dilemma," <u>Internationale wissenschaftliche Korrespondenz zur Geschichte
der deutschen Arbeiterbewegung,</u> 13, 1977, pp. 48-65.

     Kaplan, Temma. "Quality of Life and Female Mass Movements in Turin,
St. Petersburg, and Barcelona, 1917-18."

XII. Apr. 18: Women and War

     Gilbert, Sandra. "Soldier's Heart: Literary Men, Literary Women
and the Great War," <u>Signs,</u> vol, 8, no. 3, 1983, pp. 422-50.

     Burnett, John, ed. <u>Annals of Labour</u>. autobiography of Rosina Whyatt,
munitions worker, pp. 105-30.

     Rupp, Leila, "I don't Call that <u>Volksgemeinschaft</u>," in Berkin, C.R.
and Lovett, C. M., <u>Women, War and Revolution</u>, pp. 37-54.

     Riley, Denise, "The Free Mothers: Pronatalism and Working
Mothers in Industry at the End of the Last War in Britain," <u>History
Workshop Journal</u>, nr. 11, Spring 1981, pp. 59-119.

XIII. April 25: Women and Fascism

     Bridenthal, Renate, "Class Struggle around the Hearth: Women and
Domestic Service in the Weimar Republic," in Dobkowski and Walliman, ed.
<u>Towards the Holocaust,</u> pp. 243-64.

     Mason, Tim. Women in Germany, 1925-40," <u>History Workshop Journal</u>,
Part I, Issue I, Spring 1976, pp. 74-133 and Part II, Issue 2, Autumn
1976, pp. 5-32.

     Koonz, Claudia. "Mothers in the Fatherland: Women in Nazi
Germany," in Bridenthal and Koonz, <u>Becoming Visible</u>, pp. 445-73.

Bock, Gisela, "Racism and Sexism in Nazi Germany: Motherhood, Compulsory Sterilization and the State," _Signs_, 8, 3, 1983, pp. 400-21.

XIV.   May 2 :   Women, the State and Feminism

Fairbairns, Zoë.   _Benefits._   entire.

Women's History Seminar

Fall Semester 1984   T. M. McBride

There are three major requirements for this course: 1/ discussion of
significant themes in women's history in which all members of the
seminar will participate (this requires both attendance and
attention at all meetings of the seminar);
2/ an oral presentation of one's own research done in the
course of the seminar (a 15-20 minute presentation will be given by
each member of the class during the month of November); and
3/ a major research paper (minimum of 25 pages) using primary
materials as well as historical commentaries on a topic
chosen by the individual seminar participant.
  Each of these requirements will be assessed in the final
evaluation of an individual for a course grade.

Schedule of assignments:

August 29   Introduction

September 5   Family Structure and Women's Lives
                       Articles by Hufton: "Women in Revolution", Stone:
                       "Rise of the Nuclear Family"

September 12   Work and the Industrial Revolution
                       Articles in Bridenthal/Koonz,eds. Becoming
                       Visible: Women in European History by Mary Lynn
                       McDougall, "Working-Class Women" and Theresa
                       McBride, "Long Road Home"
                       America's Working Women: pp. 85-166

September 19   Education, Marriage and Women's Roles
                       Victorian Women: pp. 71-80, 134-136, 140-151,
                       177-179, 242-244, 254-260;
                       Women, Family, and Freedom: pp. 156-169

September 26   Middle-Class Women and Victorian Respectability
                       Victorian Women: pp. 335-352, 368-384;
                       America's Working Women: pp. 232-235

October 3   Sexuality and its Consequences
                       Victorian Women: pages 195-196, 199-206,
                       238-242, 292-305, 408-428;
                       Women, Family and Freedom: pp. 299-302

October 10	Domestic Feminism Hayden, The Grand Domestic Revolution, up to page 179
October 17	Women and Organization America's Working Women: pp. 187-203; Women, Family, and Freedom: pp. 73-81, 97-100
October 24	The "Woman Question" Women, Family, and Freedom: pp. 32-33, 39-50, 92-97, 136-143, 247-258, 280-282, 286-291, 420-428
October 31	Women in War and Depression Lecture by Dr. Claudia Koonz, Assoc. Prof. of History Read articles by Bridenthal, "Women between the Two World Wars", and Koonz, "Mothers in the Fatherland", in Bridenthal/Koonz, Becoming Visible: Women in European History
November 7, 14, 28	Oral presentations
December 5	Conclusion

Atina Grossmann
Spring 1989

Women in Modern Europe 1750 - 1950

Catalogue Description: This course offers an introductory survey of
the experience of women and the meaning of gender in Europe from the
onset of industrialization through the post-World II period. Focusing
on England, France and Germany, it pays particular attention to the
social construction of sexuality, the definition of separate spheres
in the Victorian era, the role of the state and the medical profession
as well as industry in defining work and family roles, the impact of
war and revolution, and the development of the welfare state.

Course Description: The course is designed as an introduction to the
economic, social, cultural and political history of women in Europe
from the mid eighteenth to the mid twentieth century. It is also
intended to acquaint students with some of the most important
scholarship and historical controversies in this rapidly developing
field. We will focus on the historical development of issues that
animate debate today: the relative importance in feminist politics of
the drive for independence verus the need for protection; the emphasis
on equality with, or difference from, men in the conception of
womanhood; the struggle to negotiate work and family roles and to
control fertility; the shifting meanings of production and
reproduction in non-industrial, proto-industrial and industrial
situations; as well as the growing importance of state and medical
intervention in defining gender and family (most dramatically in
twentieth century Germany). Throughout the course, we will be
concerned to show that there is no such as thing as "the" European
woman, but varieties of women, existing in a variety of national,
class, regional, religious, ethnic, generational and family contexts.

An important goal of women's history is to examine how it exists
within history. This course therefore requires a good general
knowledge of modern European history; if necessary, students are urged
to consult a textbook such as Chambers, McGrew et al. The course aims
both to prepare students for further study in women's history and
women's studies, and to offer them a different perspective with which
to take other courses which do not focus primarily (or at all) on the
experience of women and the meaning of gender. It should function as
an integral part of both the European and women's history program.

The length of the reading list is mitigated by its variety;
several contemporary novels as well as a document collection and
samples of some of the most exciting scholarship in the field are
included. Students are required to write an in-class midterm
examination, a take-home final in essay form and a critical book
review of Mary Barton and Germinal comparing their depictions of the
impact of industrialization and collective political action on the
nineteenth century family economy.

Course Schedule and Readings

WEEK I.   Introduction. The World We Have Lost: The Family Economy in
           Transition.

Read: Tilly and Scott, Women, Work and Family, Pt.I.
           Olwen Hufton, "Women and the Family Economy in
           Eighteenth Century France," French Historical Studies 9
           (Spring 1975):1-22.
           Jean Quataert, "The Shaping of Women's Work in
           Manufacturing: Guilds, Households and the State in Central
           Europe, 1648-1870," American Historical Review 90 (1985):
           1122-1148.

WEEK II.   Dual Revolution: Social Change and the Woman Question.

Read: Elizabeth Fox-Genovese, "Women and the Enlightenment" in
           Becoming Visible
           Levy and Applewhite, "Women and Political Revolution in
           Paris" in Becoming Visible.
           Olwen Hufton, "Women in Revolution, 1789-1796," Past and
           Present 53: 90-108.
           Barbara Taylor, "The Men are as Bad as Their Masters,"
           Feminist Studies 5, no.1 (1979).

WEEK III. A New Working Class Family in Industrial Europe.

Read: Emile Zola, Germinal;
           Tilly and Scott, Part II.
           Laura Levine Frader, "Women in the Industrial Capitalist
           Economy," in Becoming Visible.

WEEK IV.   Victorian Sex/Gender System: Double Burden and Double
           Standard in Bourgeois Society.

Read: Elizabeth Gaskell, Mary Barton.
           John Gillis, "Servants, Sexual Relations and the Rise of
           Illegitimacy in London, 1801-1900," Feminist Studies 5
           (Spring 1979): 142-73.
           Karin Hausen, "Family and Role Division: The Polarization of
           Sexual Stereotypes in the 19th Century," in The German
           Family, ed. Evans and Lee, (1981).

WEEK V.   Fertility, Sexuality and the State: Motherhood, Birth
           Control and Prostitution.

Read: Jeffrey Weeks, Sex, Politics and Society, Ch. 1-6.
           Judith Walkowitz, "The Making of an Outcast Group" in The
           Widening Sphere: Women in Victorian England, ed. Martha
           Vicinus.

Judith Walkowitz, "Male Vice and Feminist Virtue: Feminism
and the Politics of Prostitution in Nineteenth Century
Britain," History Workshop 13.
Bell and Offen, Ch.1.

WEEK VI. Feminism and Socialism: Organized Motherhood and Class
Conflict.

Read: Bell and Offen, Ch.2-6.
Charles Sowerwine, "The Socialist Women's Movement from 1850
to 1940" in Becoming Visible
Karen Offen, "Liberty, Equality and Justice for Women: The
Theory and Practice of Feminism in Nineteenth-Century
Europe," in Becoming Visible.

WEEK VII. Eugenics and Maternalism at the End of The Century:
Science, Race, Class , Imperialism and Gender.

Read: Anna Davin, "Imperialism and Motherhood," History Workshop 5
(1978):9-66.
Ellen Ross, "Labour and Love: Rediscovering London's
Working-Class Mothers, 1870-1918," in Labour and Love:
Women's Experience of Home and Family 1850-1940 (Basil
Blackwell 1986), pp. 73-98.
Jeffrey Weeks, Sex, Politics and Society, Ch. 7-9.
Margaret Strobel, "Gender and Race in the Nineteenth
Century- and Twentieth Century British Empire," in
Becoming Viusible.

Week VIII. The end of Victorianism: World War I and the Russian
Revolution.

Read: Bell and Offen, Ch. 7,8.
Alexandra Kollontai, Love of Worker Bees
Temma Kaplan, "Women and Communal Strikes in the Crisis of
1917-1922" in Becoming Visible
Richard Stities, "Women and the Revolutionary Process in
Russia," in Becoming Visible.

Week IX. The New Woman and the Rationalization of Work and Sexuality
Between the Wars.

Read: Renate Bridenthal, "Something Old, Something New: Women
Between the Two World Wars" in Becoming Visible.
Bell and Offen, Ch. 9, 10.
Bridenthal and Koonz, "Beyond 'Kinder, Küche, Kirche: Weimar
Women in Politics and Work"; Amy Hackett, "Helene Stöcker:
Left-Wing Intellectual and Sex Reformer"; Meyer-
Renschhausen, "The Bremen Morality Scandal" all in When
Biology Became Destiny.
Jeffrey Weeks, Ch.10-11.

Week X.   The Great Depression: Economic crisis, Political
          Polarization and the Politics of Reproduction.

Read: Atina Grossmann, "Abortion and Economic Crisis"; Karin
          Hausen, "Mother's Day in the Weimar Republic"; Renate
          Bridenthal, "Professsional Housewives: Stepsisters of the
          Women's Movement," in When Biology Became Destiny.
          Bell and Offen, Ch.11, 365-374.
          Tilly and Scott, Part III.

Week XI. Modern Society in Crisis: Fascism, Political
          Polarization and Selective Population Policy.

Read: Claudia Koonz, "The Fascist Solution to the Woman Question
          in Italy and Germany" in Becoming Visible.
          Bell and Offen, Ch.11, 375-399.
          Claudia Koonz, "The Competition for Women's Lebensraum,
          1928-1934"; Annemarie Tröger, "The Creation of a Female
          Assembly Line Proletariat"; Gisela Bock, "Racism and Sexism
          in Nazi Germany: Motherhood,Compulsory Sterilization, and
          the State" in When Biology Became Destiny.

Week XII. World War II and the Holocaust: Gender Specificity on Home
          and Battle Front.

Read: Sybil Milton, "Women and the Holocaust"; "The Story of
          Ruth" and Katharina Jacob,"Comrade-Woman-Resistance Fighter"
          Story of Ruth," in When Biology Became Destiny.
          Bell and Offen, Ch.11, 12, pp. 400-420.
          Denise Riley, "The Free Mothers: Pronatalism and Working
          Mothers in Industry at the End of the Last War in Britain,"
          History Workshop Journal 11.

Week XIII. Work and Family in Post-World War II Europe: Women and the
          Welfare State.

Read: Elizabeth Wilson, Only Halfway to Paradise: Women in Postwar
          Britain 1945-1968.
          Jane Jenson, "Both Friend and Foe: Women and State Welfare"
          in Becoming Visible.

The following books are required:

Susan Bell and Karen Offen, eds., Women, the Family and Freedom, Vol.
Two, 1880-1950 (Stanford)

Bridenthal, Koonz, Stuard, Becoming Visible: Women in European
History, (Houghton Mifflin,second edition.)

Bridenthal, Grossmann, Kaplan, eds., When Biology Became Destiny:
Women in Weimar and Nazi Germany (Monthly Review)

Margery Davies, <u>Maternity: Letters From Working Women</u> (Norton)

Elisabeth Gaskell, <u>Mary Barton</u>

Alexandra Kollontai, <u>Love of Worker Bees</u> (Academy)

Louise Tilly and Joan Scott, <u>Women, Work and Family</u>, (Methuen, 1988, revised edition.)

Jeffrey Weeks, <u>Sex, Politics and Society: The Regulation of Sexuality Since 1800.</u>

Elizabeth Wilson, <u>Only Halfway to Paradise:Women in Postwar Britain 1945-1968</u> (Tavistock)

Emile Zola, <u>Germinal</u> (Penguin)

Required articles will be available for purchase in a packet.

Students will also screen several films throughout the semester, including "Bed and Sofa," (USSR,1927); "Mädchen in Uniform" (Germany 1931) and "All Quiet on the Western Front." (United States, 1930).

Seminar in Women's History — 544

Spring 1987   Office: Mesa Vista 2081
Prof. Jane Slaughter

I.   REQUIRED READINGS

     Judith Friedlander, Blanche Wiesen Cook, Alice Kessler-Harris
     and Carroll Smith-Rosenberg (eds.), Women in Culture and
     Politics: A Century of Change (Indiana University Press,
     1986) available at Full Circle Books

     Additional articles for weekly readings placed on reserve in
     library

II. STRUCTURE OF THE SEMINAR

     Seminar material will be organized topically on a weekly
     basis; for each topic assigned readings will reflect the
     variety of subject matter and methodology in the field.
     The first half of each class session will be spent in dis-
     cussion of required readings; the second half will be
     devoted to oral critical reviews by class members of
     longer works related to the topic of the week (selections
     to be made from list of suggested readings which will be
     distributed).

III. SEMINAR REQUIREMENTS

     A. Oral critical reviews: each student will present three
        critical reviews (c. 15 min.) of longer works related to
        the subject of the week. At the time of the oral review
        a brief written summary of the review (2 typed pages)
        will be handed in to me.

     B. Research Project: Women's autobiographies, diaries and
        collected writings; each student will select a woman's
        autobiography, diary, etc. and use it for the focus of a
        research paper. By adding other available primary
        materials and information from secondary works dealing
        with the time period in which the woman lived you will
        assess (a) the usefulness of the autobiography, diary,
        etc. to the study of women's history, and (b) attempt
        to determine where the particular woman "fits" in the
        historical epoch in which she lived.

        Papers should be 15-20 typed pages and are due the last
        class meeting of the semester.

        Specific instructions for both of the above will be
        forthcoming.

66

C. Attendance at all class sessions is naturally expected. Should some emergency interfere with your schedule you must notify me prior to the class time.

Seminar in Women's History - 544

Spring 1987
Prof. Jane Slaughter
Office: Mesa Vista 2981

WEEKLY TOPICS AND READINGS

** (A copy on reserve by author's name and article title)

Jan. 21 Introduction

28 Reproduction: Marriage, Fertility and Family (I)

** Nancy Folbre, "Of Patriarchy Born: The Political Economy of Fertility Decisions," (from _Feminist Studies_, 9:2 Summer 1983)

** E.A. Wrigley, "The Growth of Population in 18th Century England," (from _Past and Present_ 98 February 1983)

** Lawrence Stone, "Family History in the 1980's," (from _Journal of Interdisciplinary History_ 12:1 Summer 1981)

Feb. 4 Reproduction (II)

Diana Gittins, "Between the Devil and the Deep Blue Sea," in J. Friedlander, et.al. (eds.), _Women in Culture and Politics_

** Heidi Hartmann, "The Family as the Locus of Gender, Class and Political Struggle," (from _Signs_ Spring 1981)

Nancy Tomes, "A Torrent of Abuse: Crimes of Violence Between Working Class Men and Women in London, 1840-75," _Journal of Social History_ 11:3 (Spring 1978)

11 Women and Work (I)

Alice Kessler-Harris, "Independence and Virtue in the Lives of Wage-Earning Women: The United States, 1870-1930," in Friedlander

Sonya Rose, "Gender at Work: Sex, Class and Industrial Capitalism," _History Workshop Journal_ 21 (Spring 1986)

Karen Anderson, "Last Hired, First Fired: Black Women Workers in W W II," _Journal of American History_ 69 (June 1982)

18 Women and Work (II)

Susan B. Carter and Mark Prus, "The Labor Market and the American High School Girl, 1890-1928," _Journal of Economic History_ 42:1 (March 1982)

Mary E. Cookingham, "Combining Marriage, Motherhood and Jobs Before World War II: Women College Graduates, Classes of 1905-35," _Journal of Family History_ (Summer 1984)

Claudia Goldin, "The Changing Economic Role of Women: A Quantitative Approach," _Journal of Interdisciplinary_

History 13:4 (Spring 1983)

25 Women's Community and Culture

Virginia Drachman, "Female Solidarity and Professional Suc-
    cess: The Dilemmas of Women Doctors in Late 19th C.
    America," <u>Journal of Social History</u> 15:4 (1982)
Martha Vicinus,"One Life to Stand Beside Me: Emotional
    Conflicts in First-Generation College Women in England,"
    <u>Feminist Studies</u> 8:3 (Fall 1982)
** Mary P. Ryan, "The Power of Women Networks," (from Judith
    Walkowitz, et.al. (eds.), <u>Sex and Class in Women's</u>
    <u>History</u>

Mar. 4 Private and Public Meet

Rayna Rapp and Ellen Ross, "The 1920's: Feminism, Consumer-
    ism, and Political Backlash in the United States," in
    Friedlander, et.al.
Estelle Freedman, " Separatism as Strategy: Female Institu-
    tion Building and American Feminism, 1870-1930,"
    <u>Feminist Studies</u> 5:3 (Fall 1979)
Kathryn Kish Sklar, "Hull House in the 1890's: A Community
    of Women Reformers," <u>Signs</u> 10:4 (1985)

10 Private and Public Meet (II)

Anne-Marie Sohn, "Catholic Women and Political Affairs," in
    Friedlander, et.al.
Claudia Koonz, "Some Political Implications of Separatism:
    German Women Between Democracy and Nazism," in
    Friedlander,et.al.
Judith R. Walkowitz, "The Politics of Prostitution," <u>Signs</u>
    6:1 (Autumn 1980)

SPRING BREAK

25 Women and the World of Public Politics (I)

Paula Baker, "The Domestication of Politics: Women and
    American Political Society," <u>American Historical Review</u>
    89:3 (June 1984)
Elinor Lerner, "Family Structure, Occupation Patterns and
    Support for Women's Suffrage," in Friedlander, et.al.
Nancy Cott, "Feminist Politics in the 1920's: The National
    Woman's Party," <u>Journal of American History</u> 71:1
    (June 1984)

Apr. 1 Women and the World of Public Politics (II)

Francoise Basch, "The Socialist Party of America, The Woman
    Question, and Theresa Serber Malkiel," in Friedlander
Blanche Wiesen Cook, "Feminism, Socialism and Sexual Free-
    dom: The work and Legacy of Crystal Eastman and

69

Alexandra Kollontai," in Friedlander
Maxine Molyneux, "Mobilization Without Emancipation?
    Women's Interests, the State and Revolution in Nicara-
    gua," Feminist Studies 11:2 (Summer 1985)

8   Women of Color (I)

    Suzanne Lebsock, "Free Black Women and the Question of
        Matriarchy: Petersburg, Virginia, 1784-1820," and
    Jacqueline Jones, "My Mother Was Much of a Woman: Black
        Women, Work and the Family Under Slavery," in Feminist
        Studies 8:2 (Summer 1982)
    M. Palmer, "White Women/Black Women: The Dualism of Female
        Identity," Feminist Studies 9:1 (Spring 1983)

15 Women of Color (II)

    Gisela Bock, "No Children at Any Cost: Perspectives on
        Compulsory Sterilization, Sexism and Racism in Nazi
        Germany," in Friedlander
    Mario T. Garcia, " The Chicana in American History: The
        Mexican Women of El Paso, 1880-1920," Pacific Histor-
        ical Review 49:2 (1980)
    Richard Griswold del Castillo, "Mexican American Families,
        1910-1945," Chapter 7 in La Familia by same author

22 Women and the Influence of Institutions

    Atina Grossman, "Girlkultur or Thoroughly Rationalized
        Female: A New Woman in Weimar Germany," in Friedlander
    Maureen Honey, "The 'Womanpower' Campaign: Advertising and
        Recruitment Propaganda During World War II," Frontiers
        6: 1/2 (1981)
    Catherine Scholten, "On the Importance of the Obstetrik Art:
        Changing Customs of Childbirth in America," William
        and Mary Quarterly 34:3 (July 1977)

29 The History of Sexuality (I)

    Francoise Ducrocq, "From Poor Law to Jungle Law: Sexual
        Relations and Marital Strategies (London, 1850-1870) in
        Friedlander
    Annemarie Troger, "Between Rape and Prostitution: Survival
        Strategies and Chances of Emancipation in Berlin," in
        Friedlander
** Kathy Peiss, " 'Charity Girls' and City Pleasures: Histori-
        cal Notes on Working Class Sexuality, 1880-1920," (from
        Ann Snitow, et.al. (Eds.) Powers of Desire

May 6   The History of Sexuality (II)

    George Mosse,"Nationalism and Respectability: Normal and
        Abnormal Sexuality in the 19th Century," Journal of
        Contemporary History 17:2 (April 1982)

Evelyn Blackwood, "Sexuality and Gender in Certain Native
    American Tribes: The Case of Cross-gender Females,"
    and
Estelle Freedman, et.al. "Introduction" and "Forum: The
    Feminist Sexuality Debates," in <u>Signs</u> 10:1 (Autumn 1984)

WOMEN'S HISTORY COLLOQUIUM

History 394E
Spring, 1983
Wednesday evenings, 7:00-9:30
CW 312

Deborah Hertz
LT 715
X 2503
Office Hours:
Tues. 8-9:30 a.m.
Thurs. 11:30-1:00

Course Description: In this seminar we aim to accomplish three tasks: make explicit the implicit methodological assumptions of some recent women's history; learn the basic tools of the demographic, economic, and anthrological study of women; evalute the literature on women and the industrialization process in Europe. What female behavior contributed to the modernization process in Western Europe between 1750 and 1900? How were women's lives effected by this most fundamental of transformations? Answers to these questions rest not just on facts, but on arrangement of these facts using theories and methods. This seminar will help us learn and evaluate how the facts, the theories, and the methods do and should fit together.

Class Texts: All texts (and other assigned readings) have been placed on reserve.

Burke, P., Sociology and History
McLennan, G., Marxism and The Methodology of History
Whyte, M., Status of Women in Preindustrial Societies
Wrigley, E., Population and History
Nieme, B. & Lloyd, C., The Economics of Sex Differentials
Scott, J. & Tilly, L., Women Work and Family
Rotberg & Rabb, Marriage and Fertility
Pinchbeck, I., Women Workers and the Industrial Revolution

Student Requirements: The seminar will meet once weekly for discussion of books read by all and for discussion of book reviews written by members of the seminar. Each student will be required to write three 6-page, double-spaced book reviews. One review should be devoted to a methodological or interdisciplinary topic discussed in the first or second section of the course. Two reviews should be devoted to the historical topics discussed in the third part of the course.

Books chosen for review may not be class texts. A bibliography of relevant books and articles will be distributed on the first day of class, and titles may of course be selected from other sources. Four related articles may be substituted for one book. Students who review a book in a foreign language will only be required to write two reviews.

The reviews will be due in class the week before that topic is to be discussed in class. Reviews addressing topics discussed before February 16 will be due on February 16. Each student's three topics, (but not their book choices) will be declared at the second class session. Each student will provide copies of their review for other members of the seminar. Those persons whose reviews will be discussed at a particular session will be responsible for helping to lead the discussion on that evening. Unless there is a medical or familial emergency, and approval is requested two full days before the due date, no late book reviews will be accepted. Reviews with excessive misspellings or typographical errors will be returned for rewriting.

Each review will be worth a maximum of 25 points, and a maximum of 25 points will be awarded for contribution to class discussion.

While attendance will not be recorded, everyone is expected to keep up with the reading, come to class regularly, and participate in the discussions.

Class Schedule

January 19:   Introduction

              Methodology in the History of Women

January 26:   The Philosophy of History

              Read: R. F. Atkinson, Knowledge and Explanation in History
                    Chapters three through six.

                    Gregor McLennan, Marxism and the Methodologies of
                    History, Chapter four.

              Student topics declared.

February 2:   Marxism

              Read: McLennan, Chapters one, two, and three
                    Adam Schaff, Marxism and the Human Individual,
                    Chapters one and two.

              Reviews:

              INTERDISCIPLINARY TECHNIQUES

February 9:   Sociology

              Read: Peter Burke, Sociology and History, all.

              Reviews:

February 16: Social History and the Annales Tradition

              Read: McLennan, Chapters six and seven
                    J. H. Hexter, "Fernand Braudel," Journal of Modern
                    History 44 (1972), 480-539

                    Peter Burke, "Reflections on the Historical Revolution
                    in France;" Eric J. Hobsbawm, "Comments," and "Discus-
                    sion" in Review 1 (1978), 147-164.

                    E. Fox-Genovese and E. Genovese, "The Political Crisis
                    of Social History," Journal of Social History 10
                    (1976), 205-220.

              Reviews:

February 23: Anthropology

              Read: Martin Whyte, The Status of Women in Preindustrial
                    Societies, Chapters one through seven.

              Reviews:

March 2:   Demography

            Read: E. A. Wrigley, Population and History, Chapters 1-5

            Reviews:

March 9:   Economics

            Read: C. Lloyd and B. Niemi, The Economics of Sex Differentials.
            Chapters one through four.

            Reviews:

WOMEN AND INDUSTRIALIZATION IN EUROPE: HISTORICAL WORKS

March 16:   The Early Industrial Period, 1600-1750

            Read: Alic Clark, The Working Life of Women in the Seventeenth
            Century, all

            Reviews:

March 23:   The Industrial Revolution

            Read: Ivy Pinchbeck, Women Workers and the Industrial Revolution
            Chapters

            Reviews:

March 30:   NO CLASS: HOLIDAY

April 6:   Capitalism and Sex

            Read: Rotberg and Rabb, eds., Marriage and Fertility,
            articles by Shorter, Tilly, Cohen and Scott, Fairchilds,
            Lee, Flandrin.

            Reviews:

April 13:   Integrating Work and Fertility

            Read: Louise Tilly anddJoan Scott, Women, Work and Families,
            all.

            Reviews:

April 20:   Kin Ties in the Urbanization Process

            Read: Michael Anderson, Family Structure in Nineteenth Century
            Lancashire, all

            Reviews:

April 27:   Household Formation and Family Structure in Four English
            Villages.

            Read: David Levine, Family Formation in an Age of Nascent
                  Capitalism, all.

            Reviews:

May 4:   What Have We Learned?

            Read: Carl Degler, "Women and the Family," in Michael Kammen,
                  ed., The Past Before Us, 308-326.

            "Recent United States Scholarship on the History of
            Women," AHA Pamphlet.

            Lawrence Stone, "Family History in the 1980s,"
            Journal of Interdisciplinary History 12 (1981), 51-88.

HIST 345.051   WOMEN AND SOCIETY IN VICTORIAN ENGLAND   Fall 1984

Prof. Dorothy O. Helly
History Department   **Course Requirements**
Room 1519W
Hours: **By appointment:**   Midterm Examination   30% Grade
          Tues/Thurs 4-5:30   Final Examination   30% Grade
          Other times as needed   Research Paper   25% Grade
                                  Discussion Leader   15% Grade
Phone: 772-5546 (772-5680 Afternoons, except Tues.)

Texts (all are paperbacks and available at the HC Bookstore)

Burstyn, Joan N., _Victorian Education and the Ideal of Womanhood_
    New Brunswick: Rutgers University Press, 1984)

Mill, John Stuart and Harriet Taylor Mill, _Essays on Sex
    Equality,_ ed. Alice Rossi (Chicago: Chicago University
    Press, 1972)

Murray, Janet, ed., _Strong-Minded Women and Other Lost Voices
    from Nineteenth-Century England_ (New York: Pantheon, 1982)

Showalter, Elaine, _A Literature of Their Own_ (Princeton:
    Princeton University Press, 1977)

Vicinus, Martha, ed., _Suffer and Be Still: Women in the Victorian
    Age_ (Bloomington: Indiana University Press, 1973)

Vicinus, Martha, ed., _A Widening Sphere: Changing Roles of
    Victorian Women_ (Bloomington: Indiana Univ. Press, 1977)

ASSIGNMENTS   (R)=Library Reserve
                         (HO)=Class handout; to be returned

Sep 6   Introduction

Sep 11   TOPIC 1.   WOMEN AND SOCIETY: Cultural Assumptions,
    13   Economic and Demographic Realities,
                      Literary Perspectives, and Course Themes

    (HO) Sherry B. Ortner, "Is Female to Male as Nature is to
             Culture?" in M. Rosaldo and L. Lamphere, _Woman,
             Culture and Society,_ 67-88.
    (HO) Eric Richards, "Women in the British Economy since
             about 1700," _History_ (October 1974), 337-357.
    (HO) Sheila Ryan Johansson, "Demographic Contributions to
             the History of Victorian Women," in _The Women of
             England,_ ed. Barbara Kanner, 259-295.
    (HO) Patricia Otto Klaus, "Women in the Mirror: Using Novels
             to Study Victorian Women," in _The Women of England,_
             296-344.
         Murray, _Strong-Minded Women,_ 3-16
         Burstyn, _Victorian Education,_ ch. 1

Sep 18   TOPIC 2.   PATRIARCHAL ATTITUDES: Woman's Nature,
    20   Women's Roles

Murray, Strong-Minded Women, 17-47, 75-88, 95-118,
    204-210
Burstyn, Victorian Education, ch. 2
(HO) Catherine Hall, "The Early Formation of Victorian
    Domestic Ideology," in Fit Work for Women, ed.
    Sandra Durman, 15-32.
 (R) Patricia Branca, "Image and Reality, The Myth of the
    Idle Victorian Woman," in Clio's Consciousness
    Raised, ed. Hartman and Banner, 179-191.
Elaine and English Showalter, "Victorian Women and
    Menstruation," in Suffer and Be Still, ed.
    Vicinus, 38-44.
Helene E. Roberts, "Marriage, Redundancy or Sin: The
    Painter's View of Women in the First Twenty-five
    Years of Victoria's Reign," Suffer and Be Still,
    45-76.
Jill Conway, "Stereotypes of Femininity in a Theory of
    Sexual Evolution," Suffer and Be Still, 140-154.
Sheila Ryan Johansson, "Sex and Death in Victorian
    England: An Examination of Age-and Sex-Specific
    Death Rates, 1840-1910," in A Widening Sphere,
    ed. Vicinus, 163-181.

Sep 25   TOPIC 3.   VICTORIAN LITERATURE: Women as Subjects,
Oct 2   Women as Writers

Murray, Strong-Minded Women, 89-90, 149-159, 291-294.
Sally Mitchell, "The Forgotten Woman of the Period:
    Penny Weekly Family Magazines of the 1840's and
    1850's,"A Widening Sphere, 29-51.
Carol Christ, "Victorian Masculinity and the Angel in
    the House,"A Widening Sphere, 146-162.
Elaine Showalter,A Literature of Their Own, chs. 1-3.

Oct 4   TOPIC 4.   WOMAN'S NATURE, WOMEN'S ROLES: A Feminist
    9   Perspective

John Stuart Mill and Harriet Taylor Mill, Essays on
    Sex Equality, ed. Rossi, 3-63, 67-87, 125-241.

Oct 11   TOPIC 5.   VICTORIAN WOMEN UNDER THE LAW: Marriage,
                        Divorce, Property, and Child Custody

Murray, Strong-Minded Women, 118-149.
Lee Holcombe, "Victorian Wives and Property: Reform of
    the Married Women's Property Law, 1857-1882," A
    Widening Sphere, 3-28.

Oct 16   TOPIC 6.   INDUSTRIALIZATION: Working-Class Women and
    18   Women's Work

        Murray, Strong-Minded Women, 326-337, 339-346, 350-356,
            362-383.
    (R) Theresa M. McBride, "The Long Road Home: Women's Work
            and Industrialization," Becoming Visible, 280-295.
   (HO) Sally Alexander, "Women's Work in Nineteenth-Century
            London: A Study of the Years 1820-1850," in The
            Rights and Wrongs of Women, eds. Juliet Mitchell
            and Ann Oakley, 59-111.
    (R) R. Burr-Litchfield, "The Family and the Mill: Cotton
            Mill Work, Family Work Patterns and Fertility in
            Mid-Victorian Stockport," The Victorian Family,
            ed. Anthony S. Wohl, 180-196.
    (R) Anthony S. Wohl, "Sex and the Single Room: Incest
            among the Victorian Working Classes," The
            Victorian Family, ed. Wohl, 197-216.
    (R) Theresa McBride, "'As the Twig is Bent': the Victorian
            Nanny," The Victorian Family, ed. Wohl, 44-58.
   (HO) Leonore Davidoff, "Mastered for Life," Journal of
            Social History (Summer 1974), 406-428.

Oct 23   TOPIC 7.   WOMEN AND VICTORIAN PHILANTHROPY: Workhouse
                         Visiting and Juvenile Delinquency

        Murray, Strong-Minded Women, 283-288.
   (HO) Anne Summers, "A Home from Home--Women's Philanthropic
            Work in the Nineteenth Century," in Fit Work
            for Women, 33-62.
   (HO) Harriet Warm Schupf, "Single Women and Social Reform
            in Mid-Nineteenth Century England: The Case of
            Mary Carpenter," Victorian Studies (March 1974),
            301-317.

Oct 25   **MID-TERM EXAMINATION**

Oct 30   TOPIC 8.   "SURPLUS WOMEN": Victorian Women Begin to
Nov 1   Mobilize--Employment, Emigration, Education,
                         and Nursing

        Murray, Strong-Minded Women, 48-61, 90-93, 159-166,
            193-204, 211-213, 230-236, 259-264, 266-283,
            288-289, 294-306, 318-325.
        Burstyn, Victorian Education, chs. 3 and 4.
    (R) Gorham, Deborah, The Victorian Girl and the Feminine
            Ideal, ch. 2.
        M. Jeanne Peterson, "The Victorian Governess: Status
            Incongruence in Family and Society," Suffer and
            Be Still, 3-19.
        A. James Hammerton, "Feminism and Female Emigration,
            1861-1886," A Widening Sphere, 52-71.
        Showalter, A Literature of Their Own, 153-181.

Nov 8   TOPIC 9.   EDUCATION: The Struggle to enter the
     13   University and the Professions and
                          the Legal and Judicial Response

          Murray, Strong-Minded Women, 213-230, 236-245, 264-266,
               306-318.
          Burstyn, Victorian Education, chs. 5,6,7,8 and 9.
          Rita McWilliams-Tullberg, "Women and Degrees at
               Cambridge University, 1862-1897," A Widening
               Sphere, 117-145.
     (R) Albie Sachs and Joan Hoff Wilson, Women and the Law:
               Male Beliefs and Legal Bias, 14-22, 53-66.

Nov 15   TOPIC 10.   TOWARD THE VOTE: The Constitutional
                          Suffrage Movement

    (HO) Andrew Rosen, Rise Up, Women! The Militant Campaign of
               the Women's Social and Political Union, 1903-1914, 1-13.
    (HO) Barbara Caine, "Feminism, Suffrage, and the 19th
               Century English Women's Movement," Women's Studies
               International Forum, 5:6 (1982), 537-550.
     (R) Brian Harrison, Separate Spheres: The Opposition to
               Women's Suffrage in Britain, 55-90.

Nov 20   TOPIC 11.   PROSTITUTION AND VENEREAL DISEASE: The
     27   Women's Campaign against the Contagious
                          Diseases Acts

          Murray, Strong-Minded Women, 385-437.
     (R) Judith R. Walkowitz, Prostitution and Victorian
               Society: Women, Class, and the State, 13-65,
               69-147, 246-256.
          Judith R. Walkowitz, "The Making of an Outcast Group:
               Prostitutes and Working Women in Nineteenth-
               Century Plymouth and Southampton," A Widening
               Sphere, 72-93.

Nov 29   TOPIC 12.   REPRODUCTIVE RIGHTS: Contraception and
                          Abortion Across the Classes

     (R) Patricia Branca, Silent Sisterhood, 114-141, 144-153.
    (HO) Angus McLaren, Birth Control in Nineteenth-Century
               England, 197-211, 215-252.

Dec 4   TOPIC 13.   "SOCIETY": The Rituals of Class

          Murray, Strong-Minded Women, 62-73.
     (R) Leonore Davidoff, The Best Circles: Society
               Etiquette, and the Season, 20-36, 51-57, 67,
               71-84, 90-100.
    (HO) Helene Roberts, "The Exquisite Slave: The Role of
               Clothes in the Making of the Victorian Woman,"
               Signs (Spring 1977), 554-569.
    (HO) David Kunzle, "Dress Reform as Antifeminism: A Response
               to Helene E. Roberts...," Ibid., 570-579.

Dec 6   TOPIC 14. CHARITY, SOCIAL WORK, AND DOMESTIC DUTIES:
    11   Middle-class Work and Working-class
                    Realities

         Murray, Strong-Minded Women, 167-192, 289-291,
              246-255, 338-339 346-350, 357-362.
     (HO) F.K. Prochaska, Women and Philanthropy in 19th Century
              England, 97-137.
      (R) Carol Dyhouse, Girls Growing Up in Late Victorian and
              Edwardian England, 79-114.
      (R) Laura Oren, "The Welfare of Women in Laboring
              Families: England 1860-1950," Clio's Consciousness
              Raised, 226-244.

Dec 13   TOPIC 17. END OF AN ERA: Changes in Sexual Ideology
                    and the Beginning of Militant Suffrage.

         F. Barry Smith, "Sexuality in Britain, 1800-1900: Some
              Suggested Revisions," A Widening Sphere, 182-198.
         Showalter, A Literature of Their Own, 182-215.
     (HO) Andrew Rosen, Rise Up, Women!, 24-48, 272-275.
     (HO) Jill Liddington, "Women Cotton Workers and the Suffrage
              Campaign: The Radical Suffragists in Lancashire,
              1893-1914," Fit Work for Women, 98-111.

(R) BOOKS PLACED ON LIBRARY RESERVE FOR ABOVE ASSIGNMENTS:

Branca, Patricia, Silent Sisterhood: Middle Class Women in the
     Victorian Home (Pittsburgh, 1975)
Bridenthal, Renate and Claudia Koonz, eds., Becoming Visible:
     Women in European History (Boston, 1977)
Davidoff, Leonore, The Best Circles: Society, Etiquette, and the
     Season (London, 1973)
Dyhouse, Carol, Girls Growing Up in Late Victorian and Edwardian
     England (Boston and Henley, 1981)
Gorham, Deborah, The Victorian Girl and the Feminine Ideal
     (Bloomington, 1982)
Harrison, Brian, Separate Spheres: The Opposition to Women's
     Suffrage in Britain (New York, 1978)
Hartman, Mary and Lois Banner, eds., Clio's Consciousness Raised
     (New York, 1974)
Kanner, Barbara, ed., The Women of England: From Anglo-Saxon
     Times to the Present (Hamden, 1979) ON REF: HQ 1599 .E5 W65
Walkowitz, Judith R., Prostitution and Victorian Society: Women
     Class, and the State (New York, 1980)
Wohl, Anthony S., ed., The Victorian Family: Structure and
     Stresses (London, 1978)

English 416   M. Vicinus
History 484   Autumn 1986
                        VICTORIAN WOMEN

This is an advanced, upper-division, interdisciplinary course
using history and literature to examine the position of women in
Victorian England. Since this period saw the rise of the first
organized women's movement, materials on women are extremely
rich. You are encouraged to explore widely, beyond the required
readings. The written assignments are designed to help you think
critically about Victorian literature, to assess primary sources
in the period and to speculate about the alternatives available
for women then and now. You will be graded on the following
basis: paper: 30% annotated bibliography: 40%, final
examination: 20%, in-class participation: 10%. You are expected
to come to class having done the reading for the day, prepared to
discuss and ask questions.

Office Hours: 1626 Haven, 2-4 Monday.

Required texts:

Janet Murray, Strong-Minded Women and Other Lost Voices from
     Nineteenth Century England.
Martha Vicinus, A Widening Sphere: Changing Roles of Victorian
     Women.
Charlotte Bronte, Jane Eyre.
Mary Elizabeth Braddon, Lady Audley's Secret.
Mrs. Gaskell, Mary Barton.
M. V. Hughes, A London Girl of the 1880s.
Course Pack (Albert's).

Sep 4   R: Introduction

Sep 9   T: Murray, pp. 1-39, 108-118; Vicinus, pp. ix-xix.

Sep 11 R: The Ideal Woman: Course pack: Dinah Mulock Craik,
             "Adelaide" and "The Two Houses," plus Vicinus, pp. 146-
             162 (Mitchell) and 146-162 (Christ).

Sep 16 T: The Revolt Against the Ideal Woman: Bronte, pp. vii-
             109 (preface- chap 12).

Sep 18 R: Bronte, pp. 109-261 (chap 13-24).

Sep 23 T: Bronte, pp. 261-433 (chap 25-end).

Sep 25 R: Course pack: Peterson, "The Victorian Governess:
             Status Incongruence in Family and Society."

Sep 30 T: The perils of Marriage: Murray, pp. 40-47, 62-73,
             Vicinus, pp. 3-28 (Holcombe).

Oct 2   R: Murray, pp. 77-107, 118-149. Course pack: Love letters
             of Elizabeth Barrett Browning.

Oct 7   T: Braddon, pp. 1-184.

Oct 9   R: Braddon, pp. 184-286.

Oct 14 T: FIRST PAPER DUE.

Oct 16 R: Old Maids and New Work: Murray, pp. 48-61, 159-166;
             Vicinus, pp. 52-71 (Hammerton).

Oct 21 T: New Opportunities for Middle-Class Women: Murray, pp.
             226-245; Hughes, pp. 1-127.

Oct 23 R: Hughes, pp. 128-245.

Oct 28 T: Murray, pp. 259-271, 288-325; Vicinus, pp. 94-116 (Kent).

Oct 30 R: Working-Class Women: Murray, pp. 246-255, 326-375.

Nov 4   T: Mrs. Gaskell, pp. 1-149 (chap. I-XIII).

Nov 6   R: Mrs. Gaskell, pp. 150-264 (chap. XIV-XXIV).

Nov 11 T: Mrs. Gaskell, pp. 265-381 (chap XXV-end).

Nov 13 R: Course pack: Ada Nield Chewe, "Letters of a Crewe
             Factory Girl."

Nov 18 T: Murray, pp. 167-192, Ellen Ross, "'Fierce Questions
             and Taunts': Married Life in Working-Class London,
             1870-1914."

Nov 20 R: ANNOTATED BIBLIOGRAPHIES DUE.

Nov 25 T: Sex and Sexuality Murray, pp. 283-288, 376-383, 385-
             436; Vicinus, pp. 72-93 (Walkowitz).

Dec 2   R: Murray, pp. 149-159; course pack: Martha Vicinus,
             "Distance and Desire: English Boarding-School
             Friendships."

Dec 4   R: Course pack: Christina Rossetti, "Goblin Market."

Dec 9   T: Vicinus, pp. 182-198 (Smith). Summing up.

COURSE PACK CONTENTS

1. [Dinah Mulock Craik], "Adelaide. Being Fragments from a
   Young Girl's Diary," Sharpe's London Magazine, n. s. I
   (1852), 74-80.

2. [Dinah Mulock Craik], "The Two Homes. A Story for Wives,"
   Chambers's Edinburgh Journal, 7 (17 April 1847), 242-246.

3. M. Jeanne Peterson, "The Victorian Governess: Status
   Incongruence in Family and Society," Suffer and Be Still:
   Women in the Victorian Age, ed. Martha Vicinus (Bloomington:
   Indiana University Press, 1972), 3-19, 207-211.

4. The Letters of Elizabeth Barrett Browning, ed. Frederic G.
   Kenyon. 3rd. ed. (London: Smith, Elder, 1898), I, 280-317.

5. Ada Nield Chew, The Life and Writings of a Working Woman,
   presented by Doris Nield Chew (London: Virago, 1982), pp. 75-
   91, 118-134.

6. Ellen Ross, "'Fierce Questions and Taunts": Married Life in
   Working-Class London, 1870-1914," Feminist Studies, 8/3
   (Fall, 1982), 575-602.

7. Christina Rossetti, "Goblin Market," The Pre-Raphaelites and
   Their Circle, ed. Cecil Y. Lang (Boston: Houghton Mifflin,
   1968), pp. 130-143.

8. Martha Vicinus, "Distance and Desire: English Boarding-School
   Friendships," Signs, 9/4 (Summer, 1984), 600-622.

VICTORIAN WOMEN: ANNOTATED BIBILIOGRAPHIES

This assignment is designed to introduce you to the rich and
complex debates about women during the Victorian period. It is
also an opportunity to explore primary sources beyond the
excerpts in Murray, in order to gain a fuller sense of how the
Victorians felt about themselves, what issues they considered
important, how they argued about them, and why they were
important. You should select one of the following topics for
consideration, or consult with me about a topic of your own
choosing. Please select a <u>minimum</u> of one book and five essays,
chosen from at least three different periodicals or newspapers or
anthologies, <u>published</u> <u>in</u> <u>England</u> between the years 1820 and
1900. You will find materials in the Graduate Library, the
Medical Library and some other specialist libraries. The
Graduate Library has especially rich holdings in Victorian
periodicals, which were the main vehicle of critical debates
during the period. The bulk of these are to be found under the
call number of AP4, but many are also on microfilm, and available
in the Microfilm Reading Room.

The major sources for citations on the Victorian period will be
discussed in class, but you will also find most helpful the two
bibliographies by S. Barbara Kanner in <u>Suffer</u> <u>and</u> <u>Be</u> <u>Still</u> (on
reserve) and <u>A</u> <u>Widening</u> <u>Sphere,</u> as well as the citations in
Murray. You will probably find secondary sources on your topic
useful for giving you an overview, as well as supplying you with
initial suggestions on what is available on the topic.
But remember that you need to shape your topic.   Required course
material, including Murray, American sources and secondary works
should be discussed only <u>in</u> <u>addition</u> <u>to</u> the six English primary
sources.

Do not attempt to cover all issues of a broad topic, but focus
on a particular aspect. For example, you might want to choose
the debate over whether women should attend university, selecting
and comparing the arguments of advocates for and opponents of
women's higher education. What were the main reasons for and
against?   What do both sides share, if anything? What arguments
for both sides were most convincing for the Victorians? Why do
you think these were effective? What does this tell you about
the ways in which the Victorians approached the subject?

What does an annotated bibliography look like? First, it is an
assignment which surveys and evaluates sources on a particular
topic. You should write an introduction, placing your particular
topic in the context of period, and outlining the major debates.
You should then present your sources individually (providing
complete citations for each sources); 1) give a precis of the
main arguments of the article or book, 2) explain what the
author's main assumptions are, discussing how these assumptions
are a part of the debate you are discussing (eg, are they

extremely conservative, typical middle-of-the-road, radical, etc), and 3) place this author's work in the context of your overall analysis of the topic. Your conclusion should discuss what aspects of the topic you have chosen that the Victorians concentrated upon, why, and what this means for our understanding of their approach to your topic; you might also want to address what they did not discuss and why. You will need to read widely in your topic in order to evaluate your specific sources; your task is to understand and analyze the principles underlying a contemporary debate about a specific topic.

Your paper should be 12-15 pages long; it is due Thursday, November 20 by 5:00 p. m.

<u>Suggested Topics:</u>

The concept of "The Lady" <u>or</u> "The Gentleman"
The struggle to gain entry into medicine
The debate over higher education for women
Occupations for middle-class women: governess, nurse, teacher,
          social worker, clerical worker.
Religious sisterhoods
Jewish, Irish or other immigrant women
Women and charity work/philanthropy
Family relations--sisters and brothers, daughters and mothers,
          daughters and fathers
Marriage manuals/advice books
Girls' upbringing, education
Fashion and changes in fashion
Household management, cook books
Midwifery
Motherhood
Birth control
Divorce
Middle-class women and the medical debate about their sexuality
Single Women and the "Surplus Woman" debate
Emigration
Actresses and the acting profession
Women artists, entry into art schools
Women and crime
Prostitution, white-slave trade, Contagious Diseases Acts
Occupations for working-class women: domestic service, factory
          work, cottage industries, seamstresses, laundry work,
          coal mining/surface work, argicultural work.
Elementary-school education
Household advice/management for working-class wives
Working-class family life

THE WOMAN QUESTION IN WESTERN THOUGHT IN EUROPE AND AMERICA 1750 - 1950

Susan Groag Bell and Karen Offen

History 238
Feminist Studies 238

Stanford University
Spring Quarter 1986
Thurs. 3.15 - 5.05

Course Information

This course will explore the debate in Western nations over women, their relationship to the family, and their claims to freedom, from the Enlightenment to the mid-twentieth century. Our focus is on the controversies over women's legal status, education, employment, and participation in political life. The main contributors to the debate come from Britain, France, Germany and America, but significant participants from Scandinavia, Russia and Italy will also be introduced; this was a debate of truly international scope.

The course is organized as a colloquium and informed participation in discussion is considered an essential part of the course work. Colloquium participants will be expected to completed approximately 300 pages of common reading per week. Written assignments will consist of a short analytical mid-term paper and a final examination.

Required Reading

Bell and Offen, Women, the Family and Freedom: The Debate in Documents, 1750-1950. 2 Vols. (Stanford University Press, 1983). Graduate students will also read a variety of assigned supplementary articles on reserve in Green Library.

For background in the history of Western civilization and culture, see Donald Kagan, Steven Ozment, Frank Turner, The Western Heritage Since 1648 (New York: Macmillan, 1979) and/or Edward McNeill Burns, Robert Lerner, and Standish Meacham, Western Civilizations, Their History and Their Culture (New York: Norton, 1980). See also Renate Bridenthal and Claudia Koonz, eds., Becoming Visible: Women in European History (Boston: Houghton Mifflin, 1977).

THE WOMAN QUESTION IN WESTERN THOUGHT
History 238
Spring Quarter 1985-86

April 3: Thinking About Women's History: The Implications of Gender Analysis

April 10: Women and the "Rights of Man" in the Age of Republican Revolutions,
          1750-1830

          Readings (undergraduate)
          WFF—General Introduction to Vol. I,
             Part I, Introductory Essay & chs. 1, 2, 3 (documents 1-33)

April 17: Women and Their Sphere in the Romantic Era, 1830-1848

          Readings (undergraduate)
          WFF—Part II, Introductory Essay & chs. 4, 5, 6, 7 (documents 34-68)

April 24: Women, Revolution, and Reaction, 1848-1860

          Readings (undergraduate)
          WFF—Part III, Introductory Essay and chs. 8, 9, 10, 11 (documents
             69-100)
          QUESTIONS FOR MID-TERM ESSAY WILL BE HANDED OUT

May 1:   Evolution, Education, and Economics, 1860-1880

          Readings (undergraduate)
          WFF—Part IV, Introductory Essay and chs. 12, 13, 14, 15, 16
             (documents 101-138)

          MID-TERM ESSAYS DUE, BEGINNING OF CLASS

May 8:   "New Women," Population, Socialism, and Nationalism, 1880-1914

          Readings (undergraduate)
          WFF—Vol. II, General Introduction
             Part I, Introductory Essay & chs. 1, 2, 3, (documents 1-34)

May 15:   Feminism, Women's Education and Women's Rights in the Nation State

          Readings (undergraduate)
          WFF—Vol. II, Part I, chs. 4, 5, 6 (documents 35-64)

May 22:   The Great War and Women's Issues, 1914-1925

          Readings (undergraduate)
          WFF—Vol. II, Part II, Introductory Essay and chs. 7, 8, 9,
             (documents 65-91)

May 29:   The Family, Politics, Psychology, and Fascism

          WFF—Vol II, Part II, chs. 10, 11, 12 (documents 92-120)

Karen Offen
NEH Summer Seminar for
College Teachers
Stanford University, 1986

The Woman Question in Western Thought, 1750-1950

Participants are strongly encouraged to familiarize themselves in advance of the seminar with the contents of the two-volume, 1200 page paperback documentary text, Women, the Family, and Freedom: The Debate in Documents, 1750-1950, ed. Bell and Offen (Stanford University Press, 1983), referred to hereafter as WFF. Since the book is so wide-ranging, thematically, chronologically, and geographically, advance reading should enable participants to frame their projects with a comparative dimension in mind. Assigned articles and books will be placed on reserve in Green Library. Participants who already have copies of various articles in their possession are strongly urged to bring them to Stanford.

All participants are assumed to be conversant with the history of Western civilization and culture. For those who would like to refresh their knowledge, recommended texts include Donald Kagan, Steven Ozment, Frank Turner, The Western Heritage Since 1648 (New York: Macmillan, 1979) and/or Edward McNeill Burns, Robert Lerner, and Standish Meacham, Western Civilizations, Their History and Their Culture (New York: Norton, 1980). See also Renate Bridenthal and Claudia Koonz, eds., Becoming Visible: Women in European History (Boston: Houghton Mifflin, 1977).

The organization of readings and the list of articles offered below is provisional; important new articles may be added and/or substituted as they become available. Some of the session readings may be slightly reorganized to accommodate the special interests of seminar participants.

1st meeting: **Thinking About Women's History: The Implications of Gender Analysis**
WFF--General Introduction. Vol. I.
Joan Kelly-Gadol, "The Social Relations of the Sexes: A New Methodology for Women's History," Signs (1975).
Natalie Zemon Davis, "'Women's History' in Transition: The European Case," Feminist Studies (1976).
Gerda Lerner, "The Challenge of Women's History," (1977) in The Majority Finds Its Past (1980)
Carolyn Lougee, "Women, History, and the Humanities," Women's Studies Quarterly (1981)
Carl N. Degler, At Odds, (1980) Preface & chs. 7 & 8.

2nd meeting: **Women and the "Rights of Man" in the Age of Republican Revolutions, 1750-1830.**
WFF--Part I, Introductory Essay & chs. 1, 2, 3 (documents 1-33).
Selections from Levy, Applewhite, & Johnson, Women in Revolutionary Paris
Maurice Bloch & Jean Bloch, "Women and the Dialectics of Nature in Eighteenth-century French Thought," in Nature, Culture, and Gender, ed. MacCormack and Strathern (1980)
Mitzi Myers, "Reform or Ruin: 'A Revolution in Female Manners,'" in Studies in Eighteenth-Century Culture, ed. Harry C. Payne, vol. 11 (1982).
Jane Abray, "Feminism in the French Revolution," American Historical Review (1975).
Linda K. Kerber, chapter 7 from Women and the Republic (1980)

3rd meeting: **Women and their Sphere in the Romantic Era, 1830–1848.**
WFF-- Part II, Introductory Essay & chs. 4, 5, 6, 7 (documents 34–68).
Claire Goldberg Moses, "Saint-Simonian Men/Saint-Simonian Women," Journal of Modern History (1982).
Barbara Taylor, "The Men are as Bad as Their Masters," Feminist Studies (1979).
Joan Moon, "Feminism and Socialism: The Utopian Synthesis of Flora Tristan," in Socialist Women, ed. Boxer and Quataert (1978).
Kathryn Kish Sklar, "The Storms of Democratic Liberty, 1835–37," (Ch. 9) in Catharine Beecher: A Study in American Domesticity (1973).
David Jones, "Women and Chartism," History (1983).

4th meeting: **Women, Revolution, and Reaction, 1848–1860.**
WFF--PART III, Introductory Essay and Chs. 8, 9, 10, 11 (documents 69–100).
Lee Holcombe, "Victorian Wives and Property Reform of the Married Women's Property Law, 1857–1882," in A Widening Sphere, ed. M. Vicinus (1977).
Richard Stites, "M. L. Mikhailov and the Emergence of the Woman Question in Russia," Canadian Slavic Studies (1969), or ch. 2 and pp. 89–99 of The Women's Liberation Movement in Russia (1978).
Ellen DuBois, "Introduction" and Ch. 6, "The Fifteenth Amendment and the Emergence of Independent Suffragism," in Feminism and Suffrage (1978)

5th meeting: **Evolution, Education, and Economics, 1860–1880.**
WFF--PART IV, Introductory Essay & Chs. 12, 13, 14, 15, 16 (documents 101–138).
Elizabeth Fee, "The Sexual Politics of Victorian Social Anthropology," in Clio's Consciousness Raised, ed. M. Hartman and L. Banner (1973).
Rita McWilliams-Tullberg, "Women and Degrees at Cambridge University, 1862–1897," in A Widening Sphere, ed. M. Vicinus (1977).
Judith Jeffrey Howard, "The Civil Code of 1865 and the Origins of the Feminist Movement in Italy," in The Italian Immigrant Woman in North America..., ed. Caroli, Harney, and Thomasi (1978).
Marilyn J. Boxer, "Foyer or Factory: Working Class Women in Nineteenth Century France," Proceedings of the Western Society for French History, vol. 2 (1975).
Susan Moller Okin, "John Stuart Mill's Feminism: The Subjection of Women and the Improvement of Mankind," The New Zealand Journal of History (1973).

6th meeting: **Women's Egotism versus the Nation State, 1880–1914.**
WFF--VOL. 2, Gen. Intro, Part I: Introductory Essay & chs. 1, 2, 3 (documents 1–34).
Lloyd Fernando, "The Radical Ideology of the 'New Woman,'" Southern Review: An Australian Journal of Literary Studies (1967).

Karen Honeycutt, "Socialism and Feminism in Imperial Germany,"
 Signs (1979).
Richard J. Evans, "Theory and Practice in German Social Democracy
 1880-1914: Clara Zetkin and the Socialist Theory of Women's
 Emancipation," _History of Political Theory_ (1982).
Karen Offen, "Depopulation, Nationalism, and Feminism in Third
 Republic France," _American Historical Review_ (1983).
Carl N. Degler, "Introduction" to reissue of Charlotte Perkins
 Gilman, _Women and Economics_ (1966).
Cheri Register, "Motherhood at Center: Ellen Key's Social
 Vision," _Women's Studies International Forum_ (1982).

7th meeting: **The Population Question and Women's Rights in the Nation State**
 WFF--VOL. II, PART 1, chs. 4, 5, 6 (documents 35-64).
Theodore Roszak, "The Hard and the Soft: The Force of Feminism in
 Modern Times" in _Masculine/Feminine_, ed. Roszak & Roszak (1969)
Linda L. Clark, "The Molding of the _Citoyenne_: The Image of the
 Female in French Educational Literature, 1880-1914," _Third
 Republic/Troisième République_, no. 3/4 (1977).
James C. Albisetti, "Could Separate Be Equal? Helene Lange and
 Women's Education in Imperial Germany," _History of Education
 Quarterly_ (1982).
Steven C. Hause and Anne R. Kenney, "The Limits of Suffragist
 Behavior: Legalism and Militancy in France, 1876-1922,"
 American Historical Review (1981).
Barbara Caine, "Beatrice Webb and the Woman Question," _History
 Workshop_ (1982).
Charles Sowerwine, "Women and Workers in France before 1914: The
 Debate over the Couriau Affair," _Journal of Modern History_
 (1983).
Ann Taylor Allen, "Mothers of the New Generation: Adele
 Schreiber, Helene Stocker, and the Evolution of the Idea of
 Motherhood, 1900-1914," _Signs_ (forthcoming 1985)

8th meeting: **The Great War and the Women's Issue, 1914-1925**
 WFF--VOL. II, PART II: Introductory Essay & chs. 7, 8, 9
 (documents 65-91).
Lela B. Costin, "Feminism, Pacifism, Internationalism and the
 1915 International Congress of Women," _Women's Studies Inter-
 national Forum_ (1982).
Sandra M. Gilbert, "Soldier's Heart: Literary Men, Literary
 Women, and the Great War," _Signs_ (1983).
Sheila M. Rothman, "The Politics of Protection" (ch. 4) in
 Woman's Proper Place (1978)
Beatrice Farnsworth, "Bolshevism, the Woman Question, and
 Aleksandra Kollontai," _American Historical Review_ (1976)
Claudia Koonz, "Conflicting Allegiances: Political Ideology and
 Women Legislators in Weimar Germany," _Signs_ (1976).
Jane Lewis, "In Search of a Real Equality: Women Between the
 Wars," _Class, Culture, and Social Change: A New View of the
 1930's_, ed. Frank Gloversmith (1980)

9th meeting: **The Family, Politics, Psychology and Fascism.**
WFF—VOL. II, PART II, chs. 10, 11, 12 (documents 92-120)
Leila J. Rupp, "Mother of the Volk: The Image of Women in Nazi
Ideology," Signs (1977)
Dee Garrison, "Karen Horney and Feminism," Signs (1981)

Berenice A. Carroll, "'To Crush Him in Our Own Country': The
Political Thought of Virginia Woolf," Feminist Studies (1978)
Dorothy Kaufmann McCall, "Simone de Beauvoir, The Second Sex, and
Jean Paul Sartre," Signs (1979)

Additional recommended books in English:
(Supplementing the bibliography in Women, the Family, and Freedom)

—Carol Bauer & Lawrence Ritt, eds., Free and Ennobled: Source Readings in
the Development of Victorian Feminism (1979)
—Carol R. Berkin and Clara M. Lovett, eds. Women, War & Revolution (1980)
—Patrick Kay Bidelman, Pariahs Stand Up! The Founding of the Liberal Feminist
Movement in France, 1858-1889 (1981)
—Marilyn J. Boxer and Jean H. Quataert, eds. Socialist Women: European
Socialist Feminism in the Nineteenth and Early Twentieth Centuries (1978)
—Renate Bridenthal, Atina Grossman, and Marion Kaplan, eds. Women in the
Weimar Republic and Nazi Germany (1984)
—William Chafe, The American Woman: Her Changing Social, Economic, and
Political Role, 1920-1970 (1972)
—Linda L. Clark, Schooling the Daughters of Marianne: Textbooks and the
Socialization of Girls in Modern French Primary Schools (1984)
—Carl N. Degler, At Odds: Women and the Family in America from the Revolution
to the Present (1980)
—Ellen Carol DuBois, Feminism and Suffrage: The Emergence of an Independent
Women's Movement in America, 1848-1869 (1978)
—Linda Edmondson, Feminism in Russia, 1900-17 (1983)
—Richard J. Evans, The Feminist Movement in Germany 1894-1933 (1976)
—John C. Fout, ed. German Women in the Nineteenth Century: A Social History
(forthcoming)
—Brian Harrison, Separate Spheres: The Opposition to Women's Suffrage in
Britain (1978)
—Steven C. Hause, with Anne R. Kenney, Women's Suffrage and Social Politics
in the French Third Republic (1984)
—Dolores Hayden, The Grand Domestic Revolution (1981)
—Erna O. Hellerstein, Leslie Parker Hume, and Karen M. Offen, eds. Victorian
Women: A Documentary Account of Women's Lives in Nineteenth Century England,
France, and the United States (1981)
—Marielouise Janssen-Jurreit, Sexism: The Male Monopoly on History & Thought
(1982)
—Linda K. Kerber, Women of the Republic: Intellect and Ideology in
Revolutionary America (1980)
—Gerda Lerner, The Majority Finds Its Past (1980)
—Darline Gay Levy, Harriet Branson Applewhite, Mary Durham Johnson, eds.,
Women in Revolutionary Paris 1789-1795 (1979)
—William R. Leach, True Love and Perfect Union: The Feminist Reform of Sex
and Society (1980)
—Eleanor S. Riemer and John C. Fout, eds., European Women: A Documentary
History, 1789-1795 (1980)

--Katharine M. Rogers, _Feminism in Eighteenth-Century England_ (1982)
--Andrew Rosen, _Rise Up, Women! The Militant Campaign of the Women's Social and Political Union, 1903-14_ (1974)
--Rosalind Rosenberg, _Beyond Separate Spheres: Intellectual Roots of Modern Feminism_ (1982)
--Sheila M. Rothman, _Woman's Proper Place: A History of Changing Ideals and Practices, 1870 to the Present_ (1978)
--Janet Sayers, _Biological Politics_ (1982)
--Samia I. Spencer, _French Women and the Age of Enlightenment_ (1984)
--Richard Stites, _The Women's Liberation Movement in Russia: Feminism, Nihilism, and Bolshevism, 1860-1930_ (1978)
--Barbara Taylor, _Eve and the New Jerusalem: Socialism and Feminism in the Nineteenth Century_ (1983)
--Louise A. Tilly and Joan W. Scott, _Women, Work, & Family_ (1978)
--Martha Vicinus, ed. _Suffer and Be Still_ (1973)
--Martha Vicinus, ed. _A Widening Sphere_ (1977)
--Judith R. Walkowitz, _Prostitution and Victorian Society_ (1980)

ALSO

--American Historical Association, _Recent United States Scholarship on the History of Women_ (1980)
--Gerda Lerner, _Teaching Women's History_ (1981)
--Carolyn Lougee, "Women, History, and the Humanities: An Argument in Favor of the General Curriculum," _Women's Studies Quarterly_ (1981)
--Gilbert Allardyce, Carolyn C. Lougee, Morris Rossabi, William F. Woehrlin, "The Rise and Fall of the Western Civilization Course," _American Historical Review_ (1982)
--Joan Hoff Wilson, "A Grand Illusion: Continuing the Debate on General Education," _Women's Studies Quarterly_ (1981)
--Joan W. Scott, "Women in History: The Modern Period," _Past and Present_ (1983)

Office hours: RUTGERS UNIVERSITY
409 Hickman Hall M 1-2   Ziva Galili y Garcia
101D Van Dyck Hall Th 2-3   Fall 1982
and by appointment

01 510 358

WOMEN, FAMILY, AND EDUCATION IN THE SOVIET UNION

Course description:

This course will consider the transformation of Russian society by industrialization, revolution, and socialist "reconstruction," through a study of the interrelated questions of the status of women, the role of the family, and state responsibility for the education of the young. Readings, films, and discussions will be used to explore the evolution of the women's movement in pre-revolutionary Russia and its ties with revolutionary socialism; to document the changes brought about by the revolution in the legal-political status of women, in their economic activity, and sexual behavior; and, finally, to assess the success of Soviet society in creating the social institutions and social norms necessary for female equality.

Course requirements:

1. Students should complete all reading assignments, attend all lectures, discussions, and film presentations.

2. Several class periods will be set aside for discussion (Specific sessions are indicated in the class schedule below). Students should have completed the relevant readings and be prepared to discuss the questions under consideration.

3. There will not be an in-class examination in this course. Instead, students will be required to write 3 short papers on topics assigned by the instructor. (Students wishing to write on topics of their own selection may do so only after discussing their proposed topic with the instructor). The papers will be based on the assigned readings and lecture notes. The purpose of these papers is to allow students to express their understanding of key questions in Russian and Soviet history without time pressure and while the material is still fresh in their minds.

Readings:

1. An effort has been made to avoid repetitive reading and to provide the students with a wide variety of sources through which they may reach a fuller understanding of the topic. These considerations, as well as the relative novelty of the subject, require that we rely heavily on materials collected by the instructor from various sources in multiple copies. Packets of   materials (containing close to 700 pages of articles, short stories, a play, and contemporary documents) will be sold to students for $7. One packet will be placed on reserve.

2. In addition, the following books are available in paperback editions at the Cooperative Student Bookstore and are recommended for purchase:

   D. Atkinson, A. Dalin, G. Warshofsky-Lapidus, eds., Women in Russia.

   Alexandra Kollontai, A Great Love.

   Fyedor V. Gladkov, Cement: A Novel.

   Urie Bronfenbrenner, Two Worlds of Childhood.

   These books will also be put on Reserve.

3. Students are encouraged to consult the following reference book which is on Reserve for my history course 510:460 sec. 6:

   Riasanovsky, N., A History of Russia.

Class Schedule:

I. WOMEN AND THE WOMAN QUESTION IN PRE-REVOLUTIONARY RUSSIA

   September 8   Introduction: Questions and Methodology.

   Deptember 13   The historical background.
                    Atkinson, 3-38.

   September 15   Women and family in 19th century Russia

                    Articles by Engel ("Mothers and Daughters"), Tovrov, and Stillman in packet.

   September 20   The Woman Question and the Social Question

                    Article by Engel ("From Separatism to Socialism") in packet.

   September 22   Discussion: Women in the revolutionary movement

                    Article by Engel ("The Personal and the Political") in packet.

                    Portraits of Vera Figner and Elizaveta Kovalskaia (from Engel & Rosenthal, Five Sisters) in packet.

   September 27   On the eve of revolution: modernization, social change, and the split in the women's movement.

                    Atkinson, 39-84
                    Article by Bobroff in packet.

September 29   Film: Revolutionists
Vera Stroeva, 1936, 106 minutes.
The film, documenting the history of the Russian
revolutionary labor movement from its origins in
the 1890's to its defeat on the barricades of
Moscow in 1905, is one of the first feature
films by a woman director.

Begin reading A Great Love

October 4   Marxism and the Woman Question

Atkinson, 85-115
Article by Kollontai in packet.

October 6   Discussion: Women in the Bolshevik Party

Finish reading A Great Love
Article by Clements in packet.

***   Paper topics haded out. Due on October 13.

II. THE REVOLUTIONARY ERA: 1917-1939

October 11   Civil War (1918-1921): A break with the past.

Schlesinger, 30-71, in packet.
Begin reading Cement.

October 13   Film: Bed and Sofa
Room, 1927, 100 minutes.
This silent classic is a Soviet variation on
the old "triangle" theme and demonstrates the
effects of overcrowded housing and female
unemployment on the family life of Soviet
workers.

October 18   The NEP period (1921-1928): Revolutionary
ideals in the test of Soviet reality.

Atkinson, 139-65.
Article by Fitzpatrick in packet.
Continue reading Cement.

October 20   Discussion: Women's equality and sexual
behavior in the early Soviet period.

Schlesinger, 172-87, in packet.
Finish reading Cement.
Also review readings for October 11, 13, 18.

October 25   Education: The collective and the state take over

        Bowen, 27-134, in packet.

October 27   **Film:** **The Road to Life**
Eck, 1929, 100minutes.
Life in a "Children's Republic" and the educational
ideas of its founder, Anton Makarenko (based on
his memoirs).

November 1   The Stalinist Industrialization:
Economic and demographic revolution.

        Article by Mitchison (1933) in packet.

        Atkinson, 167-73, 189-204 (sections relating
         to the pre-WW II period).

November 3   **Discussion:** The impact of industrialization
             on the status of women.

        A. Glebov, "Inga" (a play) in packet.

***   Paper topics are handed out. Due on November 10.

November 8   Stalin's "Great Retreat."
(The Family Laws of 1936 and 1944)

        Schlesinger, 251-79; 348-77, in packet.

        Article by Dunham in packet.

November 10   **Film:** **Zoya**
Arnshtein, 1944, 86 minutes.
True life story of the partisan-heroine of
World War II Zoya Kosmodemianskaia, one of the
more than one million Soviet women volunteers
who fought against the Nazi invaders.

III. THE BALANCE SHEET FOR SOVIET WOMEN

November 15   Women in production

        Atkinson, 189-204 (review), 205-239.

November 17   Women in society; the family. (**Discussion**)

        Atkinson, 243-332.

November 22   The special case of peasant women and Eastern
               minority women.

                Atkinson, 167-188.

                Schlesinger, 188-223, in packet.

November 24   Film: Spring
               Alexandrov, 1947, 106 minutes.
               Musical comedy about a film-maker and the woman
               scientist whose life story he is trying to film
               and who doesn't want a film made about her life:
               Typical of the many career women who figure in
               Soviet works of art of the immediate post-World
               War II era.

November 29   The Woman Question in the Soviet Union Today

                Atkinson, 333-374

December 1   Soviet Feminism

                Stories by Baranskaia (excerpted in Our Soviet
                Sister) and Grekova, in packet.

December 6   Children and education in the Soviet Union today.

                Bronfenbrenner

***   Paper topics handed out. Due on December 13.

December 8   Film:

December 13   Discussion: Summation, assessment, and comparison
               with the American experience.

LOVE, MARRIAGE, AND THE FAMILY

1983 ACM/GLCA Newberry Library Seminar in the Humanities

Penny Gold (History, Knox College) and Warren Rosenberg (English, Wabash College)

****

Since 1979, I have been teaching a course at Knox on "Love and Marriage in Western History," a course beginning with the Romans and ending with the 1980s. The course is designed for students without previous course work in history. In 1983 I had the opportunity to do a similar course as an interdisciplinary seminar at the Newberry Library for students from the member schools of the Associated Colleges of the Midwest and the Great Lakes College Association. The assignments were changed to include material on the family, and to reflect the expertise in American Literature of Warren Rosenberg, with whom I taught the seminar. The reading assignments given below are those from the Newberry seminar, with the addition of a few from my Knox course, which had broader chronological limits.

I prepared for this course a 20-page bibliography on "Love, Marriage, and Family," arranged topically. I will be happy to send out copies for cost ($2.00). My address:
                                                                        Department of
History, Knox College, Galesburg, IL 61401.
****

General Course Goals

Our aim in the course is to open for study an area that in most college course offerings is considered peripheral, but which is central to our lives--love, marriage, and family. Almost by definition such a study will be interdisciplinary. We will read a variety of texts in juxtaposition, so that a particular period and issue will be illuminated from a number of directions. The course will be cumulatively historical, building our knowledge from period to period. But it will also be dialectical, in that we will be constantly comparing concepts within and between periods. We hope that studying this relatively unexplored field will expand your view of what knowledge is and what is worth knowing. We also hope it will show you that scholarship and life need not occupy separate realms.

An Historical Overview
Lawrence Stone, _Family, Sex and Marriage in England_
Carl Degler, _At Odds: Women and the Family in America from the Revolution to the Present_,
    pp. v-x, 3-30, 66-85

Ancient Society
Keith Hopkins, "The Age of Roman Girls at Marriage," _Population Studies_ 18 (1964-65): 309-27
Ovid, _The Art of Love:_
    The Loves, Bk. I, entire
      Bk. II: 4, 7, 8, 10, 13-15, 17
      Bk. III: 7, 11A, 11B, 14
    The Art of Love, entire; _The Remedies for Love_, entire

Medieval Love Poetry and Critical Perspectives
selected medieval lyric poetry
C. S. Lewis, The Allegory of Love, pp. 1-43
D. W. Robertson, "The Concept of Courtly Love as an Impediment to the Understanding of Medieval
    Texts," In The Meaning of Courtly Love, ed. F. X. Newman, pp. 1-18
John F. Benton, "Clio and Venus: An Historical View of Medieval Love," in The Meaning of Courtly
    Love, pp. 19-42

Romance and Reality
Orderic Vitalis, The Ecclesiastical History (selections)
George Homans, English Villagers of the Thirteenth Century, pp. 3-14, 144-76
letter of Archbishop Theobald to Pope Alexander III, in The Letters of John of Salisbury, vol. 1
    (London, 1955), pp. 227-37
Tristan and Isolt, in Medieval Romances, pp. 88-232

The Early Modern Period: Historical Sources
Scott and Wishy, America's Families, pp. 1-171
"The Return of Martin Guerre" (film)

The Early Modern Period: Literature
selected sonnets (Sidney, #1 from Astrophel and Stella; Shakespeare, #18, 116, 129, 130, 138,
    144; Milton, "Methought I Saw My Late Espoused Saint"
J. Bunselmeyer, "Appearances and Verbal Paradox: Sonnets 129 and 238," Shakespeare Quarterly
    25 (1974): 103-8
Old Testament: Genesis, 1-3
New Testament:
    1 Corinthians, 7:1-11, 25-40; 11:1-16; 14: 26-35
    Galatians, 3:26-29
    Ephesians, 5:21-6:9
    1 Timothy, 2:8-15
    1 Peter, 3:1-7
Milton, Paradise Lost, Books 4, 5, 8, 9, 10 (lines 1-162, 719-1104), 11 (lines 1-370),
    12 (lines 605-649)

Courtship and Marriage
Scott and Wishy, pp. 173-80, 198-212, 235-70
Jane Austen, Pride and Prejudice

Love, Marriage and Family in Nineteenth-Century America
Scott and Wishy, pp. 181-97, 213-34, 271-309, 335-89
C. Smith-Rosenberg, "The Female World of Love and Ritual: Relations between Women in
    Nineteenth-Century America," Signs 1 (1975): 1-29

The Family under Slavery
Scott and Wishy, pp. 310-34
Linda Brent, Incidents in the Life of a Slave Girl

Male Literary Imagination--Nineteenth Century
Hawthorne, "Wakefield"
Melville, "I and My Chimney"
Fiedler, Love and Death in the American Novel, pp.. 336-91 (chp. 11)
Flaubert, Madame Bovary

Female Literary Imagination--Nineteenth Century
Kate Chopin, The Awakening
Scott and Wishy, pp. 391-400
Annette Kolodny, "Dancing through the Minefield: Some Observations on the Theory, Practice and
    Politics of a Feminist Literary Criticism," Feminist Studies 6 (1980)

Twentieth Century
Scott and Wishy, 436-40, 450-504, 514-23, 569-78, 605-26, 635-53
Marge Piercy, Woman on the Edge of Time

(**N.B.** The next time I teach this course, I expect to use selections from Susan Groag Bell and Karen
M. Offen, Women, the Family and Freedom: The Debate in Documents, 2 vols. (Stanford University
Press, 1983)

Atina Grossmann   History Department
Fall 1988   Tuesday 2:10-4:00

The New Woman in Interwar Europe

Catalogue Description: This seminar explores why and how the
struggle to reconcile modernity and maternity in the figure of
the "New Woman" became such a central problem in Europe after the
first World War. We shall use a wide variety of sources including
films, novels, and sociological surveys to investigate the
relationship between social experience and cultural meaning, and
to analyze the impact of rationalization, Americanization,
Bolshevism and fascism on workplace, household, and sexuality.

Course Description: This seminar seeks to understand the social
and cultural history of interwar Europe by focusing on a set of
problems that might be called the "Gender of Modernity." We will
interrogate the figure of the "New Woman" by analyzing the role
of women both as the bearers of modernity -- on the cutting edge
of rationalization as workers on the assembly line, saleswomen in
department stores, users of birth control, doctors in public
clinics, consumers of urban commercial culture -- and the
defenders of tradition in housewives and mothers organizations,
religious associations, and fascist mobilizations. We will
concentrate on three areas for analysis: the application of (and
resistance to) bureaucratized and streamlined managerial models
to the household, bedroom and public welfare system; commercial
culture and how women represent themselves and are represented in
moments when conventions and codes are undergoing rapid change;
and notions of social welfare entitlements and female
citizenship, in the face of great anxiety over population rates
and the breakdown of traditional female roles as reproducers and
nurturers.

An introductory session on "new women" at the turn of the
cnetury raises the question of periodization and how profound the
impact of the first World War and the Russian Revolution (second
and third sessions) really was. A primary focus on England and
Germany, and a secondary focus on France, Italy and Russia raises
questions about national difference and the particular importance
for example of Catholicism, communism or fascism. Particular
attention to population policy, the conflict between work and
family,. and the political mobilization of women raises questions
about the relationship between gender, class and race (or
ethnicity).

Each session will require reading and evaluating both
primary and secondary sources. A lengthy list of memoir
literature is appended; it seems that contemporaries, rather than
historians, have written more about women in this period!
Additional source lists, especially in foreign languages, will be
available from the instructor. Students will be expected to

prepare a ten-minute oral presentation of the key issues and areas of controversy raised in one week's reading. They will write a brief (5-7 pages) paper which analyzes the use of a novel, memoir or eyewitness account as a historical source. Oral history is a definite possibility and should be discussed with the instructor. Students will also prepare a research paper (15 to 20 pages) pages which both discusses the information gathered, and the sources and methodologies (probably including those discussed in the first paper) required to further pursue the topic. Ideally, the seminar requires a good background knowledge of modern European and modern European women's history (although the latter is probably not realistic the first year).

Course Schedule and Readings:

"Housewife, mother and career woman. The synthesis of these three life styles is the problem of the age."

German fashion magazine, 1930.

"Yes, all things concerning women have taken a turn for the worse since the war."

Physician responding to sex survey, 1930.

"For a married working woman it is hardly possible anymore to find a quiet moment and feel like her own person."

Textile worker, 1930.

"In the atmosphere of the twenties one breathed the permissiveness of freedom...Heaven was not somewhere above us, but on earth...in the metropolis."

Charlotte Wolff's memoirs, 1980.

WEEK I. NEW WOMEN AND OLD WOMEN at the Turn of the Century. Introduction.

Margaret Llewelyn Davies, ed. Life as We have Known It (Norton, 1931, 1975).

Anna Davin, "Imperialism and Motherhood," History Workshop 5 (1978): 9-66.
Martha Vicinus, "Male Space and Women's Bodies: The English Suffragette Movement," in Women in Culture and Politics: A Century of Change (WCP).
Martha Vicinus, Independent Women (University of Chicago, 1986), selections.

WEEK II. WAR. World War I and the end of the 19th century.

Vera Brittain, Testament of Youth
Radclyffe Hall, The Well of Loneliness, pp.264-295.

Gail Braybon, Women Workers in the First World War, Ch.2-4.

Sandra Gilbert, "Soldiers' Hearts, Literary Men, Literary Women and the Great War," Signs 8, no.3 (1983): 422-450.
Margaret Higgonet, Behind the Lines: Gender in Two World Wars (Yale, 1987), selections.
Klaus Theweleit, Male Fantasies: Women, Floods, Bodies, History (University of Minnesota, 1987), selections.

WEEK III. REVOLUTION. Bolshevism, Americanism, New Women and New Men.

Alexandra Kollontai, Love of Worker Bees (Academy).

Barbara Evans Clements, "Working-Class and Peasant Women in the Russian Revolution, 1917-1923," Signs 8, no.2 (1982): 215-235.
Beatrice Farnsworth, "Bolshevism, the Woman Question and Alexandra Kollontai," American Historical Review (1976).
Christine Faure, "The Utopia of the "New Woman'" in WCP
Temma Kaplan, "Women and Communal Strikes in the Crisis of 1917-1922," in Becoming Visible, second edition, ed. Bridenthal, Koonz, Stuard (Houghton Mifflin, 1987), pp. 429-450.

WEEK IV. POLITICS. Old and New Feminists in Public.

Hugh Wiley Puckett, Germany's Women Go Forward (Columbia, 1930)

Jane Boak, "Women in Weimar Germany: The 'Frauenfrage" and the Female Vote," in Social Change and Political Development in Weimar Germany, ed. Bessel and Feuchtwanger (Barnes and Noble, 1981), pp.155-173.
Jane Lewis, "Beyond Suffrage: English Feminism in the 1920s," Maryland Historian 6 (1973): 1-17.
Bridenthal, "Professional Housewives" in When Biology Became Destiny (Monthly Review), WBBD.
Jane Lewis, "In Search of Real Equality: Women Between the Wars," in Class, Culture and Social Change: A New View of the 1930s., ed. Frank Gloversmith (1980).
Annemarie Sohn, "Catholic Women and Political Affairs," in WCP.
Mieke Aerts, "Catholic Constructions of Femininity" in WCP.

WEEK V. CULTURE AND REPRESENTATIONS: The New Woman as Cultural Icon.

Siegfried Kracauer, "The Little Shopgirls Go the Movies," (Trans. Tom Levine, 1988).

John Willett, Art and Politics in the Weimar Period: The New Sobriety 1917-1933 (Pantheon).

Music and slide presentation.

WEEK VI.   PAID WORK. Rationalization, Consumerism and the Double
            Burden.

Judith Grunfeld, "Rationalization and the Employment and Wages of
Women in Germany," International Labor Review 29, no. 5 (1934).

Bridenthal and Koonz,"Beyond Kinder, Küche, Kirche," in (WBBD).
Atina Grossmann, "'Girlkultur' or Thoroughly Rationalized Female:
A New Woman in Weimar Germany?" in WCP.
N. Ferguson, "Women's Work, Employment Opportunities and Economic
Roles, 1918-1939," Albion 7 (1975): 55-68.
Tim Mason, "Women in Germany, 1925-1940: Family, Welfare and
Work, Part I," History Workshop 1 (1976).

WEEK VII   HOUSEWORK, MARRIAGE, MOTHERHOOD.

Margery Spring Rice, Working Class Wives (1939, Virago, 1981).
Erich Fromm, "An Investigation of Labourers and Salaried
Employees in Germany on the Eve of the Third Reich," 1929.
Siegfried Giedion, "Mechanization Encounters the Household," in
Mechanization Takes Command (Norton, 1969), pp. 512-627.

Pat Ayers and Jan Lambertz, "Marriage Relations, Money and
Domestic Violence in Working-Class Kuverpoool, 1919-1939," in
Labour and Love: Women's Experience of Home and Family 1850-1940,
ed. Jane Lewis (Basil Blackwell, 1986), pp. 195-222.
Stefan Bajohr, "Illegitimacy and the Working Class: Illegitimate
Mothers in Brunswick, 1900-1933," in The German Working Class,
ed. Richard Evans.
Renate Bridenthal, "Class Struggle Around the Hearth: Women and
Domestic Service in the Weimar Republic," in Dobkowski and
Wallimann, Towards the Holocaust (Greenwood, 1983), pp. 243-264.
Elizabeth A. M. Roberts, "'Women's Strategies', 1890-1940," in
Labour and Love, pp. 249-267.

WEEK VIII. SEX. Sex Reform and the Rationalization of
           Sexuality.

Antonio Gramsci, "Americanism and Fordism" in Selections from the
Prison Notebooks (International, 1971),pp. 277-627.
Radclyffe Hall, The Well of Loneliness.
Wilhelm Reich, "Politicizing the Sexual Problem of Youth" (1932)
in Sex-Pol, Essays 1929-1934, ed. Lee Baxandall (Vintage, 1972),
pp.75-88.
Th. Van de Velde, Ideal Marriage (1930), selections.

Atina Grossmann,"The New Woman and the Rationalization of
Sexuality" in Powers of Desire, ed. Snitow, Stansell, Thompson,
(Monthly Review, 1983).
Ellen Holtzmann, "The Pursuit of Married Love: Women's Attitudes
Toward Sexuality and Marriage in Great Britain, 1918-1939,"

Journal of Social History 16, no.2 (1982): 39-51.
Gudrun Schwarz, "Viragos in Male Theory" in WCP.
Meyer-Renschhausen, "Bremen Morality Scandal" in WBBD.

WEEK IX. BIRTH CONTROL AND POPULATION POLICY: Crisis and Family
        Strategies.

D.V. Glass, Population Policies and Movements in Europe (1940),
selections.

Michael Freeden, "Eugenics and Progressive Thought: A Study in
Ideological Affinity," The Historical Journal 22 (1979): 645-671.
Atina Grossmann, "'Satisfaction is Domestic Happiness': Mass
Working-Class Sex Reform Organizations in the Weimar Republic,"
in Towards the Holocaust, ed. Dobkowski and Wallimann (Greenwood,
1983), pp.265-293.
Amy Hackett, "Helene Stoecker" in WBBD.
Karin Hausen, "Mother's Day" in WBBD.
Greta Jones, "Eugenics and Social Policy Between the Wars," The
Historical Journal 25, no. 3 (1982): 717-728.
Jane Lewis, "The Ideology and Politics of Birth Control in
Interwar England," Women's Studies International Forum 2 (1979):
33-48.

WEEK X: LEFT AND RIGHT. Economic Crisis and Family
          Politics.

Sheila Rowbotham, A New World for Women: Stella Browne -
Socialist Feminist (Pluto, 1977).

Atina Grossmann, "Abortion and Economic Crisis" in WBBD;
Marion Kaplan, "Sisterhood Under Siege" in WBBD;
Claudia Koonz, "Women's Lebensraum" in WBBD;
Claudia Koonz, "Some Political Implications of Separatism" in
WCP.
Claudia Koonz, Mothers in the Fatherland: Women, the Family and
Nazi Politics (St. Martin's, 1987), Ch. 1-4.

WEEK XI. THE NEW WOMAN AND FASCISM.

Documents on "Women, The Family , and Population Policy," in
Nazism 1919-1945, Vol.2 Sate, Economy and Society 1933-1939, ed.
Noakes and Pridham (Exeter, 1984), pp. 448-470.

Gisela Bock, "Racism and Sexism: Motherhood, Compulsory
Sterilization, and the State" in WBBD.
Gisela Bock, 'No Children at Any Cost'"in WCP.
Lesley Caldwell, "Reproducers of the Nation: Women and the Family
in Fascist Policy," in Rethinking Italian Fascism: Capitalism,
Populism and Culture (Lawrence and Wishart, 1986).
Alexander de Grand, "Women Under Italian Fascism," Historical
Journal 19 (1976): 947-68.

Claudia Koonz, Mothers in the Fatherland, Ch. 5–11.
Annemarie Tröger, "The Creation of a Female Assembly-Line Proletariat," in WBBD.

WEEK XII. MODERNITY. The New Woman and What Happened to Her.
Conclusions and discussion of research papers.

Virginia Woolf, Three Guineas

The following books are required (on reserve and/or available for purchase):

Bridenthal, Grossmann, Kaplan, When Biology Became Destiny: Women in Weimar and Nazi Germany (WBBD) (Monthly Review)
Margery Llewelyn Davies, Life as We Have Known It (Norton)
Judith Friedlander et al, Women in Culture and Politics (WCP) (Indiana University Press)
Radclyffe Hall, The Well of Loneliness
Alexandra Kollontai, Love of Worker Bees (Academy)
Claudia Koonz, Mothers in the Fatherland: Women, the Family and Nazi Politics (St. Martins)
Margery Spring Rice, Working Class Wives (Virago)
Sheila Rowbotham, A New World for Women: Stella Browne – Socialist Feminist (Pluto)
John Willett, Art and Politics in the Weimar Period: The New Sobriety 1917–1933 (Pantheon)
Virginia Woolf, Three Guineas

We will also screen several films including "Bed and Sofa" (Soviet Union, 1927), "The Blue Angel" (Germany, 1930), "Kuhle Wampe (Germany 1932).

History 190E
Judith Walkowitz
Winter, 1983
Office hours: Tu, Th, 11:30-12:15

HISTORY OF SEXUALITY

We will study the history of sexual attitudes and practices in nineteenth century and twentieth century America, England, and France. We will look at the social world of prostitutes and other sexual minorities, as well as the political mobilizations over sexuality by middle-class reformers and feminists. A variety of documents, novels, medical writings, oral histories, and manifestoes will illustrate how historical participants experienced the transformations of sexual practices and values over the past two centuries. There will be two critical essays, the first due February 3.

Readings available at the bookstore:

> Charlotte Perkins Gilman, Herland
> Claude Jaget, ed., Prostitutes, Our Lives
> Judith Walkowitz, Prostitution and Victorian Society
> Jeffrey Weeks, Sex, Politics, and Society
> Oscar Wilde, Picture of Dorian Gray

In addition, a packet of xeroxes has been prepared and should be available by the second week.

Week 1   Introduction
         Theories of Sexuality and Prostitution

         Reading: Weeks, ch. 1, "Sexuality and the Historian"

Week 2   Victorianism
         Sexual Style and Sexual Symbolism: Victorian Dress and Homosocial
             Rituals

         Reading: Carroll Smith Rosenberg, "Female World of Love and Ritual"(xerox)
                   Weeks, ch. 2 and 3
                   Walkowitz, introduction

Week 3   The Victorian Family and its Radical Critics
         Working Class vs. Middle-class Realities
         Critics of Victorian Sexual Arrangements: Socialists and Utopians

         Reading: Weeks, chs. 3 and 4
                   Louis Kern, "Ideology and Reality: Sexuality and Women's
                       Status in Oneida Community"
                   Barbara Taylor, "Socialist Feminism: Utopian or Scientific?"

                   Recommended: Walkowitz, ch. 2 (for evangelical opponents of
                       the socialists)

Week 4   The World of Prostitution
         Prostitution in Victorian England
         Prostitution in Progressive-Era America

         Reading: Walkowitz, ch. 1, 8, 10
                   Rosen, "Commercialization of Prostitution,""Subculture of
                       Prostitution" Epilogue

Week 5   Doctors and Women: Diseased Prostitutes and Hysterized Ladies
Feminist Virtue and Male Vice

        Reading: Carroll Smith Rosenberg, "The Hysterical Woman: Sex Roles
                and Role Conflict"
                Theorists and Rescuers
                Walkowitz, ch. 3, 4, 11
                              6, 7, epilogue
                Weeks, ch. 5

Week 6 (Feb. 8, 10)   The New Woman and the Fallen Man

        Reading: <u>Herland</u>
                Walkowitz, "Jack the Ripper and the Myth of Male Violence"
                "English Collective of Prostitutes: Manifestoes" (xerox)

Week 7   Construction of Homosexuality

        Reading: Weeks, ch. 6
                Adrienne Rich, "Compulsory Heterosexuality and Lesbian
                  Existence"
                Wilde, <u>Picture of Dorian Gray</u>

Week 8 (Feb. 22, 24)   The New Sexuality and the New Sexology
Affluence and Sexual Liberation

        Reading: Weeks, ch. 7, 8, 13
                Linda Gordon and Ellen Dubois, "Seeking Ecstasy on the
                  Battlefield"
                Leslie Fishbein, "Harlot or Heroine"
                Amber Hollibaugh, et al., "Talking Sex"
                "Untangling Eros and Emotions," "In the Heart of the
                Mineshaft"

Week 9   Prostitution Today
Prostitutes Rights Organizers and Interviews with French Prostitutes
    on Strike

        Reading: <u>Prostitutes, Our Lives</u>, pp. 7-115, and afterword by Margo
                St. James
                163-175

Week 10   The New Right and Reproductive Rights
Women against Pornography

        Reading: Ros Petchesky, "Antiabortion, Antifeminism and the Rise of
                the New Right"
                Ellen Willism, "Lust Horizons"
                "Women Against Pornography Manifestoes"
                "Tempers Flare over the Sexuality Conference"
                Irene Diamond, article on pornography
                Kathy Barry and Adrienne Rich on pornography

rb
1/6/83
15 copies

HISTORY OF SEXUALITY - 320/495

Spring 1988   Prof. Jane Slaughter
Office: Mesa Vista 2081   Office Hours:
                                                   M 1-2, W 1-3

I.   REQUIRED READINGS

      Pat Caplan (ed.), The Cultural Construction of Sexuality
      Joel Schwartz, The Sexual Politics of Joan Jacques Rousseau
      Herculin Barbin: Being the Recently Discovered Memoirs of
         a 19th Century Hermaphrodite
      Jeffrey Weeks, Sexuality and Its Discontents

      These books are available at Full Circle Books, 2205 Silver
         SE (near corner of Yale and Silver).

II.   COURSE CONTENT

      We will examine the same topics and themes --the social
   context, sexual behavior, identity, ideology and politics
   -- through the following time periods:
         The Pre-Industrial Western World; 1800-90;   1890-1920;
         1920-60; 1960-Present

III. COURSE REQUIREMENTS

      A. Critical Reviews: You will read two works in the area
   of the History of Sexuality, one for the time period to 1890, one
   for the period 1890-Present, and will write a 700 word critical
   analysis of each. First Review due March 2: Second Review
   due April 20. Instructions for the reviews and a list of sugges
   ted readings will be forthcoming. Each review will be worth 50
   points.

      B. Mid Term Exam: Will be a take-home written exam: you
   will receive the questions on March 2; Exam will be due March 9.
   Exam is worth 100 points.

      C. Research Project: You will select a research topic of
   interest to you, but within a series of topics to be provided.
   Your paper should be 10-12 pages (typed, double-spaced). plus a
   complete bibliography. Topics and instructions will be forthcoming. Paper is worth 100 points. Papers due last day of class
   May 4.

      For all written requirements, late papers drop 1/2 letter
   grade for each class day late. No exceptions.

      It is also assumed you will have read and be prepared to
   discuss the above listed readings on days assigned.

HISTORY OF SEXUALITY - 320/495

Spring 1988   Prof. Jane Slaughter

Course Outline and Assignments

Date	Topic	Assignment
Jan. 20	Introduction	

27   Methodology and Themes   DISCUSSION, Caplan, The
         Cultural Construction of Sexuality, Introd.,
         Chaps. 1, 7; Weeks, Sexuality and Its Discontents
         Chaps. 1, 2.

Feb. 3 The Pre Industrial Western World READ Caplan, Chap. 5

10   " " "   DISCUSSION, Schwartz,
         The Sexual Politics of Jean Jacques Rousseau;
         Caplan, Chap. 3.

17   1800-1890 The Industrial Revolution and Sexuality

24   " " "   DISCUSSION, Herculin
         Barbin; Caplan, Chap. 9.

Mar. 2   " " "   DISCUSSION, Caplan,
         Chaps. 6, 10
         First Critical Review Due

9   1890-1920 The First Sexual Revolution
         Mid Term Essays Due

23   " " "   DISCUSSION, Weeks,
         Chap. 4; Caplan, Chap. 2, pp. 52-59.

30   " " "   DISCUSSION, Caplan,
         Chap. 8

Apr. 6 1920-60 Sex as "Normal" and Necessary
                               DISCUSSION, Weeks,
         Chaps. 5,6,7; Caplan, Chap. 2, pps. 59-79

13   " " "

20   1960 to the Present. A Second Revolution
         Second Critical Review Due

27   " " "   DISCUSSION, Weeks,
         Chaps. 3,8,9

May   4 Current Issues and Conclusions
         Research Papers Due

INTRODUCTION
Week 1:

EARLY MODERN EUROPE--THE BACKGROUND

Week 2:
Richard S. Dunn, The Age of the Religious Wars

THE ORIGINS OF WITCHCRAFT

Week 3:
William E. Monter, "The Historiography of European Witchcraft:
Progress and Prospects," Journal of Interdisciplinary History 2
(1972).
European Witchcraft, ed. Wm. Monter, pp. 1-109.
E. Le Roy Ladurie, "The Aiguillette: Castration by Magic," in The
Mind and Method of the Historian pp. 84-96.
First written assignment: Hand in carefully worked out
definitions of "heresy", "orthodoxy", "witchcraft."

TWO THEORETICAL BASES FOR UNDERSTANDING THE WITCH CRAZE

Week 4:
Margaret Murray, The God of the Witches

Week 5:
Norman Cohn, Europe's Inner Demons
Second Written Assignment: Hand in an analytic book
review of no more than 4 pages of either Murray or Cohn.
State the central thesis of the author; then examine his or
her methodological and historical techniques; finally,
present your judgment of the author's success in
supporting and defending the thesis.

WAS "THE WITCH" A WOMAN?

Week 6:
Robert Muchembled, "The Witches of the Cambresis," in Religion and
the People, 700-1700, ed. James Obelkevitch.

Week 7:
Carlo Ginzburg, The Night Battles: Witchcraft and Agrarian Cults
in the Sixteenth and Seventeenth Centuries tr. John & Anne
Tedeschi.

Week 8:
    Read one of these three area studies:
Christina Larner, Enemies of God: The Witchhunt in Scotland (1981).
H. C. Erik Midelfort, Witch Hunting in Southwestern Germany,
    1562-1684 (1972).
William E. Monter, Witchcraft in France and Switzerland (1976).
        Third Written Assignment: Write an essay of 6 to 8 pages
        which analyzes (1) the role of gender in the witch
        hunting of early-modern Europe and (2) historians'
        perceptions of gender as an element in the witch hunts.
        This is due in class.

THE DECLINE OF THE WITCH HUNTS

Week 9:
European Witchcraft, pp. 111-143.
H. D. Erik Midelford, "Witch Hunting and the Domino Theory,"
    in Religion and the People, 800-1700, ed. Jas Obelkevich.
Thomas Forbes, "Midwifery and Witchcraft," Journal of the History
    of Medicine, 17 (1962), 264-283.

CAN THE WITCH HUNTS BE EXPLAINED?

Week 10:
European Witchcraft, pp. 145-172.
Richard Horsley, "Who Were the Witches? The Social Roles of the
    Accused in European Witch Trials," J.I.H. 9 (1979).
Richard Kieckhefer, European Witch Trials: Their Foundations in
    Popular and Learned Culture, 1300-1500.
        Fourth Written Assignment: A carefully considered and
        reasoned discussion in no more than 8 pages is due in
        class of the following question: Taking the position
        either that witchcraft never actually existed, or that
        it was a real phenomenon, how can you explain the witch-
        hunting craze of early modern Europe?

A MODERN CASE

Week 11:
Jeanne Favret-Saada, Deadly Words: Witchcraft in the Bocage tr.
    Catherine Cullen (Cambridge, 1980).

STATE UNIVERSITY OF NEW YORK
at Stony Brook

DEPARTMENT OF HISTORY

HIS 316: THE HEALER AND THE WITCH IN HISTORY
SPRING 1985

> Instructor: Helen Lemay
> Office Hours: Mon., Wed., 11-1
> Office: SBS S-317
> Telephone: 246-6511, 246-6500

COURSE REQUIREMENTS:

1. The major written requirement for this course is a
    fifteen-page research paper on a topic approved by
    the instructor. This paper will make up 40% of
    your final grade.

    Students are to choose their paper topics early in
    the semester. Attached to this syllabus is a list
    of topics that have been selected by students in
    the past. Bibliographies for these topics are on
    reserve for this course under "Lemay Bibliography,"
    and you may consult this document and xerox
    materials that interests you. You are encouraged
    to choose your own topic, provided that it pertains
    to the matter of the course (women and medicine
    from the Greeks to the present). Your paper does
    not have to deal with women; if you wish to pursue
    research on a topic on the SOCIAL history of
    medicine, this will be considered appropriate.
    Please be aware that you may not hand in one paper
    for two courses without first receiving the
    permission of both instructors.

    The project should be prepared in three stages. On
    March 4-8 you should hand in a statement of the
    topic you have chosen and a bibliography of 10
    items that you have already consulted with a
    statement about the content of each item. These
    should come from 10 different sources which have
    given you a general idea of the basic material in
    the field and the shape of your future research.
    This is not intended to be a "book report" to prove
    that you did the reading, but rather a progress
    report which gives the instructor an idea of what
    kind of information you have been collecting so
    that she can make constuctive suggestions to help
    you. Along with the above information, you should
    list possible questions that your paper might
    address.

Although you will receive suggestions on
bibliography, you are responsible for developing a
good collection of references pertinent to your
topic, and you should ask the help of the reference
librarian. Please remember that the quality of
your bibliography will determine in large measure
the quality of your final paper. If you do your
research in general works on women's history, your
paper will be general in nature and not very good.
If you research a specific aspect of your topic, on
the other hand, you will have a good grasp of it.
For this reason, the bulk of your research will
most likely be done in periodical literature. This
means journals that give serious, scholarly
treatment of the subjects under discussion not
popular magazines. Family Health, Prevention,
Parents, Glamour, Newsweek and similar magazines
should not have a prominent place in your
bibliography. You will search for periodical
literature in bibliographical sources such as the
Cumulated Index Medius and the Bibliography of the
History of Medicine put out by the National Library
of Medicine, and not in the Reader's Guide. More
detailed instuctions on bibliography are found
later on in this syllabus. You should plan to do
some work in the Health Sciences Center Library
they have a good collection of periodicals in this
field, and a respectable collection of monographs
as well.

On April 1-6 you should hand in stage 2 of your
paper. At this point you should write down a
statement of the point that you intend to make in
your paper, and you should give your final
bibliography. Please note that your research is
supposed to have direction, that you are supposed
to be investigating the answer to a question or
testing a hypothesis that you have formulated
during your preliminary reading. Thus your paper
will have a thesis and will present, expound, and
prove the validity of your point of view on your
chosen subject. For example, you will not simply
write a paper on "Nursing reform under Florence
Nightingale" and state that she cleaned up the sick
rooms, listened to the doctors, and emphasized
morals and ladylike behavior in her nurses.
Rather, your paper would discuss what you think is
SIGNIFICANT about what she did, for example that
Florence Nightingale's ideal for a nurse embodied
the value of ladylike submissiveness found in
Victorian society and emphasized aristocratic
values instead of technical expertise. You must

not only do research, therefore; you must THINK
about what is important about the information you
have uncovered.

Try to pick a topic that interests you, or one that
has meaning for your life. There is much
fascinating material in this field, all of it with
contemporary relevance. You are urged to explore
it, and you may certainly include in your paper a
discussion of the contemporary significance of the
issue you have chosen--to carry out the example
above, the nursing profession and its relation to
the feminine ideal of the past decades.

Please remember that this is a 300-level course
that satisfies the University's upper-level
requirement for undergraduates, and that therefore
you are expected to do a respectable term paper.
Your final bibliography should have a minimum of 15
items, and you should be knowledgeable in your
chosen field. You should footnote your sources in
the standard manner; if you are not sure how to do
this consult the MLA style sheet, Turabian's
manual, or another guide. It is NOT sufficient
simp[ly to list your sources at the end in a
bibliography; your paper should have footnotes as
well.

Your final paper is due on April 22. The schedule
above by which you turn in two preliminary stages
of your paper or criticism, is designed to aid the
student in preparing a good piece of work. If, for
some reason, you choose not to take advantage of
it, you will not be penalized if you hand in an A
paper on April 22. Some students do not need
guidance. However, if you are not a solid A
student, and quality and promptness of these
reports will be taken into account in determining
your final grade. Further, if your topic or your
treatment of it is unsatisfactory and you have not
turned in the preliminary statements you will not
find this out until it is too late.

2.   Participation in discussion. Discussions of
      course topics and their contemporary significance
      are scheduled throughout the semester. Students
      are expected to prepare for these discussion by
      doing reading on the topic, and by taking turns as
      discussion leaders in class. Topics are announced
      on the syllabus, and you are encouraged to look in
      Reader's Guide course bibliographies, or Women's
      Studies bibliographies for pertinent articles and

to bring your findings to class. In addition,
specific articles will be assigned on a rotating
basis for oral class reports. Performance in
discussion counts as 20% of your grade.

3.   Two essay examinations, a midsemester and a final.
The final will be held during finals week. It is
not cumulative. Each makes up 20% of your grade.

REQUIRED BOOKS:

Norman Cohn, <u>Europe's Inner Demons</u>, Meridian Book,
New American Library
Richard Wertz and Dorothy Wertz, <u>Lying In: A
History of Childbirth in America</u>, Schocken Books
Judith Walzer Leavitt, ed. <u>Women and Health in
America</u>, University of Wisconsin Press.

SUGGESTIONS FOR PREPARING YOUR BIBLIOGRAPHY

1. Go to the reserve room and request to see the
    reserve list for HIS 316. From the books and
    articles listed, you should be able to get a start
    on researching your topic. Look at the footnotes
    and bibliographies in these volumes for further
    direction.

2. The following entries in the subject catalogue of
    the library are pertinent to material covered in
    this course and might cover the topic of your
    paper:

            Women in Medicine
            Women Dentists
            Women Physicians
            Medical Education
            Medical Students
            Discrimination in Education
            Sex discrimination against women -- U.S.
            Midwives
            Obstetrics
            Witchcraft
            Hysteria

    The material in the SUBJECT catalogue of the main
    library does not list Health Sciences Center books.
    Therefore, when researching in the SUBJECT
    catalogue, you must go to the HCC library.

    The AUTHOR catalogue, however, does list HCC
    books.

3. Look in the Reference Room for the following books
    which will help you in your research. THEY DO NOT
    CIRCULATE, SO THEY WILL BE THERE.

            Chaff, S.L. Women in Medicine: A Bibliography
            of the Literature on Women Physicians.
            Metuchen, N.J.: Scarecrow Press, 1977.

            Call no: Ref. R692, W65

            Faunce, Patricia, Women and Ambition

            Call no: Ref. HQ 1206 F28

            Een, Joanne D., Women and Society. Beverly
            Hills: Sage Publications, 1978

            Call No: Ref. HQ 1399 .E4

Women's Eduicational Equity Comm. Network,
Resources in Women's Educational Equity

Call no: Ref. HQ 1154 R45

In the Reference Room, look at the Women's Studies
Reference Collection, HQ 1115 to HQ 1883. This
should be helpful in preparing bibliography for
your paper.

An EXCELLENT reference tool for this course can be
found in the third floor of the stacks. It does
NOT circulate. Call no: 26660 B 582. National
Library of Medicine. Bibliography of the History
of Medicine.

4.   When you have narrowed down your topic, you might
be able to arrange for a computer search with the
reference librarian. DO NOT LEAVE THIS FOR THE DAY
BEFORE YOUR STATEMENT OF TOPIC IS DUE. You must
make an appointment for this service.

If you have difficulties, ask the reference
librarians for help.

Also, take a trip to the Health Sciences Center to
see what kind of material they have. This is
especially helpful for your research in
periodicals, because the periodicls are out on the
shelves, arranged alphabetically.

Try for example:

Journal of the American Medical Women's
    Association
Bulletin of the History of Medicine
Journal of Health Politics, Policy and Law
Linacre Quarterly: Journal of Philosophy and
    Ethics of Medical Practice
Milbank Memorial Fund Quarterly: Health and
    Society
Perspectives in Biology and Medicine
Social Science and Medicine
Social Policy
Science for the People

TOPICS FOR WHICH BIBLIOGRAPHIES HAVE BEEN COMPILED;
THEY ARE ON RESERVE

> Witchcraft (You should choose only one ASPECT of
>   this topic)
> Demonic Possession
> Witchcaft at Salem
> Ergotism and the Witch Trials at Salem
> Witchcraft Today and Its Origins
> Arican Witchcraft
> African Herbalists
> Herbal Medicine of the North American Indians and
>   its Uses with Women
> Nursing (one aspect of this topic)
> Midwifery (one aspect of this topic)
> Birthing Centers
> Hospitals Doctors, Medicine: Their Invation into
>   Childbirth
> Role of Father at Child's Birth
> Obstetrics in Modern America
> Sexual Surgery
> Gynecology
> Self-Help Movement in Gynecological Care
> The Schism in Gynecology: Psychological/
>   Physiological Issues
> Women and Drugs
> Psychiatric Health Seekers: Women in the Market of
>   Mental Health
> Rape
> Fertility
> Surrogate Mothering: The Myths and Controversies
> Sterilization
> The Pill and its Side Effects
> Women Against the Women's Movement
> Women and Aging
> Right to Life Propaganda
> Alternative Therapies or Cancer: Laetrile
> Menstrution: The Medial Perspective
> Effects of Discrimination during Residencies and
>   Internships on Women Physicians
> Anorexia Nervosa and Bulimia
> Neurasthenia and Victorian Women
> Animal Experimentation and the Biology of Women
> Contraception
> "Menopause Syndrome" as Social Control
> Benign Breast Disease
> Surrogte Mothers
> Women and Sports
> Vaginitis
> Herbal Medicine in 19c America
> Natural Childbirth
> Role of Father in Childbirth

TOPICS FOR WHICH BIBLIOGRAPHIES HAVE BEEN COMPILED;
cont'd

Dental Care for the Handicapped
Chiropractic
Couvade Syndrome
Informed Consent
Mesothelioma: The Carcinogenic Manifestation of
    Asbestos Exposure
Effects of Phenylketonuria
Female Infanticide in China
Child Growth Disorders
Teenage Pregnancies
Prostitution and the Medical Profession
Male Nursing
Patient Confidentiality
Biofeedback
Stress in Medical School
Chinese Medicine
The Woman Physician Today
Death
Sexual Surgery and Electroconvulsive Therapy--A
    Parallel
Black Women in Medicine
Holistic Medicine
Obstacles Faced by Female Physicians in 19c America
Pharmacological Influences on Witchcraft
Hysteria Compared with Anorexia Nervosa
Effects of Alcohol on the Fetus
Teratogenic Effets of Salicylates
Health Effects of Agent Orange
Effect of Feminist Movement on Women's Admissions
    to Medical School, Mid 1960's to present
Birth Control in Nineteenth Century
Birth in the Future
Yellow Fever
Religious and Psychic Healing
Retrolental Fibroplasia
Herbal Medicine
Therapeutic Effects of Music on Autistic Children
Masturbation

LECTURE SCHEDULE AND READING ASSIGNMENTS

Jan. 21, 23   Introduction, Early Biological Views of Women,
                Ancient Mystical Healing
                        Reading: Begin Norman Cohn, Europe's Inner
                        Demons
                Discussion: Women and Biological Inferiority
                (Naomi Weisstein, "Tired of Arguing About
                Biological Inferiority?" Ms Nov. 1982 Mystical
                Healing
                (S. Kakar, Shamans, Mystics and Doctors)

Jan. 28, 30   Women and Medieval Medicine
                        Reading: Continue reading Norman Cohn
                Discussion: Witchraft and Madness: The
                Szasz Thesis (Thos Szasz, Manufacture of
                Madness)
                Witchcraft today
                (Margot Adler, Drawing Down the Moon)

Feb. 4, 6   Witchcraft and Healing
                        Reading: Finish Norman Cohn
                Discussion: Norman Cohn, Europe's Inner Demons

Feb. 11, 13   Battle of Man Midwife: Embryotomy and Instruments
                        Reading: J.W. Leavitt, Women and Health in
                        America pp. 141-174, Wertz and Wertz, Lying
                        In, pp. 1-76
                Discussion: Obstetrical Intervention Today
                (Michelle Harrison, A Woman in Residence
                Women and Health, Vol. 7, 1982: Brigitte Jordan
                "External Cephalic Version"
                Paul Doering, "Obstetrical Analgesia and
                Anesthesia"
                S. Thacker and H. Banta, "Benefits and Risks of
                Episiotomy"

Feb. 18, 20   Battle of Man Midwife: Modesty and Training for
                Midwives
                        Reading: Leavitt, pp. 299-326
                        Wertz and Wertz, pp. 76-108
                Discussion: Midwifery Today
                (Brigitte Jordan, Birth in Four Cultures,
                Janet Ashford, Birth Stories)

Feb. 25   MIDSEMESTER EXAMINATION IN CLASS

Feb. 27   Battle Against Sectarianism
                   Reading: Leavitt 246-269, 359-389
               Discussion: Alternative Medicine Today
               (Ivan Illich, Medical Nemesis, J. K. Van Fleet,
               Extraordinary Healing Secrets From A Doctor's
               Private Files

Mar. 4, 6   Battle Against Sectarianism
               Discussion: Holistic Medicine, Alternative
               Medicine (K.R. Pelletier, Holistic Medicine,
               Norman Cousins "Anatomy of an Illness"
               Norman Gevitz, The DO's: Osteopathic Medicine
               in America

       STAGE ONE OF PAPER DUE IN DISCUSSION GROUP BEFORE SPRING
       VACATION. SEE DETAILS UNDER "COURSE REQUIREMENTS."

Mar. 11, 13   NO CLASS. SPRING VACATION.

Mar. 18, 20   Med Schools vs. Women: Political Action
               (Samuel Gregory and Elizabeth Blackwell)
                   Reading: Leavitt, pp. 391-452
               Discussion: Women and Medical Schools (Mary
               Campbell, Why Would A Girl Go Into Medicine
               Jane Leserman, Men and Women in Medical School)

Mar. 25, 27   Medicine vs. Women: Propaganda (Nevrasthenia
               and Sexual Surgery)
                   Reading: Leavitt, pp. 220-284, Wertz and
                   Wertz, pp. 109-131
               Discussion: Sexual Surgery
               (Penny Wise Budoff, No More Menstrual Cramps,
               Fran Hosken, Hosken Report

Apr. 1, 3   Nursing and the Professionalization of Medicine
                   Reading: Leavitt, pp. 453-506, 327-344
               Discussion: Women and Other Health Professions
               (NY State Dental Journal, Jan. 1983: "The Dentist
               is a Lady"
               Freshmen Interested in the Health Prfessions,
               Vol. I of Women and Minorities in Health Fields:
               A Trend Analysis of College Freshman, U.S. Dept.
               of Health, Education, and Welfare, 1977

       STAGE TWO OF PAPER DUE THIS WEEK IN DISCUSSION GROUP. SEE
       DETAILS UNDER "COURSE REQUIREMENTS."

Apr. 8, 10   Nursing and the Professionalization of Medicine
               No reading. You should be working on your
               paper.
               Discussion: Nursing Today
               (Myra Macpherson, "Vietnam Nurses," Ms, June 1984
               Bullough, Bullough and Soukup, Nursing Issues and
               Nursing Strategies for the Eighties)

Apr. 15, 17   Women and Medical Education in the Post-Flekner Era
               No reading. Begin reading for next topic.
               Discussion: The Careers of Women Physicians
               (Morantz, Pomerleau, Fenichel In Her Own Words,
               D. R. Mandelbaum, Work, Marriage and Motherhood:
               The Career Persistence of Female Physicians)

Apr. 22   FINAL PAPER DUE IN CLASS

Apr. 22, 24   Gynecology and Obstetrics in the Twentieth Century
               Reading: Leavitt, pp. 175-184, Wertz and
               Wertz   132-246
               Discussion: Contemporary Women's Health Issues
               (Hilde Bruch, Eating Disorders
               Katharina Dalton, Premenstrual Syndrome)

Apr. 29, May 1 Birth Control and Abortion
               Reading: Leavitt, pp. 175-184
               Discussion: Birth Control and Abortion
               (Barbara Seaman, The Doctors' Case Against the Pill
               Linda Bird Francke, The Ambivalence of Abortion)

May   6, 8   Contemporary Women's Health Issues, The Women's
               Health Movement
               Discussion: Contemporary Women's Health Issues
               (Snowden, Mitchell and Snowden, Artificial
               Reproduction: A Social Investigation
               B. Seaman and G. Seaman, Women and the Crisis in
               Sex Hormones)

       FINAL EXAMINATION TO BE HELD DURING FINALS WEEK ACCORDING
       TO UNIVERSITY-WIDE SCHEDULE.

Department of History
Columbia University

Undergraduate Seminar

Robert Moeller

Case Studies in Women's Collective Action in
Modern Europe, 1750-1945

This course is intended as a systematic, comparative
investigation of the forms of women's collective action in modern
Europe. Case studies have been carefully chosen both to allow us
to develop a typology of forms of collective action, and also to
make comparisons over time and between different national
contexts. Our studies will include: 1) the French Revolution of
1789; 2) forms of feminist politics within the 19th century
British parliamentary system (Owenite feminism, organized
opposition to the regulation of prostitution and the fight for
women's suffrage); 3) socialist feminism in Russia and women's
participation in the Russian Revoluion of 1917; 4) the
'conservative feminism' of women's groups in the Weimar Republic
and under the National Socialist regime. The success of our
attempts at national comparisons will be contingent on a thorough
knowledge the larger context within which each of our case
studies are located. Reading will thus include not only
materials on the specific varieties of women's collective action
but in addition a general introduction to the national political
history in each case. This comparative approach and long-term
perspective will allow us to raise several important questions:
How have the forms of women's collective action changed over
time? How can we identify and specify a uniquely feminist
politics and how have its dimensions changed in modern Europe?
What influence do particular state forms, paths of industrial
development, and national 'political cultures' have on the forms
and possibilities of women's collective action? What forces and
conditions shape the potential success of women's collective
action?

Course requirements will include:

1) presentation of a framework for the discussion of one week's
readings. This should not be recapitulation of the readings but
rather should identify key points of controversy or interest for
our discussion. The presentation should last no longer than ten
minutes and will serve to get our discussion started. A set of
questions for discussion should be prepared and circulated to
class members before your presentation.

2) a brief paper (6-8 typed pages) which offers a discussion of a
book which addresses an important element of historical context
in the course but which does not specifically discuss women. You
wil be asked to summarize the information of relevance for our
discussion and also to suggest the points at which women and
feminist concerns might be integrated into such a text.

3) a brief paper (6-8 pages) which discusses a monograph relevant to the course or a memoir or contemporary eyewitness account.

4) a term paper (15 pages) which develops one aspect of one of the cases covered in the course or treats another instance of women's collective action which can broaden our comparative framework.

All readings are on reserve in the College Library. In addition, the following books have been ordered in the University Bookstore:

- George Lefebvre, The Coming of the French Revolution

- Carol R. Berkin and Clara M. Lovett, Women, War and Revolution

- Darline Gay Levy, Harriet Branson Applewhite, Mary Dunham Johnson, Women in Revolutionary Paris 1789-1795

- Barbara Taylor, Eve and the New Jerusalem: Socialism and Feminism in the Nineteenth Century

- Judith Walkowitz, Prostitution and Victorian Society: Women, Class and the State

- Ray Strachey, The Cause: A Short History of the Women's Movement in Great Britain

- Jill Liddington and Jill Norris, One Hand Tied Behind Us

- Alexandra Kollontai, Selected Writings, ed. Alix Holt

- Victoria Bonnell, ed., The Russian Worker: Life and Labor under the Tsarist Regime

- Richard Stites, The Women's Liberation Movement in Russia

- Gail Lapidus, Women in Soviet Society

- David Schoenbaum, Hitler's Social Revolution

- Lydia Sargent, ed., Women and Revolution

- Zillah R. Eisenstein, The Radical Future of Liberal Feminism

WEEK I - GENERAL INTRODUCTION

WEEK II - SOCIETY IN 18TH CENTURY FRANCE AND THE COMING OF REVOLUTION

- George Lefebvre, *The Coming of the French Revolution*

- Abby R. Kleinbaum, "Women in the Age of Light," in R. Bridenthal and Claudia Koonz, eds., *Becoming Visible*, pp. 217-36

- Olwen H. Hufton, "Women and the Family Economy in Eighteen Century France," *French Historical Studies* (Spring 1975), 1-22

- Louise A. Tilly, "The Food Riot as a Form of Political Conflict in France," *Journal of Interdisciplinary History* 2 (1971): 23-57

WEEK III - WOMEN IN REVOLUTIONARY FRANCE

- Jane Abray, "Feminism in the French Revolution," *American Historical Review* 80 (1975): 43-62

- Olwen Hufton, "Women in the French REvolution," *Past & Present* Nr. 53 (1971): 90-108

- Darline Gay Levy and Harriet Branson Applewhite, "Women of the Popular Classes in Revolutionary Paris, 1789-1795," in Carol R. Berkin and Clara M. Lovett, *Women, War, and Revolution*, 9-36

- Darline Gay Levy, Harriet Branson Applewhite, Mary Dunham Johnson, *Women in Revolutionary Paris 1789-1795* (selections)

WEEK IV - LIBERY, EQUALITY AND FRATERNITY FOR WHOM?

- Margaret George, "The 'World Historical Defeat' of the Republicaines-Revolutionnaires," *Science and Society* 40 (Winter 1976-77): 410-37

- Barbara Corrado Pope, "Revolution and Retreat: Upper-Class French Women after 1789," in *Women, War and Revolution*, 215-36

- Mary Dunham Johnson, "Old Wine in New Bottles: The Institutional Chances for Women of the People During the French Revolution," in *Women, War and Revolution*, 107-45

- Scott Lyle, "The Second Sex (September 1793)," *Journal of Modern History* 26 (1955): 14-26

- Roderich Phillips, "Women and Family Breakdown in Eighteenth Century France: Rouen 1780-1800," *Social History* 1 (1976): 197-218

WEEK V - UTOPIAN VISIONS AND EARLY SOCIALIST FEMINISM

- R.K. Webb, *Modern England from the 18th Century to the Present* (1971), pp. 152-63, 178-83, 193-201, 205-14, 233-52

- Barbara Taylor, *Eve and the New Jerusalem: Socialism and Feminism in the Nineteenth Century* (New York, 1983)

WEEK VI - SEXUAL POLITICS? THE FIGHT FOR THE REPEAL OF THE CONTAGIOUS DISEASE ACTS

- Webb, *Modern England*, 258-89, 318-27, 379-412

- Judith Walkowitz, *Prostitution and Victorian Society: Women, Class and the State* (New York, 1980)

WEEK VII THE SUFFRAGE MOVEMENT (I)

- Webb, *Modern England*, 448-61, 465-69, 473-75

- Ray Strachey, *The Cause: A Short History of the Women's Movement in Great Britain* (selections)

WEEK VIII THE SUFFRAGE MOVEMENT (II)

- Jill Liddington and Jill Norris, *One Hand Tied Behind Us*

WEEK IX WORKING WOMEN AND SOCIALIST FEMINISM: RUSSIA BEFORE THE REVOLUTION

- J.P. Nettl, *The Soviet Achievement* (selections)

- Rose L. Glickman, "The Russian Factory Woman, 1880-1914," in D. Atkinson, A. Dallin and G. Lapidus, *Women in Russia* (Stanford, 1977), 63-84

- Anne Bobroff, "Russian Working Women: Sexuality in Bonding Patterns and the Politics of Daily Life," in A. Snitow, C. Stansell and S. Thompson, eds., *Powers of Desire: The Politics of Sexuality* (New York, 1983), 206-27

- Alexandra Kollontai, *Selected Writings*, ed. A. Holt, 13-74, 127-39

- Victoria Bonnell, ed., *The Russian Worker: Life and Labour under the Tsarist Regime* (Berkeley and Los Angeles, 1983), 113-50, 185-208

WEEK IX - WOMEN IN THE REVOLUTION OF 1917

- Nettl, *Soviet Achievement*

- Anne Bobroff, "The Bolsheviks and Working Women," *Soviet Studies* (October 1974): 540-76

- Barbara Evans Clement, "Working-Class and Peasant Women in the Russian Revolution, 1917-1923," *Signs* 9 (1982): 215-35

- Richard Stites, *The Women's Liberation Movement in Russia. Feminism, Nihilism and Bolshevism, 1860-1930* (Princeton, 1978), 233-77

- Gail W. Lapidus, *Women in Soviet Society: Equality, Development and Social Change* (Berkeley and Los Angeles, 1978), 17-53

WEEK X - UTOPIAN DREAMS, REVOLUTIONARY NIGHTMARES?

- Lapidus, *Women in Soviet Society*, 54-94

- Kolontai, *Selected Writings*, 216-92

- Carol Eubanks Hayden, "The Zhenotdel and the Bolshevik Party," *Russian History* 3 (1976): 156-73

- Stites, *Women's Liberation Movement*, 317-422

- Beatrice Brodsky Farnsworth, "Communism Feminism: Its Synthesis and Demise," in *Women, War and Revolution*, 145-64

- Farnsworth, "Bolshevik Alternatives and the Soviet Family: The 1926 Marriage Law Debate," in Atkinson, Dallin, Lapidus, *Women in Russia*, 139-66

WEEK XI - 'CONSERVATIVE FEMINISM'? WOMEN'S ORGANIZATIONS IN THE WEIMAR REPUBLIC

- AJ Nicholls, *Weimar and the Rise of Hitler*

- Claudia Koonz, "Conflicting Alliances: Political Ideology and Women Legislators in Weimar Germany," *Signs* 1 (1975/76), 663-83

- Renate Bridenthal, "Beyond Kinder, Küche, Kirche: Weimar Women at Work," *Central European History* 6 (1973): 148-66

- Richard Evans, *The Feminist Movement in Germany 1894-1933* (Beverly Hills, 1976) (selections)

WEEK XII - WOMEN AND NATIONAL SOCIALISM

- David Schoenbaum, *Hitler's Social Revolution*, ci-72, 178-92, 234-88

- Tim Mason, "Women in Nazi Germany," *History Workshop*, 1-2

- Claudia Koonz, "Mothers in the Fatherland: Women in Nazi Germany," in *Becoming Visible*, 445-73

- Gisela Bock, "Racism and Sexism in Nazi Germany: Motherhood, Compulsory Sterilization and the State," *Signs* 8 (1983): 400-21

WEEK XIII - EQUALITY OF THE BOMB SHELTERS?

- Leila Rupp, "I Don't Call that Volksgemeinschaft," in *Women, War and Revolution*, 37-54

- Jill Stephenson, *The Nazi Organization of Women*

- Leila Rupp, *Mobilizing Women for War: German and American Propaganda 1939-1945* (Princeton, 1978)

WEEK XIV - TOWARD A TYPOLOGY OF WOMEN'S COLLECTIVE ACTION: HOW CAN HISTORY INFORM THEORY

- Lydia Sargent, ed., *Women and Revolution* (Boston, 1981)

- Zillah R. Eisenstein, *The Radical Future of Liberal Feminism* (New York, 1981), 89-114

Penny Gold, Fall 1985
Office hours: MW 2:00–3:15 or
by appointment
Phone: office x328; home 342–0232

History 323: HISTORY OF FEMINISM

An introduction to feminist theory and to feminism as a political and social movement, from the late Middle Ages to the present, with a focus on the nineteenth and early twentieth centuries.

Goals: To learn about:

> one of the largest, most successful social movements of modern times
> the diversity of goals that feminism has embraced
> the class, racial, sexual, gender, and religious tensions within the movement
> the variety of strategies used to bring about social change
> the extent of change and the extent of continuity over time
> the connections of feminism to other political, cultural, and social developments

> To further skills in:
>> analysis of historical source materials
>> group discussion
>> historical research
>> writing
>> oral presentation

Books available for purchase:

Richard Evans, The Feminists: Women's Emancipation Movements in Europe 1840–1920 (Barnes and Noble)

Alice Rossi (ed.), The Feminist Papers: from Adams to de Beauvoir (Bantam)

Susan Groag Bell and Karen Offen, Women, the Family and Freedom: The Debate in Documents, 2 vols. (Stanford University Press)

Alexandra Kollontai, Love of Worker Bees (Academy Chicago)

Th 9/12   Introduction

Tu 9/11   **WHAT IS FEMINISM?** The problem of definition
> WFF, vol. 1, p. 2, n. 3
> Rossi, pp. xii–xiii (the paragraph beginning "A second critical issue..."
> Andreas Capellanus, The Art of Courtly Love
> Jean de Meun, Romance of the Rose
> Christine de Pizan, The Book of the City of Ladies, xix–xxii, Part I, chps. 1, 2,
> 8, 9, 11, 27, 33, 37; Part II, chps. 7, 13, 30, 36, 44, 53, 66, 69;
> Part III, chps. 1, 19 (about 50 pages altogether) (on reserve)

Th 9/19   **CHRONOLOGICAL SURVEY**: Enlightenment thought
> Evans, preface and Chap. 1 (pp. 13–43)
> WFF, pp. 42–49 (Rousseau)
> Rossi, pp. 25–85 (Wollstonecraft)

II Tu 9/24   The French Revolution
> WFF, pp. 1–23, 97–109, 119–22

Th 9/26   Liberalism
            Rossi, pp. 183–238 (J. S. Mill)
            WFF, pp. 391-2, 399-408

III Tu 10/1   Social Reform
            Evans, Chap. 2 (pp. 44-143; you may skim pp. 69-102)
            Rossi, pp. 241-311 (Grimké sisters)
            Rossi, pp. 323-55 (Blackwell family)

Th 10/3   Socialism
            Evans, Chap. 3 (pp. 144-88)
            Rossi, 473-516
            WFF, vol. 2, 73-4, 87-91

            [Hand in choice of oral report topic and tentative reading list.]

IV Tu 10/8   Suffrage
            Evans, Chap. 4 (pp. 189-245)
            Rossi, 378-96, 407-470
            Virgil Thompson/Gertrude Stein, The Mother of Us All (opera about Susan B.
              Anthony; on reserve in Seymour Library)

Th 10/10   MIDTERM (option of in-class midterm during class time on Thursday or take-home
            exam due by noon Friday)

Tu 10/15 to Tu 11/4 **THE ISSUES AND THE PEOPLE**
            For the next seven classes our schedule will be determined by what issues people in
            the class would like to explore. Each student will be responsible for choosing an issue
            from the list below. You will prepare an oral report on that issue, focusing on one
            person who identified her/himself with that issue. Together with the instructor, you
            will also put together a reading list for the class on that issue; readings from WFF
            and/or Rossi are the most obvious choice for such readings, but material to be put on
            reserve may also be used.

            ISSUES (other issues possible, on consultation with instructor)
            birth control   personal relationships
            child custody   property rights
            church/religion/anti-clericalism   prostitution
            class issues   race issues
            critique of male culture   sexuality
            divorce   suffrage
            education   temperance
            entry to professions   working conditions

VIII W 11/6   Public lecture: Diane Worzala, "Days of Glory: The British Woman's Suffrage
            Campaign, 1904-1914", 7:00 p.m., Round Room, CFA

Th 11/7   Feminism in the inter-war period (Diane Worzala will be our guest today)
            WFF, vol. 2 (selection to be announced)

IX Tu 11/12 **CONTEMPORARY FEMINISM IN HISTORICAL PERSPECTIVE**
            Jo Freeman, "The Women's Liberation Movement in the United States" (reserve)
            Adrienne Rich, "Compulsory Heterosexuality and Lesbian Existence" (reserve)

Th 11/14   Cherrié Moraga and Gloria Anzaldúa (eds.), <u>This Bridge Called My Back:</u>
            <u>Writings by Radical Women of Color</u> (reserve; selection to be announced)

X   Tu 11/19 Conclusion

<u>GRADE</u>: Your grade will be based on the following:

Midterm exam	20%
Oral report	10%
Critique of another's oral report	10%
Paper	20%
Final exam	20%
Class participation	20%

<u>MIDTERM EXAM</u>: The midterm will be an essay exam aimed at a review of the readings assigned
        during the first four weeks. You will have the option of taking an in-class exam during class
        on Thursday, November 10 or of doing a take-home exam due at noon on Friday, November 11;
        questions for the take-home exam will be handed out on Tuesday, November 9.

<u>ORAL REPORT</u>: See description above at 10/15. Your oral report should be 15-20 minutes long. You
        should speak from an outline or organized set of notes, copies of which will be given to the
        instructor and to the student assigned to critique your report.

<u>CRITIQUE OF ANOTHER'S ORAL REPORT</u>: Each student will critique the oral report of another. (I will
        assign the critiques, taking into account the scheduling and your interests.) Your critique
        should be a written document of about 500 words. Critique due by class following the report.

<u>PAPER</u>: Your paper should be an expansion of your oral report, building on the comments received in
        class and the critique of the student and the instructor. Length: about 15 pages.

<u>FINAL EXAM</u>: The final exam will be held during the regularly scheduled examination period. I will
        pass out a document not previously studied in the class and ask you to analyze the issues raised
        in the text , in the context of material covered in the course.

<u>PENALTY FOR LATENESS</u>: Late written assignments will be graded down, with more points taken off
        for each successive day late. If you have a legitimate reason for an extension without penalty
        (e.g., illness), discuss your situation with me as soon as possible so that we can arrange an
        extension.

<u>COLLEGE ATTENDANCE POLICY</u>: "Students are expected to attend class regularly and to participate
        fully in class activities. Students who are absent from class, for whatever reason, are still
        responsible for all assigned work."

Please do not smoke in class.

132

MEDITERRANEAN WOMEN
(Italy, Spain, Greece and Portugal)

I.   Cultural background

Peristiany, J.G. (ed.). Honour and shame: the values of
     Mediterranean Society (London, 1965)
Kenny, Michael and Kertzer, David. Urban life in Mediterranean
     Europe: anthropological perspectives (Urbana, 1983)
Cornelisen, Ann. Torregreca: life, death miracles (N.Y., 1962)
Gage, Nicholas. Eleni (N.Y., 1983)
Pescatello, Ann. Power and pawn: the female in Iberian families,
     societies and cultures (Westport, 1976)
Silverman, Sydel. Three bells of civilization: the life of an
     Italian hilltown (N.Y., 1975)
Sarti, Roland. Long live the strong: a history of rural society
     in the Apennine mountains (Amherst, 1985)

II. Marriage and the family

Kirschner, J. and Molho, A. "Dowry fund and the marriage market
     in early quattrocento Florence," Journal of Modern History,
     50 (1978), 403-38
Schneider, Jane. "Of vigil and virgins: honor, shame and access
     to reason in Mediterranean society," Ethnology, 10 (1971),
     1-24
Hirschon, Renee. "Under one roof: marriage, dowry and family
     relations," Urban life in Mediterranean Europe, ed. by M.
     Kenny and D. Kertzer (Urbana, 1983), pp. 299 323
Campbell, J. Honor, family and patronage: a study of institutions
     and moral values in a Greek mountain community (Oxford, 1964)

III. Work: agricultural and industrial

Friedl, Ernestine. Vasilika: village in modern Greece (N.Y., 1962)
Malefakis, Edward. Agarian reform and peasant revolutions in
     Spain (New Haven, 1973)
Martinez-Alier, Juan. Labourers and landowners in southern Spain
     (London, 1971)
Riegelhaupt, Joyce, "Saloio women: an analysis of informal and
     formal political and economic roles of Portuguese peasant
     women," Anthropology Quarterly, 40 (1967), 95-126
Brown, J. and Goodman, J. "Women and industry in Florence,"
     Journal of Economic History, 40 (1980), 73-80
Cornelisen, Ann. Women of the shadows (N.Y., 1974)
Tilly, Louise. "Occupational structure, women's work and industry
     in Milan, 1880-1910," Journal of Urban History, 3 (1977),
     467-84
Bandettini, Pierfrancesco. "Employment of women in Italy, 1881-
     1951," Comparative Studies of Society and History, 2 (1959-60)
     369-74
Lambiri, Joanna. "Impact of industrial employment on the position
     of women in a Greek country town," Contributions to
     Mediterranean Society, ed. by J.-G. Peristiany (1963),
     pp. 261-68

Balbo, L. "Women's access to intellectual work: the case of
    Italy," _Signs_, 6 (1981), 763-70

IV. _Migration and emigration_

Brettell, Caroline. _Men who migrate: Women who wait: Population_
    and history in a Portuguese parish (Princeton, 1986)
Simon, Rita and Brettell, Caroline. _International Migration:_
    the female experience (N.Y., 1986)
Buechler, M.H. "Something funny happened on the way to the agora:
    a comparison of Bolivian and Spanish Galician female
    migrants,"_Anthropology Quarterly_, 49 (1976), 62-8
Ets,Marie Hall. _Rosa: the life of an Italian immigrant_
    (Minneapolis, 1970)
Caroli, Betty B. (ed.) _Italian immigrant women in North America_
    (Toronto, 1977)
Kessner, T. and Caroli, B. "New immigrant women at work: Italians
    and Jews in New York City 1880-1905," _Journal of Ethnic_
    Studies, 5 (1978), 19-32
Cornelisen, Ann. _Strangers and Pilgrims: the last Italian migration_
    (N.Y., 1980)

V. _Political and social issues_

Birnbaum, Lucia C. _Liberazione della donna: feminism in Italy_
    (Middletown, 1986)
Gibson, Mary S. _Prostitution and the state in Italy_ (New Brunswick,
    1986)
Slaughterm M. Jane. _A sense of oneself: women and the Italian_
    resistance (Denver, 1987)
Hellman, Judith. _Journey among women: feminism in five Italian_
    cities (Oxford, 1987)
Daniels, Elizabeth. _Jessie White Mario: Risorgimento revolutionary_
    (Athens, 1972)
De Grand, Alexander. "Women under Italian fascism," _Historical_
    Journal, 19 (1976), 947-68
Pankhurst, E.S. "Women under fascism," _Hibbert Journal_, 34 (1936)
    219-34, 450-53, 602-12
Kaplan, Temma. "Spanish anarchism and women's liberation,"
    Journal of Contemporary History, 6 (1971), 101-10
Ergas, Y. "1968-79 feminism and the Italian party system: women's
    politics in a decade of turmoil," _Comparative Politics_,
    14 (1982), 253-79
Swidler, L. "Discussion with Giglia Tedesca: woman, communist
    and catholic," _Christianity and crisis_, 39 (L979), 311-15

VI. _Folk-culture; music_

Farrer, Claire. _Women and folklore_ (Austin, 1976)
Caraveli-Chaves, A. "Bridge between worlds: the Greek women's
    lament as communicative event," _Journal of American Folklore_,
    93 (1980), 129-57
McLeod, N. and Herndon, M. "Bormliza: Maltese folksong style
    and women," _Journal of American Folklore_, 88 (1973), 81-100
Constable, M.V. "Figlie del coro: fiction and fact," _Journal of_
    European Studies, 11 (1981), 111-39
_____. "Venetian figlie del coro: their environment and
    achievement," _Music and letters_, 63 (1982), 181-212

CRJ 790.03
Spring, 1988

Prof. Gibson
Office: 4307N; x5032

THE FEMALE OFFENDER IN WESTERN SOCIETY

COURSE OBJECTIVES: This course examines the female offender in Europe and the United States, with the emphasis on the nineteenth and twentieth centuries. It seeks to give students the opportunity to familiarize themselves with the burgeoning new literature on female crime. Often neglected in the past, female offenders are now recognized by historians, sociologists, and criminologists to constitute a group whose behavior cannot always be explained by traditional theories of male deviance. Women often commit different crimes than men or commit similar crimes for different reasons. Once apprehended, their experience within the criminal justice system often divurges from that of the male majority. This course is organized topically; each class will focus on one type of crime and consider both historical and contemporary examples. We will conclude with a review of the major theorists of female criminality and an evaluation of each in light of the earlier empirical studies.

Final Grade: Papers (2): Two-page book review   40%
                            Twenty-page research
                              paper
               Exams (2)   Midterm and final   30%
               Oral presentations, discussion and   30%
                 attendance

REQUIRED READING:

D. Kelly Weisberg, ed., Women and the Law: The Social Historical Perspective, vol. 1 (1982)
N. H. Rafter and E. A. Stanko, eds., Judge, Lawyer, Victim, Thief: Women, Gender Roles, and Criminal Justice (1985)
C. Smart, Women, Crime, and Criminology: A Feminist Critique (1976)
Additional articles on reserve (see syllabus)

SYLLABUS

Feb. 1   Introduction: The Female Offender in Historical and Comparative Perspective

Feb. 8   Witchcraft
           Reading: Wm. Monter, "The Pedestal and the Stake: Courtly Love and Witchcraft," in Bridenthal and Koonz, eds., Becoming Visible, pp. 119-136*
           "Judgement of Witch Walpurga Hausmannin" in Wm. Monter, ed., European Witchcraft, pp. 75-81*

Feb. 22   Infanticide
           Reading: R. Trexler, "Infanticide in Florence: New Sources and First Results," Hist. of Childhood Quarterly, v. 1 (Summer, 1973),pp. 98-11*
           P. Hoffer and N.E.H. Hull, Murdering Mothers: Infanticide in England and New England, 1558-1803, Intro. (pp. ix-xix); Chap. 3, 4(65-109)*

Feb. 29   Prostitution
           Reading: M.E. Perry, "'Lost Women' in Early Modern Seville," _Feminist Studies_
           v. 4, n. 1 (1978)*
                     Rosenbaum, "Work and the Addicted Prostitute," in Rafter and
           Stanko, pp. 131-150

Mar. 7   Murder
           Reading: M. Hartman, _Victorian Murderesses_, Intro. (pp. 1-9); chap. 4
           (pp. 130-173); conclusion (pp. 255-269)*
                     "Murdering Women and Women Who Murder: A Critique of the Literature,
           in Rafter and Stanko, pp. 151-181

Mar 14   Property Crime
           Reading: E. Crane, "Dealing with Dependence: Paternalism and Tax Evasion
           in Eighteenth-Century Rhode Island," in Weisberg, pp. 27-44
                     P. O'Brien, "The Kleptomania Diagnosis: Bourgeois Women and Theft
           in Late Nineteenth-Century France," _J. of Social History_, v. 17 (Fall, 1983)
           pp. 65-77*

Mar. 21   Abortion
           Reading: A. McLaren, "Women's Work and Regulation of Family Size," _History
           Workshop_, n. 4 (1977)*
                     N. Davis, _From Crime to Choice: The Transformation of Abortion_
           in America, chap. 3 (pp. 3-64; chap. 11 (pp. 237-252)*

Mar. 28   Political Crime
           Reading: O. Hufton, "Women in the French Revolution, 1789-1796," _Past and
           Present_, v. 56 (1971) pp. 90-108*
           *Midterm

Apr. 11   Juvenile Justice
           Reading: Scholssman and Wallach, "The Crime of Precocious Sexuality: Female
           Juvenile Delinquency and the Progressive Era," in Weisberg, pp. 45-84.
                     Mahoney and Fenster, "Female Delinquents in a Suburban Court,"
           in Rafter and Stanko, pp. 221-236

Apr. 18   Variable of Gender in Criminal Statistics
           Reading: B. Hanawalt, "The Female Felon in Fourteenth-Century England," in
           Weisberg, pp. 165-196
                     Beattie, "The Criminality of Women in Eighteenth-Century England,"
           in Weisberg, pp. 197-238
                     Parisi, "Exploring Female Crime Patterns: Problems and Perspectives,
           in Rafter and Stanko, pp. 111-130

Apr. 25   Female Offenders in Court
           Reading: NEH Hull, "The Certain Wages of Sin: Sentence and Punishment of
           Female Felons in Colonial Massachusetts, 1673-1774," in Weisberg, pp. 7-26
                     Nagel et al., "Sex Differences in the Processing of Criminal Defenden
           in Weisberg, pp. 259-282
                     Parisi, "Are Females Treated Differently? A Review of the Theories
           and Evidence on Sentencing and Parole Decisions," in Rafter and Stanko, pp. 205
           236.

May 2   Female Offenders in Prison
            Reading: E. Freedman, "Nineteenth-Century Women's Prison Reform and Its
            Legacy," in Weisberg, pp. 141-158
                       Rafter, "Hard Time: Custodial Prisons for Women and the Example of
            the New York State Prison for Women at Auburn, 1893-1933" in Rafter and Stanko,
            pp. 237-260
                       Shaw, "Female Patients and the Medical Profession in Jails and
            Prisons: A Case of Quintuple Jeopardy," in Rafter and Stanko, pp. 261-273
                       Jensen, "The Incarceration of Women: A Search for Answers," in
            Weisberg, pp. 239-258

May 9   Theories of Female Criminality: Historical
            Reading: Smart, pp. 1-108

May 16   Theories of Female Criminality: Contemporary
            Reading: Smart, pp. 109-185

Final Examination :   Date set by registrar

BIBLIOGRAPHY: THE FEMALE OFFENDER

Historical Works

Beattie, J.M., "The Criminality of Women in Eighteenth-Century England," J. of Social Hist, v. 8 (1984).

Bristow, E., Prostitution and Prejudice: The Jewish Fight Against White Slavery (N.Y., 1983).

Connelly, Mark Thomas, The Response to Prostitution in the Progressive Era (Chapel Hill, 1980).

Finnegan, Frances, Poverty and Prostitution: A Study of Victorian Prostitutes in York (Cambridge, Eng., 1979).

Freedman, Estelle, Their Sisters' Keepers: Women's Prison Reform in America, 1830-1930 (Ann Arbor, 1981).

Gibson, Mary, Prostitution and the State in Italy, 1860-1915 (New Brunswick, N.J., 1986).

Hanawalt, Barbara, "The Female Felon in Fourteenth-Century England," Viator, v.5 (1974).

Harsin, Jill, Policing Prostitution in Nineteenth-Century Paris (Princeton, N.J.:1985).

Hartman, Mary, Victorian Murderesses (New York, 1976).

Helmholz, R.H., "Infanticide in the Province of Canterbury during the Fifteenth Century," Hist. of Childhood Q., v. 2 (1975).

McHugh, Paul, Prostitution and Victorian Social Reform (New York, 1980).

McLaren, Angus, "Abortion in France, 1800-1914," Fr. Historical Studies, v. 10, (1978).

O'Brien, Patricia, "The Kleptomania Diagnosis: Bourgeois Women and Theft in Late Nineteenth-Century France," J. of Social Hist., v. 17 (1983).

Perry, Mary Elizabeth, "Deviant Insiders: Legalized Prostitutes and a Consciousness of Women in Early Modern Seville," Comp. Studies in Soc. and Hist., v. 27 (1985).

Rafter, Nicole Hahn, Partial Justice: Women in State Prisons, 1800-1935 (Boston, 1984).

Rosen, Ruth, The Lost Sisterhood: Prostitution in America, 1900-1918 (Baltimore, 1982).

_____, ed., The Maimie Papers (New York, 1977).

Schlossman, S. and Wallach, S., "The crime of precocious sexuality: Female juvenile delinquency in the Progressive era," Harvard Edu. Review, v. 48 (1978).

Trexler, Richard, "Infanticide in Florence: New Sources and First Results," Hist. of Childhood Q., v. 1 (1973).

Walkowitz, Judith R., Prostitution and Victorian Society: Women, class and the state, (New York, 1980).

Weisberg, D. Kelley, ed., Women and the Law: The Social Historical Perspective, 2 vols. (Cambridge, Mass., 1982).

Wiener, Carol Z., "Sex Roles and Crime in Late Elizabethan Hertfordshire," J. of Social Hist., v. 8 (1975).

Hoffer, Peter C. and Hull, N.E.H., Murdering Mothers: Infanticide in England and New England, 1558-1803 (New York, 1981).

Contemporary Society

Adler, Freda and Simon, Rita J., eds., The Criminology of Deviant Women (Boston, 1979).

Adler, Freda, ed., The Incidence of Female Criminality in the Contemporary World (New York, 1985)

Bowker, Lee H., Women, Crime, and the Criminal Justice System (Lexington, Mass., 1978).

Brodsky, Annette, The Female Offender (Beverly Hills, Calif., 1975).

Bullough, Vern, et al., A Bibliography of Prostitution (New York, 1977).

Carlen, Pat, ed., Criminal Women: Autobiographical Accounts (Cambridge, Eng., 1985).

Carmen, Arlene and Moody, Howard, Working Women: The Subterranean World of Street Prostitution (New York, 1985).

Chapman, Jane Roberts, Economic Realities and the Female Offender (Lexington, Mass., 1980).

Cohen, Bernard, Deviant Street Networks: Prostitution in New York City (Lexington, Mass., 1985).

Crites, Laura, ed., The Female Offender (Lexington, Mass., 1976).

Edwards, Susan, Female Sexuality and the Law (Oxford, 1981).

Gora, JoAnn Gennaro, The New Female Criminal: Empirical Reality or Social Myth? (New York, 1982).

James, Jennifer, et al., The Politics of Prostitution (Seattle, 1975).

Jones, Ann, Women Who Kill (New York, 1980).

Kuncl, Tom and Paul Einstien, Ladies Who Kill (New York, 1985).

Leonard, Eileen B., Women, Crime, and Society: A Critique of Criminological Theory (New York, 1982).

Mann, Coramae Richey, Female Crime and Delinquency (University, Al., 1984).

Millett, Kate, The Prostitution Papers (New York, 1971).

Moyer, Imogene, ed., The Changing Roles of Women in the Criminal Justice System: Offenders, Victims, and Professionals (New York, 1985).

Parker, Tony, Women in Crime: Five Revealing Cases (New York, 1965).

Price, Barabara Raffel and Sokoloff, Natalie, eds., The Criminal Justice System and Women (1982).

Rafter, Nicole Hahn, and Stanko, Elizabeth Anne, eds., Judge, Lawyer, Victim, Thief: Women, Gender Roles, and Criminal Justice (Boston, 1985).

Reckless, W., and Kay, B., The Female Offender: Report to the U.S. President's Commission on Law Enforcement and the Administration of Justice (Washington, D.C., 1967).

Sereny, Gitta, The Invisible Children: Child Prostitution in America, West Germany and Great Britain (New York, 1985).

Simon, Rita James, The Contemporary Woman and Crime (Washington, D.C., 1975).

Smart, Carol, Women, Crime, and Criminology: A Feminist Critique (Boston, 1976).

Sturgeon, Susan and Rans, L., The Woman Offender: A Bibliographic Sourcebook (1975).

Symansky, Richard, The Immoral Landscape: Female Prostitution in Western Societies (Toronto, 1981).

Vadder, Clyde B., and Somerville, Dora B., The Delinquent Girl (Springfield, Ill., 1973).

Warren, Marguerite Q., ed., Comparing Male and Female Offenders (Beverly Hills, Calif. 1981).

This is a select bibliography limited to English-language sources and mostly books.

WOMEN AND WORLD CULTURES (WoSt 1102)

Spring, 1988
  Office: 494 Ford Hall
6:20-8:50 (W)
Ford 55

Instructor: Susan Geiger

Office: 494 Ford Hall
Phone: 624-7502, or 624-6006 (messages)

Office hours: T., 10-12; W., 4-5.
(or by appointment)
T.A.: Tania Ripoll
  Office: 476a Ford Hall
  Phone: 624-8506
  Office hrs.:

REQUIRED READING:

Domitila Barrios De Chungara with Moema Viezzer, Let Me Speak!
New York: Monthly Review Press, 1978.

Betsy Hartmann, Reproductive Rights and Wrongs. New York:
Harper & Row, 1987.

Ann Olson and Joni Seager, Women in the World: An International
Atlas. New York, Simon and Schuster. 1986.

--and articles, short stories and book chapters available for
purchase at BECKWITH copy center, 700 Washington Ave. S.E.
(378-1433) and on reserve under WoSt. 1102 in Wilson Library.

COURSE DESCRIPTION:

We will examine the major factors affecting women's lives
throughout the world, with careful attention to both the diversity
of experiences and shared features within an historical framework.
Course objectives include: a) an increased understanding of the lives
of women in cultures other than our own; b) a greater awareness of
the problems of bias and ethnocentrism in generalizations about
'women;' and c) acquisition of intellectual skills related to both
comprehension and analysis of information about women in the world.

COURSE REQUIREMENTS AND EXPECTATIONS:

1. Students are expected to attend class regularly and to complete
the required reading in preparation for the class period for which it
is assigned. Please bring with you to class the relevant book(s) or
articles assigned for the session so that we can refer together to
specific passages for discussion or questions.

2. Students are strongly urged to pay regular attention to one
or more forms of media (newspapers, radio, T.V., news magazines)
in order to become more aware of:
    a. the absence or presence of women in articles or news
reports on "international affairs," or Third World countries;
    b. the possible consequences for women of U.S. foreign aid
and related decisions made by our government;
    c. the impact of major economic, health or population
control issues/decisions on women;
    d. the particular problems of women with respect to war,
revolution, famine or natural disasters;
    e. "success stories" and their details.

3. Students are also strongly urged to keep a "log" or "journal" reflecting on the required reading and films. This log is a useful learning tool in the course and especially for preparing thoughtful responses to exams and written assignments. It might include:

a. major points of information you wish to remember from readings and films;

b. questions you want to raise, whether about certain "facts," or for clarification or because you find the material especially interesting and would like to know more. (These questions can be raised in class discussion.)

c. your criticisms of the approach, terms or apparent bias in the readings, films, etc.;

d. changes in your own understanding of women's lives, of major issues and problems, and of how women perceive their own situations and conditions.

To get the most effective use out of a log, it is best to write regularly, while you are reading or immediately after finishing an assignment or viewing a film. This conscious process will help to insure that you are thinking about and absorbing information and ideas. Such a log can either be kept in a separate notebook or integrated into your lecture/discussion notes.

4. Course grades will be based on the following:

a. A mid-quarter in-class exam (May 4) based on readings, films, lectures and discussions to date (30%);

b. TWO film critiques (2-4 typed pages each) demonstrating your awareness of the major points or issues brought out in the film you are writing about, and relating what you have learned from the film to relevant readings, class discussions, etc. While your opinion of the film is welcome, it should go beyond "I really liked..." or "I didn't like..." to a clear and thoughtful explanation of your views (30%);

c. A final (take-home) essay exam (40%).

COURSE SESSIONS AND REQUIRED READINGS

WEEK I
3/30

THE STUDY OF WOMEN IN WORLD CULTURES: APPROACH AND ISSUES
Intro. to course content, requirements and expectations.
Preliminary "test" and self-correction, discussion.
Issues and Problems in the Study of Women. Factors and conditions shaping women's experience.

WEEK II
4/6

WORK -- FOR WHAT, FOR WHOM, AND UNDER WHAT CONDITIONS?
What constitutes "women's work" and how do we understand changes in the gender division of labor? Unpaid family labor; agricultural labor; "service" and "alternative" sectors.
Film: "With These Hands"
Required Reading:
ATLAS, Introduction; 1, 13-21 (With all ATLAS assignments, be sure to read the "Notes" in the back of the book that correspond to the assignment).
Christian Science Monitor reprints: "The Neglected Resource," etc.,

WEEK III   EDUCATION -- FOR WHAT, FOR WHOM, AND UNDER WHAT
            CONDITIONS?
4/13   What determines the kind of education girls receive,
            the numbers of girls who have access to it, and the extent
            to which such education is useful to them?
            Required Reading:
            ATLAS, 22-24; LET ME SPEAK! 9-61, and Okot p'Bitek,
            "Song of Lawino," in Naomi Katz and Nancy Milton (eds.)
            FRAGMENT FROM A LOST DIARY, 135-254,

WEEK IV   CHANGING FAMILIES AND SOCIAL CHANGE
4/20   Family forms and family ideology; daughter, wife,
            mother and mother-in-law; "relational" politics.
            Film: "Small Happiness"
            Required Reading:
            ATLAS, 2-6,12, 27,28, 34-37; Lu Hsun, "Benediction" & An
            Su-Gil, "The Green Chrysanthemum," in FRAGMENTS..., 3-22,56-71

            excerpts from Madru Kishwar & Ruth Vanita (eds.),IN SEARCH OF
            ANSWERS, etc. and from K. Berry & C. Bunch (eds.)INTERNATIONAL
            FEMINISM

WEEK V   RELIGION
4/27   Women's experiences of organized religion in
            comparative contexts.
            Required Reading:
            LET ME SPEAK! 61-89
            Excerpts from Diana Eck & Devaki Jain (eds), SPEAKING
            OF FAITH,

WEEK VI   SEX, GENDER AND WOMEN'S HEALTH   ***AND MID-QUARTER EXAM***
5/4   Why do women have "too many" children? Issues: primary health
            care, maternal mortality, female infanticide.
            Required Reading:
            ATLAS, 7-11, 25, 26, 33; REPRODUCTIVE RIGHTS AND
            WRONGS, 3-88
                    *** Mid-Quarter Exam, c. 1 hour ***

WEEK VII   POLITICS: FOCUS SOUTH AFRICA
5/11   Race, class, sex and gender - the intersecting bases of
            women's oppression.
            Film: "South Africa Belongs to Us."
            Required Reading:
            Alex La Guma,"Coffee For the Road," Ezekiel Mphalele,
            "Mrs. Plum," in FRAGMENTS, 244-253, 273-310; Ellen
            Kuzwayo, "Hungry in a Rich Land, from Ann Oosthuizen (ed.),
            SOMETIMES WHEN IN RAINS, 99-108; and "South Africa," in Robin
            Morgan (ed), SISTERHOOD IS GLOBAL, 600-620
*****   *****
       ALL STUDENTS MUST HAND IN A FIRST FILM CRITIQUE BY 5/18

WEEK VIII   WOMEN AND "DEVELOPMENT"
5/18   Myths and realities of women's "progress;" sources of
            control over decision-making regarding women.
            Film: "The Global Assembly Line".
            Required Reading:
            ATLAS, 29-34; LET ME SPEAK! 89-165; REPRODUCTIVE RIGHTS
            AND WRONGS,111-175.

WEEK IX   WOMEN AND "DEVELOPMENT" REVISITED
5/25   Pinpointing sources of women's oppression; identifying
            examples of and conditions for women's empowerment.
            Film: "The Double Day."
            Required Reading:
            ATLAS, 38-40; LET ME SPEAK! 165-235; REPRODUCTIVE
            RIGHTS AND WRONGS,176-296.
*****   *****
        SECOND FILM CRITIQUE DUE FROM ALL STUDENTS BY 6/1

WEEK X   INTERNATIONAL FEMINISM(S): PROBLEMS AND POSSIBILITIES
6/1   Looking to the future; toward global feminism; local,
            national and international organizing; understanding
            difference.
            Required Reading:
            Audre Lourde, excerpts from SISTER OUTSIDER, 114-133, and
            Charlotte Bunch, "Bringing The Global Home," in PASSIONATE
            POLITICS, 328-345

            ***** Questions and instructions for TAKE HOME FINAL
                  handed out during last class session (6/1);   Final
                  Exam due back by 12 NOON, JUNE 8. *******

EXAM/ASSIGNMENT DUE DATES AT A GLANCE:

May 4   Mid-Quarter Exam, in class.

May 18   1st film critique DUE by this date, at the latest.

June 1   2nd film critique DUE by this date, at the latest;
            Instructions and Questions for Take-home Essay
            Final distributed.

June 8   Take-home final due, 12 NOON, (box across from
            494 Ford Hall).

144

Cal State, Long Beach

WOMEN IN CROSS-CULTURAL PERSPECTIVE

W/ST 401 IC
T, TH - 11-12:30
Rm LA1-312
Ticket #54165, Fall, 1985
Final Exam: Dec. 19, 10:15-12:15

Dr. Sondra Hale
Office: FO2-213 or 226
Phones: 498-4839 (W/ST) or
-5798 (Hale's)
213-836-5121 (H)
Office Hrs.: T, TH 9:30-11
and by appointment

Course Description: This course is an attempt to look at the roles and positions of women throughout the world. In part of the course we will examine the traditional views and roles of women. In the rest of the course we will explore women's challenge to those traditional ideas. The course is designed to combine anthropology, sociology, history, and the humanities to give students information on the experience of women in other cultures. Although the emphasis is on "Third World" women, the aim is to produce an integrated view of women internationally.

Requirements: Your final grade in this course will be an average of three grades, two essay-type exams in class and one project which you will select from the list of choices at the back of the syllabus. The mid-term is in class on Oct. 22; the final is Dec. 19, 10:15-12:15. The projects are due before Nov. 12. Points will be removed for every day after that.

Readings:

A. Required: M. Rosaldo and L. Lamphere, Woman, Culture and Society
              S. Rowbotham, Women, Resistance, and Revolution
              M. Davies, Third World, Second Sex

B. Recommended (for term paper use and as lecture supplements)

                S. Sievers, Flowers in Salt (Japan)
                E. Fernea, Guests of the Sheik (novel, Iraq)
                O. Sembene, God's Bits of Wood (novel, West Africa)
                S. Urdang, Fighting Two Colonialisms (Africa - Guinea-Bissau)
                Latin American and Caribbean Women's Collective, Slaves of Slaves
                N. El Saadawi, Hidden Face of Eve (Middle East)
                E. Croll, Feminism and Socialism in China
*Note: This is the A. Walker, The Color Purple (novel, U.S. Black society)
list of books to   M. Randall, Sandino's Daughters (Nicaragua)
help you on your   M. Randall, Women in Cuba
term project;   D. DeChungara, Let Me Speak (Bolivia)
others must be   J. Minces, The House of Obedience: Women in Arab Society
approved by the   A. Tabari and N. Yeganeh, The Shadow of Islam: The Women's
instructor   Movement in Iran
                I. Bendt and J. Downing, We Shall Return: Women of Palestine
                U. Wikan, Behind the Veil in Arabia: Women in Oman
                D. Dwyer, Images and Self-Images: Behind the Veil in Morocco
                P. Strobel, Women of Mombasa (Africa)

(List continues on next page)

145

B. Lindsay, Comparative Perspectives on Third World Women (general)
H. Bernstein, For Their Triumphs and for Their Tears: Women in
   Apartheid South Africa
A. Moody, Coming of Age in Mississippi (Black, U.S.)
F. Mernissi, Beyond the Veil: Male-Female Dynamics in a Modern
   Muslim Society
P. Jeffery, Frogs in a well: Indian women in Purdah
C. Moraga and G. Anzaldua, This Bridge Called My Back: Writings
   by Radical Women of Color (U.S.)
M. Wilson and D. Rosenfelt, Salt of the Earth (Chicanas, U.S.)
E. Fernea, A Street in Marrakech (Morocco)
A. Cornelisen, Women of the Shadows: The Wives and Mothers
   of Southern Italy
M. Hong Kingston, The Woman Warrior (Chinese-America)
J. and D. Terrell, Indian Women of the Western Morning: Their
   Life in Early America

Reading Schedule:

(1) Read Rosaldo/Lamphere text first. Should have read pp. 1-15; 17-42;
    67-87; 97-112; 129-156; and 263-280 by mid-term on Oct. 22.

(2) From mid-term to final, read R/L articles by Sanday, Paul, O'Laughlin,
    and Wolf; all of the Rowbotham book; and all of the Davies book. You
    should read these books for general ideas and arguments, not for
    specific recall.

Lecture Schedule

Below is an approximate schedule. There will be a number of films shown which
may not always be in sequence because of ordering difficulties. After the first
two week you will be given a verbal film schedule. Tentatively the films are
among: "Kypseli", "Some Women of Marrakech", "Double Day", "N!ai", "Rosie the
Riveter", "A Veiled Revolution", "Asante Market Women", "Nellie and Mitsuye",
and "Price of Change".

	Section I

Sept. 3-12   Introduction

A. Conceptual and Philosophical Framework. (Read Rosaldo/
   Lamphere text, pp. 1-14).

Sept. 12   B. The Situation for Women throughout the World (overview)
Film: "N!ai"

Section II

Sept. 17-26   Some Historical and Anthropological Questions (Read Rosaldo/Lamphere
                      Theoretical Overview, pp. 17-42).

A. The Myth of Woman the Gatherer/Man the Hunter and Myth of
   Matriarchy
Sept. 26   B. The Origins of Inequality (Read Sacks' article in R/L text,
"Kypseli"   pp. 207, 222)
                   C. Is Female to Male as Nature is to Culture? (Read Ortner
                      article in R/L text, pp. 67-87)
                   D. Issues around Kinship (Read R/L articles by Tanner, Lamphere,
                      and Bamberger)

Section III

Oct. 1-17

Oct. 3 - "Some
Women of Marrakech"
Oct. 15 "Asante
Market Women"

Women in the Economy: The Different Modes of Production

A. Hunting and Gathering/Horticultural Societies
B. Pastoral Societies
C. Agrarian Societies

OCTOBER 22 - MID-TERM

Section IV

Oct. 24-
Nov. 7

Oct. 29 "Double Day"

Nov. 5 "Rosie the
Riveter"

Women and Work (Read R/L articles by Paul, Sanda)

A. Women's Work -- History and Definitions
B. The Double Day
C. Films: "Double Day" and "Rosie the Riveter"

PROJECTS DUE NOVEMBER 12

Section V

Nov. 12-14

Nov. 12 "Veiled
Revolution:

Women and Religion -- The Modern World (Read O'Laughlin article in R/L)

A. Women in Judeo-Christianity
B. Middle Eastern Women and Fundamentalist Assumptions
C. Sudanese Women and Islam

THANKSGIVING - NOVEMBER 28

Section VI

Nov. 19-
Dec. 10

Women and Socio-Political Movements (Resistance and Revolution)

A. General Theoretical Discussion
B. China and Russia (Read Wolf article in R/L text)
C. Algeria: Nationalism vs. Women's Concerns
D. Cuba/Nicaragua/El Salvador
E. Africa (Angola, Mozambique, Guinea-Bissau) and the Middle
East (Palestine, Iran, and Israel)

Section VII

Dec. 12

Dec. 12 "Price of
Change"

Conclusion/Overview

A. Relationship of Western Feminism to Movements in Other Areas and
Social Movements in the U.S.
B. The Future: "The Rising of the Women Means the Rising
of the Race"
C. The Price of Change

The Projects: Suggestions for Term Papers/Projects:

These papers or projects must be approved by me. Hand in a written
paragraph about your topic. If I do <u>not</u> indicate otherwise, then assume
it is approved. You may write a 10-page conventional term paper (with
bibliography) on a topic such as "The Women's Movement in (<u>e.g.</u> Spain)".
Or, "Family Structure in the Philippines"; "Women's Crafts in Africa";
"Films about Women"; "The Economic Status of Women in the Third World";
"Women in Iran", etc. As you will be told you may also interview (on
tape) a woman from a country outside the U.S. about the role/status of
women in her country or about the women's movement there. You should tran-
scribe, edit, and introduce the interview and turn it in in written form with
the tape. Be certain the interviews are relevant to the topics of the
course. You may <u>not</u> write a paper or interview someone from your own
culture or ethnic group. This is an attempt to learn something about a
culture different from your own. If you are doing the interview, you need
to read at least one book or article as background.

Other suggestions are film reviews (must be more than one film,
<u>e.g.</u> comparing the role of women in Turkey from the film "Yol" to the
role of women in another area using film). You may <u>not</u> use the documen-
taries shown in class. <u>Note</u>: You should use the books on the recommended
list for your term project. You have the choices of Africa, Middle East,
China, Latin America, the U.S., Japan, Italy, and India. These are <u>not</u>
to be book reports, but a discussion of topics covered in class and <u>in</u>
your texts, but supplemented by at least <u>two</u> recommended books. Or, you
may use the recommended books as a <u>starting</u> point for your topic.

Women's Studies 401IC   Office in FOB 2:
Women in Cross Cultural Perspective   Rm.213,x5798 (MWF
Fall Semester, 1985   11:00-11:50 a.m.)
Cal State U. Long Beach   message:FOB-226
Dr. Norma Chinchilla, Instructor   x4839 (WS office)
MW 2:00-3:30,   Office in SSPA:
Ticket No. 52625   RM. 232,x4760
                                                         messaage:Rm. ,x 4602
                                                         Wed, 5:30-6:30
                                                         and by appointment

                                SYLLABUS
Required Reading
Ruth Leger Sivard, Women...A World Survey (Available at bookstore)
Charlotte O'Kelly, Women and Men in Society (available in xerox
        form at Kinko's Copy Center, Palo Verde and Atherton)
various short articles on Third World women in movements for
social change (packet II, available at Kinko's Copy Center)

Choice Reading:
Choose one of the following (or another book approved by the
instructor) for a book report project described elsewhere in
this syllabus:

    S. Sievers   Flowers in Salt (Japan)

    E. Fernea   Guests of the Sheik (Iraq)
    O. Sembene   God's Bits of Wood (novel, West Africa)
    S. Urdang   Fighting Two Colonialisms (Africa-Guinea Bissau)
    Latin American and Caribben Women's Collective, Slaves of Slaves
    N. El Saadawi   Hidden Face of Eve (Middle East)
    E. Croll   Feminism and Socialism in China
    A. Walker   The Color Purple (novel, U.S. Black society)
    M. Randall   Women in Cuba
    M. Randall   Sandino's Daughters (Nicaragua)
    D. DeChungara   Let Me Speak (Bolivia)
    J. Minces   The House of Obedience: Women in Arab Society
    A. Tabari and N. Yeganeh The Shadow of Islam: The Women's Movement in Iran
    I. Bendt & J. Downing We Shall Return: Women of Palestine
    U. Wikan   Behind the Veil in Arabia: Women in Oman
    D. Dwyer   Images and Self-Images: Behind the Veil in Morocco
    H. Bernsetin   For Their Triumphs and for Their Tears: Women in Apartheid
                            South Africa
    A. Moody   Coming of Age in Mississippi (Black, U.S.)
    F. Mernissi   Beyond the Veil: Male-Female Dynamics in a Modern Muslin Society
    P. Jeffery   Frogs in a Well: Indian Women in Purdah
    C. Moraga and G. Anzaldus This Bridge Called My Back:Writings by Radical Women
                            of Color (U.S.)
    M. Wilson and D. Rosenfelt Salt of the Earth (Chicanas, U.S.)
    E. Fernea   A Street in Marrakech (Morocco)
    A. Cornelisen   Women of the Shadows: The Wives and Mothers of Southern Italy
    M. Hong Kingston   The Woman Warrior (Chinese-America)
    J. and D. Terrell   Indian Women of the Western Morning: Their Life in Early
                            America

      E. Burgos,   I...Rogoberta Menchu

                                  149

WK/DATE			TOPIC	READING DUE
I. Sept.	4	W	Introduction to the Course	
II.	9	M	Introduction to the Situation of Women Around the World	Sivard (all)
	11	W	Biases in the Social Science Study of Women and Other Cultures: Ethnocentrism and Sexism	O'kelly, pp.1-39
III.	16	M	Explaining How and Why The Situation of Women Varies: Some Theories and Concepts	O'Kelly, pp.40-73
	18	W	Theories and Concepts (con.)	
IV.	23	M	The Concept of Mode of Production; Types of Modes of Production	O'Kelly, pp.74-106
	25	W	Hunting and Gathering Societies: Economy, Social Structure, Division of Labor by Sex	
V.	30	M	(continued)	
Oct.	2	W	(continued)(One or two page chart due, outlining characteristics of Hunting and Gathering Societies and Sex Roles in Them)	
VI.	7	M	Horticultural Societies	O'Kelly, pp.107-131
	9	W	Pastoral Societies	O'Kelly, pp.132--15
VII.	14	M	Chart Due on Horticultural and Pastoral Societies	
	16	W	In-Class Exam	
VIII.	21	M	Agrarian Societies	begin reading
	23	W	" "	for book review project;
				O'Kelly, 152-192
IX.	28	M	" "	
	30	W	Women and Early Capitalist Industrialization.	
X. Nov.	4	M	" "	O'Kelly, 226-258
	6	W	Advanced Industrialization Under Capitalism	
				O'Kelly, 259-292
XI.	11	M	" "	
	13	W		
XII.	18	M	Underdeveloped Peasant Societies	O'Kelly, 193-225
	20	W	" "	
XIII.	25	M	Socialist Societies: USSR; the Kibbutz	O'Kelly,292-316
	27	W	" "	
XIV.Dec.	2	M	Written Book Report Due (4-7 pages) Women and Change in the World Today: Women in Revolutionary Movements (National Liberation and Socialist)	(various readings
	4	W	in a short packet that will be available later at Kinkos)	
XV.	9	M		
	11	W	Last day of Class	

Final Exam Date:

PLEASE NOTE THAT IN THIS SYLLABUS, READING IS LISTED ON THE DATE
IT IS DUE. IT IS VERY IMPORTANT FOR THE LEARNING PROCESS THAT
YOU TRY TO COME TO CLASS HAVING DONE THE READING.

Requirements (see also sheet entitled " Expectations"):
Two Exams 25% each   = 50%
Book Report 25%   = 25
Attendance, Class Parti-
  cipation and Written
  Exercises   = 25

TOTAL GRADE   100%

Written Exercises include those assigned plus three reports on
movies that we see in class. (You choose which three.) Exercises
are given   ,   , or   rather than letter grades. Movies
are used to illustrate the ideas we study in this class and should
be considered an integral part of the course.
Ask youself after each movie: Can I sumarize what this
movie is about in a few concise sentences or a paragraph? Does
this movie reflect male-female differences in a particular type
of society (i.e., mode of production)? If so, which type? Does
this movie illustrate any of the concepts or theories we have studied?
Does this movie or the people in it take one side or another in
any debates or controversies we have discussed?

Goals of the Course
The goals of this course are to survey and compare the status of
women in different cultures of the world and different historical periods,
with emphasis on non-Western, non-industrialized cultures and societies.
We will try to explain these differences by relating them to the
type of society or mode of production in which they occur as well
as to other factors such as kinship and family structure,
political system, religion, etc. The basic theory we will use is
developed in O'Kelly in the first few chapters. We will end the
course by discussing the role of women in movements for change in
"less developed" countries, particularly their role in movements
seeking fundamental or "revolutionary" change.
Another goal is to challenge existing prejuidices and
ethnocentric views that we might have regarding the rest of the
world.

Methods:
Class meetings will be a combination of lecture, discussion,
films, and occasional group exercises. Students are strongly
encouraged to participate in class by contributing questions,
ideas from the readings, their own experiences or information
related to the topic that they discover outside of class. Though
the amount of class discussion possible is always limited by
size, we will have as much participation as possible since it has
been my experience that students learn much more when they are

actively involved.

Our approach will be interdisciplinary, drawing principally on the traditions of sociology, anthropology and political science. Many of the "choice" books use biography, oral history, and fiction to tell their stories. Some of the "choice" books will be available at the campus bookstore and I will ask Chelsea Books, (2121 E. Broadway, tele:434-2220) also to try to have them in stock.

DARTMOUTH COLLEGE
Women's Studies Program

Spring Term 1984   Women's Studies 24   Professors Navarro & Spitzer

Women and Social Change in the Third World

Employing a comparative interdisciplinary approach, this course will
explore the theory and practice of women's participation in social and
political upheavals--their role in evolutionary, reformist, as well as
revolutionary movements for change. Focusing on three case studies in
detail--Algeria, Senegal, and Cuba--the major themes pursued will include:
the pre-independence and pre-revolutionary status of women and emerging
political consciousness; their visibility, expectations, and participation
during nationalist and revolutionary struggles; tensions in post-revolutionary
and post-colonial societies between patriarchical and egalitarian values;
and redefinition of women's roles in the aftermath of revolution and national
liberation.

Books indicated by a (B) on the syllabus are available in the Bookstore,
with additional copies on Reserve in Baker Library; those indicated by
an (R) are available on Reserve only. The following books will be read
in large part or in their entirety and you may find it convenient to purchase
them:

> Fanon, Franz, The Wretched of the Earth
> Randall, Margaret, Women in Cuba
> Rowbotham, Sheila, Women, Resistance & Revolution
> Sembene, Ousmane, God's Bits of Wood

COURSE REQUIREMENTS

Either:
  A) Four essays (5-7 pp. each) addressing a discussion topic in
      each of the four units into which the course is divided.
      Topics for each of the units will be suggested by the
      instructors.

  B) Four essays: one for each of the first three topics, and a
      fourth which addresses any of the topics using a comparative
      approach, and which might include an area of inquiry of your
      own choosing.

CLASS SCHEDULE

PART I: Theoretical Considerations and European Paradigms

  March 26   Introductory Overview

  March 28   The Rights of Women, The Rites of Men
               Assignment: S. Rowbotham, Women, Resistance & Revolution,
                               pp. 1-58 (B)
                            Mary Wollstonecraft in A. Rossi (ed.), The
                               Feminist Papers, pp. 25-85 (R)

153

March 30   Paradigm I: The French Revolution (Prof. Darrow)
                    Assignment: K. Marx, Part II of Communist Manifesto in
                                R.C. Tucker, ed., The Marx-Engels Reader,
                                pp. 345-353 (R)
                            F. Engels, "The Origin of the Family" in Rossi,
                                The Feminist Papers, pp. 478-495 (R)
                            S. Rowbotham, Women, pp. 59-77
                            H. Draper, "Marx & Engels on Women's Liberation"
                                in International Socialism, July/August
                                1970 (R)

April 4   Marx & Engels, continued

April 6   Anarchists, Socialists & the 'Woman Question'
                  Assignment: S. Rowbotham, Women, pp. 78-98
                            Emma Goldman in Rossi, Feminist Papers
                            pp. 506-516 (R)

April 9   Paradigm II: The Russian Revolution (Prof. Whelan)
                  Assignment: S. Rowbotham, Women, pp. 134-169
                            Basile Kerblay, "The Family" in Modern Soviet
                            Society, pp. 110-145 (R)

April 11   Violence and Liberation: Fanon (I)
                  Assignment: Frantz Fanon, The Wretched of the Earth,
                            pp. 7-106 (R)

April 13   Fanon (II)

PART II: Algeria

*** April 16   Cultural & Historical Background (I)
                  Assignment: Alistair Horne, A Savage War of Peace, pp. 23-79 (R)

April 18   Cultural & Historical Background (II)
                  Assignment: "The Koran on the Subject of Women: Selections"
                            in E.W. Fernea & B.G. Bezirgan, eds.,
                            Middle Eastern Muslim Women Speak,
                            pp. 251-262 (R)
                          D. Waines, "Through a Veil Darkly: The Study
                            of Women in Muslim Societies. A Review
                            Article" in Comparative Studies in Society
                            and History, vol. 24, No. 4 (October 1982),
                            pp. 642-659 (R)

*** April 18   FILM: THE BATTLE OF ALGIERS (Fairbanks, 8:30)

April 20   The Battle of Algiers & The Algerian War
                  Assignment: A. Horne, A Savage War, pp. 183-207 (R)

April 23   Algeria Unveiled
                  Assignment: F. Fanon, A Dying Colonialism, pp. 35-67 (R)
                          S. Rowbotham, Women, pp. 200-206 & 233-247

April 25   Post-Colonial Algeria (I)
              <u>Assignment</u>: "Interviews with Jamilah Buhrayd, Legendary
                                 Algerian Hero" in Fernea & Bezirgan,
                                 <u>Middle Eastern Women Speak</u>, pp. 251-262 (R)
                        Fadela M'rabet, Excerpts from "Les Algeriennes"
                                 in Fernea & Bezirgan, pp. 319-358 (R)
                        Juliette Minces, "Women in Algeria" in N.L.
                                 Keddie & L. Beck, eds., <u>Women in the Muslim</u>
                                 <u>World</u>, pp. 159-171 (R)

April 27   Post-Colonial Algeria (II)

PART III; <u>Senegal</u>

*** April 30   Cultural & Historical Background (I)
              <u>Assignment</u>: G. Wesley Johnson, "African Political Activity
                                 in French West Africa, 1900-1940" in
                                 J.F.A. Ajayi & M. Crowder, eds., <u>History</u>
                                 <u>of West Africa</u>, vol. 2, pp. 542-567 (R)

May 2   Cultural & Historical Background (II)
              <u>Assignment</u>: A. LeBeuf, "The Role of Women in Traditional
                                 Political Organization," in D. Paulme, ed.,
                                 <u>Women of Tropical Africa</u>, pp. 93-119 (R)
                        M. Dobkin, "Colonization and the Legal Status of
                                 Women in Francophone Africa," in <u>Cahiers</u>
                                 <u>d'Etudes Africaines</u>, vol. 8, no. 3, 1968,
                                 pp. 390-403 (R)

*** May 3   FILM: <u>EMITAI</u> (Fairbanks, 6:30)

May 4   Reformism or Nationalism?
              <u>Assignment</u>: Ousmane Sembene, <u>God's Bits of Wood</u> (B)

May 7   Reformism or Nationalism: The Role of Women
              <u>Assignment</u>: K. Sacks, "Women and Class Struggle in Sembene's
                                 <u>God's Bits of Wood</u>," in <u>Signs</u>, vol. 4,
                                 no. 2 (1978), pp. 363-370 (R)

May 9   Post-Colonial Senegal (I)
              <u>Assignment</u>: Achola O. Pala, "Definitions of Women and
                                   Development: An African Perpsective,"
                                 in <u>Signs</u>, vol. 3, no. 1 (1971), pp. 9-13 (R)
                        L. Mullings, "Women and Economic Change in
                                 Africa," in N.J. Hafkin & E. Bay, <u>Women in</u>
                                 <u>Africa</u>, pp. 239-265 (R)

May 11   Post-Colonial Senegal (II)
              <u>Assignment</u>: D.L. Barthel, "The Rise of a Female Professional
                                   Elite: The Case of Senegal," in <u>African</u>
                                   <u>Studies Review</u>, vol. 18, no. 3 (1975),
                                 pp. 1-17 (R)

PART IV: Cuba

*** May 14   Cultural & Historical Background (I)
                    Assignment: B. Keene & M. Wasserman, A Short History of
                                   Latin America, pp. 404-431 (R)

*** May 14   FILM: LUCIA, [Part I] (Fairbanks, 6:30)

      May 16   Background (II): Women in Pre-Revolution Cuba
                    Assignment: W. MacGaffey & C. Barnett, Twentieth Century
                                   Cuba, chap. 2, pp. 34-67 (R)

*** May 17   FILM: LUCIA, [Part II & III] (Fairbanks, 6:30)

      May 18   LUCIA/Women in the Cuban Revolution
                    Assignment: S. Rowbotham, Women, pp. 220-233

      May 21   Revolutionary Transformations?
                    Assignment: C. Bengelsdorf & S. Hageman, "Emerging from
                                   Underdevelopment: Women and Work in Cuba,"
                                   in Z. Eisenstein, ed., Capitalist Patriarchy
                                   and the Case for Socialist Feminism
                                   pp. 271-295 (R)
                             M. Randall, "Introducing the Family Code,"
                                   in Eisenstein, ed., Capitalist Patriarchy,
                                   pp. 296-298 (R)

*** May 22   FILM: PORTRAIT OF TERESA (Fairbanks, 8:30)

      May 23   Revolutionary Transformations? (II)
                    Assignment: M. Randall, Women in Cuba (B)

      May 25   Wrap-Up

Women and Social Change in the Third World
History 50-09
Macalester College
Spring 1988

Prof. Elizabeth Schmidt

This course analyzes the impact of social, economic, and political change on women in Africa, Latin America, and Asia. In particular, it explores the differential effect of colonization, wage labor, and cash crop production on women and men, resulting in new forms of exploitation as well as opportunity. Women's innovative response to opportunity and resistance to negative social change, and their position in emerging socialist societies are also considered. Written assignments include two short essays based on class readings and a 12-15 page research paper. Class participation will be an important aspect of the course, as the most fruitful comparisons will be developed through intensive discussion.

Resources:

Elvia Alvarado; Medea Benjamin, ed. and trans. Don't Be Afraid, Gringo; A Honduran Woman Speaks from the Heart. San Francisco: Institute for Food and Development Policy, 1987.

Lourdes Beneria. "Reproduction, Production, and the Sexual Division of Labor." Cambridge Journal of Economics 3, 3 (Sept. 1979): 203-225.

Lourdes Beneria and Gita Sen. "Accumulation, Reproduction, and Women's Role in Economic Development: Boserup Revisited." Signs 7, 2 (Winter 1981): 279-298.

Iris Berger. "Sources of Class Consciousness: South African Women in Recent Labor Struggles." In Women and Class in Africa, pp. 216-236. Edited by Claire Robertson and Iris Berger. New York: Africana Publishing Co., 1986.

Ester Boserup. Woman's Role in Economic Development. New York: St. Martin's Press, 1970.

Susan C. Bourque and Kay B. Warren. "Campesinas and Comuneras: Subordination in the Sierra." Journal of Marriage and the Family 38, 3 (Nov. 1976): 781-788.

Susan C. Bourque and Kay B. Warren. Women of the Andes; Patriarchy and Social Change in Two Peruvian Towns. Ann Arbor: University of Michigan Press, 1981.

Janet M. Bujra. "Women 'Entrepreneurs' of Early Nairobi," Canadian Journal of African Studies 9, 2 (1975): 213-234.

Martin Chanock. "Making Customary Law: Men, Women, and Courts in Colonial Northern Rhodesia." In African Women and the Law: Historical Perspectives, pp. 53-67. Edited by Margaret Jean Hay and Marcia Wright. Boston University Papers on Africa, No. 7. Boston: Boston University, 1982.

George Chauncey Jr. "The Locus of Reproduction: Women's Labour in the Zambian Copperbelt, 1927-1953." Journal of Southern African Studies 7, 2 (April 1981): 135-164.

Domitila Barrios de Chungara. Let Me Speak! Testimony of Domitila, a Woman of the Bolivian Mines (New York: Monthly Review Press, 1978).

Jane Fishburne Collier. "Women in Politics." In Woman, Culture, and Society, pp. 89-96. Edited by Michelle Zimbalist Rosaldo and Louise Lamphere. Stanford: Stanford University Press, 1974.

Elisabeth Croll. "The Sexual Division of Labor in Rural China." In Women and Development: The Sexual Division of Labor in Rural Societies, pp. 223-247. Edited by Lourdes Beneria. New York: Praeger, 1982.

Delia Davin. Woman-Work: Women and the Party in Revolutionary China (Oxford: Oxford University Press, 1976).

Carmen Diana Deere and Magdalena Leon de Leal. "Peasant Production, Proletarianization, and the Sexual Division of Labor in the Andes." Signs, 7, 2 (Winter 1981): 338-360.

Jane Deighton, Rossana Horsley, and Sarah Stewart. Sweet Ramparts: Women in Revolutionary Nicaragua (London: War on Want and the Nicaraguan Solidarity Campaign, 1983).

Patricia Draper. "!Kung Women: Contrasts in Sexual Egalitarianism in Foraging and Sedentary Contexts." In Toward an Anthropology of Women, pp. 77-109. Edited by Rayna R. Reiter. New York: Monthly Review Press, 1975.

Neela D'Souza and Ramani Natarajan. "Women in India: The Reality." In Women in the World: 1975-1985, The Women's Decade, pp. 359-380. Edited by Lynne B. Iglitzin and Ruth Ross. 2nd ed. Santa Barbara: ABC-Clio, 1986.

Diane Elson and Ruth Pearson. "The Subordination of Women and the Internationalisation of Factory Production." In Of Marriage and the Market: Women's Subordination in International Perspective, pp. 144-166. Edited by Kate Young, Carol Wolkowitz, and Roslyn McCullagh. London: CSE Books, 1981.

Cynthia H. Enloe. "Women Textile Workers in the Militarization of Southeast Asia." In Women, Men, and the International Division of Labor, pp. 407-425. Edited by June Nash and Maria Patricia Fernandez-Kelly. Albany: State University of New York Press, 1983.

Maria Patricia Fernandez-Kelly. "Mexican Border Industrialization, Female Labor Force Participation and Migration." In Women, Men, and the International Division of Labor, pp. 205-223. Edited by June Nash and Maria Patricia Fernandez-Kelly. Albany: State University of New York Press, 1983.

Geoffrey E. Fox. "Honor, Shame, and Women's Liberation in Cuba: Views of Working-Class Emigre Men." in Female and Male in Latin America, pp. 273-290. Edited by Ann Pescatello. Pittsburgh: University of Pittsburgh Press, 1973.

Nancy J. Hafkin and Edna G. Bay. Women in Africa: Studies in Social and Economic Change. Stanford: Stanford University Press, 1976.

Margaret Jean Hay. "Luo Women and Economic Change During the Colonial Period." In Women in Africa: Studies in Social and Economic Change, pp. 87-109. Edited by Nancy J. Hafkin and Edna G. Bay. Stanford: Stanford University Press, 1976.

Noeleen Heyzer. "From Rural Subsistence to an Industrial Peripheral Work Force: An Examination of Female Malaysian Migrants and Capital Accumulation in Singapore." In Women and Development: The Sexual Division of Labor in Rural Societies, pp. 179-202. Edited by Lourdes Beneria. New York: Praeger, 1982.

Kay Johnson. "Women's Rights, Family Reform, and Population Control in the People's Republic of China." In Women in the World: 1975-1985, The Women's Decade, pp. 434-462. Edited by Lynne B. Iglitzin and Ruth Ross. 2nd ed. Santa Barbara: ABC-Clio, 1986.

Temma Kaplan. "Female Consciousness and Collective Action: The Case of Barcelona, 1910-1918." Signs 7, 3 (Spring 1982): 545-566.

Maureen Mackintosh. "Gender and Economics: The Sexual Division of Labour and the Subordination of Women." In Of Marriage and the Market: Women's Subordination in International Perspective, pp. 1-15. Edited by Kate Young, Carol Wolkowitz, and Roslyn McCullagh. London: CSE Books, 1981.

Maxine Molyneux. "Women in Socialist Societies: Problems of Theory and Practice." In Of Marriage and the Market: Women's Subordination in International Perspective, pp. 167-202. Edited by Kate Young, Carol Wolkowitz, and Roslyn McCullagh. London: CSE Books, 1981.

June Nash. "Aztec Women: The Transition from Status to Class in Empire and Colony." In Women and Colonization: Anthropological Perspectives, pp. 134-148. Edited by Mona Etienne and Elanor Leacock. New York: Praeger, 1980.

Kamene Okonjo. "The Dual-Sex Political System in Operation: Igbo Women and Community Politics in Midwestern Nigeria." In Women in Africa: Studies in Social and Economic Change, pp. 45-58. Edited by Nancy J. Hafkin and Edna G. Bay. Stanford: Stanford University Press, 1976.

Jane L. Parpart. "The Household and the Mine Shaft: Gender and Class Struggles on the Zambian Copperbelt, 1926-1964." Journal of Southern African Studies 13, 1 (Oct. 1986): 36-56.

Margaret Randall. Sandino's Daughters: Testimonies of Nicaraguan Women in Struggle. Vancouver: New Star Books, 1981.

Claire Robertson. "Ga Women and Socioeconomic Change in Accra, Ghana." In Women in Africa: Studies in Social and Economic Change, pp. 111-133. Edited by Nancy J. Hafkin and Edna G. Bay. Stanford: Stanford University Press, 1976.

Michelle Zimbalist Rosaldo. "Woman, Culture, and Society: A Theoretical Overview." In Woman, Culture, and Society, pp. 17-42. Edited by Michelle Zimbalist Rosaldo and Louise Lamphere. Stanford: Stanford University Press, 1974.

Helen Safa. "Runaway Shops and Female Employment: The Search for Cheap Labor." Signs 7, 2 (Winter 1981): 418-433.

Janet W. Salaff. "Women, the Family, and the State: Hong Kong, Taiwan, Singapore--Newly Industrialized Countries in Asia." In Women in the World: 1975-1985, The Women's Decade, pp. 325-357. Edited by Lynne B. Iglitzin and Ruth Ross. 2nd ed. Santa Barbara: ABC-Clio, 1986.

Peggy R. Sanday. "Female Status in the Public Domain." In Woman, Culture, and Society, pp. 189-206. Edited by Michelle Zimbalist Rosaldo and Louise Lamphere. Stanford: Stanford University Press, 1974.

Elizabeth S. Schmidt. "Gender Ideology, Economics, and the Social Control of African Women." In Ideology, Economics, and the Role of Shona Women in Southern Rhodesia, 1850-1939, Ph.D. Dissertation, University of Wisconsin-Madison, 1987.

Gita Sen. "Women Workers and the Green Revolution." In Women and Development: The Sexual Division of Labor in Rural Societies, pp. 29-64. Edited by Lourdes Beneria. New York: Praeger, 1982.

Marjorie Shostak. Nisa; The Life and Words of a !Kung Woman. New York: Vintage Books, 1983.

Irene Silverblatt. "Andean Women Under Spanish Rule." In Women and Colonization: Anthropological Perspectives, pp. 149-185. Edited by Mona Etienne and Elanor Leacock. New York: Praeger, 1980.

Mary F. Smith. Baba of Karo; A Woman of the Muslim Hausa. New Haven: Yale University Press, 1981.

Patricia Stamp. "Perceptions of Change and Economic Strategy Among Kikuyu Women of Mitero, Kenya." Rural Africana 29 (Winter 1975/76): 19-43.

Louise A. Tilly. "Paths of Proletarianization: Organization of Production, Sexual Division of Labor, and Women's Collective Action." Signs 7, 2 (Winter 1981): 400-417.

Stephanie Urdang. "The Last Transition: Women and Development." In A Difficult Road: The Transition to Socialism in Mozambique, pp. 347-388. Edited by John S. Saul. New York: Monthly Review Press, 1985.

Judith Van Allen. "'Aba Riots' or Igbo 'Women's War'? Ideology, Stratification, and the Invisibility of Women." In Women in Africa: Studies in Social and Economic Change, pp. 59-85. Edited by Nancy J. Hafkin and Edna G. Bay. Stanford: Stanford University Press, 1976.

Luise White. "Women in the Changing African Family." In African Women South of the Sahara, pp. 53-68. Edited by Margaret Jean Hay and Sharon Stichter. New York: Longman, 1984.

Luise White. "Prostitution, Identity, and Class Consciousness in Nairobi during World War II." Signs 11, 2 (Winter 1986): 255-273.

Ann Whitehead. "'I'm Hungry, Mum': The Politics of Domestic Budgeting." In Of Marriage and the Market: Women's Subordination in International Perspective, pp. 88-111. Edited by Kate Young, Carol Wolkowitz, and Roslyn McCullagh. London: CSE Books, 1981.

Aline K. Wong. "Planned Development, Social Stratification, and the Sexual Division of Labor in Singapore." _Signs_ 7, 2 (Winter 1981): 434-452.

Kate Young. "Modes of Appropriation and the Sexual Division of Labour: A Case Study from Oaxaca, Mexico." In _Feminism and Materialism: Women and Modes Of Production_, pp. 124-154. Edited by Annette Kuhn and AnnMarie Wolpe. London: Routledge and Kegan Paul, 1978.

Week 1:   "Introduction"

    Th Feb 4

Week 2:   "Production and Reproduction: Defining Women's Roles"

    T Feb 9
        Readings: Mackintosh, Beneria.
    Th Feb 11
        Readings: Draper.

Week 3:   "The Gender Division of Labor in Selected Societies"

    T Feb 16
        Readings: Shostak.
    Th Feb 18
        Readings: Boserup, pp. 15-52; Deere and Leon de Leal.

Week 4:   "Gender Hierarchy within the Household"

    T Feb 23
        Readings: Whitehead; White, "Women in the Changing African Family..." (Recommended: Smith)
    Th Feb 25
        Readings: Fox; D'Souza and Natarajan.

Week 5:   "Gender Hierarchy in the Public Sphere"

    T March 1
        Readings: Rosaldo; Bourque and Warren, "_Campesinas_..."
    Th March 3
        Readings: Sanday, Collier, Chanock.

Week 6:   "Colonial Capitalism and the Subordination of Women"

    T March 8
        Readings: Hay, Robertson.
    Th March 10
        Readings: Chauncey, Schmidt.

Week 7:

    T March 15
        Readings: Bujra; White, "Prostitution..."
    Th March 17
        Readings: Bourque and Warren, Women of the Andes...
           (Recommended: Nash, Silverblatt)

Week 8: "Women, Community, and Collective Action"

    T March 22
        Readings: Kaplan, Alvarado.
    Th March 24
        Readings: Okonjo, Van Allen.

Week 9: Spring Break

Week 10: "Women in Rural Development"

    T April 5
        Readings: Beneria and Sen, Young.
    Th April 7
        Readings: Stamp, Sen.

Week 11: "Women in the New International Division of Labor"

    T April 12
        Readings: Elson and Pearson, Safa.

    Th April 14
        Readings: Fernandez-Kelly; Heyser.

Week 12:

    T April 19
        Readings: Salaff, Wong.
    Th April 21
        Readings: Enloe.

Week 13: "Working Class Women and Collective Action"

    T April 26
        Readings: de Chungara, whole book.
    Th April 28
        Readings: Parpart, Berger. (Recommended: Tilly)

Week 14: "Gender Relations Under Socialism"

    T May 3
        Readings: Molyneux.

Th May 5
    Readings: Davin, pp. 1-20; Croll, Johnson.
    (Recommended: Davin, whole book)

Week 15:

T May 10
    Readings: Urdang; Randall, pp. 1-93. (Recommended:
    Deighton)
Th May 12 "Summary Session"

Colloquium in Comparative and Cross-Cultural History

Women in the Modern World Economy

WSS 399 / His 485

Students will be expected to purchase the following books:

Alice Kessler-Harris, Women Have Always Worked
Ann Oakley, Woman's Work: The Housewife, Past and Present
Eli Zaretsky, Capitalism, the Family and Personal Life
Ester Boserup, Woman's Role in Economic Development
Christine Obbo, African Women: Their Struggle for Economic Independence
Margaret Llewelyn Davies, Life As We Have Known It: By Co-operative Working Women
Linda Lim, Women Workers in Multinational Corporations

Other readings will be available in the Reserve Room of the Library or will be handed out in class.

Since this a small, upper-division colloquium students should do the readings prior to the class for which they are assigned. Classroom attendance and participation in discussion are essential and will count toward your final grade.

September 15: Introduction - Issues in the Comparative Study of Women and Work

September 22: American Women at Work

Kessler-Harris, Women Have Always Worked

September 29: Kitchen and Kids - Perspectives on Household labor

Oakley, Woman's Work, pp. 1-155.

October 6: The Texture of Women's Lives - Working Class Women in 19th Century England

Davies, Life As We Have Known It, pp. 1-101

October 13: The Personal and the Political: Family Life Under Capitalism

Zaretsky, Capitalism, the Family and Personal Life

October 20: Colonialism, Capitalism and Women's Labor

Boserup, Woman's Role in Economic Development

October 27: Uganda: A Third World Case Study

Obbo, African Women

November 3:   The Perception of Domestic Workers

Jacklyn Cock, <u>Maids and Madams</u>, pp. 26-124 (on reserve)

November 10:   Prostitution: Degradation or Independence?

Luise White, "Women's Domestic Labor in Colonial Kenya:
Prostitution in Nairobi, 1909-1950"

Judith R. Walkowitz and Daniel Walkowitz, "We are Not Beasts
of the Field"

November 17:   Workers Struggles or Women's Struggles?

Barbara Wertheimer, "Women in the Industrial Workers of the World:
The Lawrence Strike, 1912" in <u>We Were There</u>, pp. 353-376

I. Berger, "Sources of Class Consciousness: Women Workers in
South Africa, 1973-1980," <u>International Journal of
African Historical Studies</u>, 16, 1 (1983)

Norma Chincilla, "Mobilizing Women: Revolution in the Revolution"

November 24:   What Is "Development" for Women?

Barbara Rogers, <u>The Domestication of Women</u>, pp. 121-193

Linda Lim, <u>Women Workers in Multinational Corporations</u>

December 1:   The Taylorization of Clerical Work: For Whose Benefit?

Margery Davies, "Women's Place Is at the Typewriter: The
Feminization of the Clerical Labor Force," Z. Eisenstein,
ed., <u>Capitalist Patriarchy and the Case for Socialist
Feminism</u>

Harry Braverman, <u>Labor and Monopoly Capital</u>, pp. 292-358

December 9:   How Does Socialism Transform Women's Labor?

Marjorie King, "Cuba's Attack on Women's Second Shift, 1974-1976,"
in Eisenstein, pp. 118-131

C. Bengelsdorf and A. Hagemen, "Emerging From Underdevelopment:
Women and Work in Cuba," in Eisenstein, pp. 271-291

Hilda Scott, "Why Women Work - And Should They?" in <u>Women and
Socialism</u>, pp. 117-137, 191-220

Margaret Randall, "Introducing the Family Code," in Eisenstein

December 15:   Reports and wrap-up session

History 781   Women, Class and Colonialism
                                   Claire Robertson
                                   Office: 230 Dulles Hall
                                   Office Hrs: TW 3-4 or
                                        by appointment
                                   Phone: 422-2174
                                   Home Phone: (812) 336-3696

Content:

This is a reading course intended to explore the relationship of

gender to class formation in the context of colonialism. We will be

adopting a cross-cultural comparative viewpoint, exploring

colonialism wherever it occurs, from Latin America to Soviet Central

Asia and many points between, and in many different forms—from

formal political control to spheres of influence. We will move

chronologically from early forms of colonialism to later ones, and

we will deal only with various forms of Europeon colonialism which

were crucial to the establishment of European dominance in the

nineteenth and twentieth centuries.

Required books available in SBX bookstore (these and all other
readings on reserve in library).

Text: M. Etienne and E. Leacock, eds. Women and Colonization:
            Anthropological Perspectives

       Pruitt, I. Daughter of Han

       De Chungara, Domitila Let Me Speak! Testimony of a Woman of
            the Bolivian Mines

       Bernstein, H. For Their Triumphs and for Their Years: Women
            in Apartheid South Africa

       N. Hafkin and E. Bay, eds. Women in Africa Studies in Social
            and Economic Change

       Mies, M. The Lacemakers of Narsapur: Indian Housewives
            Produce for the Market

<u>Procedure</u>

The critical features of participation in this seminar are doing the reading of approximately 200 pages a week and then discussing it in class. There will be no exams or papers, but you will be expected to keep a notebook including brief outlines of all the readings and a critical summary of the relationship of each book to course materials. Attached you will find a set of questions for you to use in your critical summary to sum up the relevance of each article. During the term we may be revising these questions as we find it appropriate to refine them. This may be the first course ever offered on this topic anywhere, and we bear the responsibility of pioneering the way. In compensation, it should be exciting! The notebooks must be kept up to date at all times (readings are due on the date listed on the syllabus) and are subject to instant recall (I may ask to have them at any time without warning). Your grade will depend 60% on the notebook, 40% on class participation. Notebooks should be legible and the notes kept in the order in which they are due in class. In a different color ink or set off in some other manner highlight entries that convey your opinions or comments and queries on the readings.

<u>Questions</u>: to be answered in notebook to summarize each reading after you have outlined and commented on its contents.

1. What is the central thesis of the author(s)? What is she/ she/he trying to prove?

2. Do you find any particular bias in the reading? To what do you attribute this bias?

3. What theoretical framework is being employed?

4. What form of colonialism is being presented? What is the framework for it in relation to industrialization?

5. Are there significant differences in the impact of colonialism in this case on women and men? What are they?

6. What is the relationship of gender to class position or class formation in this case?

You may put your answers in outline form; don't spend more than one page each on an article in answering all six questions. If you have problems with a question you may respond to it with further questions instead. That may be the best response in some cases.

Schedule

April 4   Introduction and Organization

April 11   What is colonialism? Theories regarding colonialism/ imperialism.

                  Readings: Roxborough, Theories of Underdevelopment Chs. 4-5 (pp. 42-69).

                  Fei and Ranis, "Economic Development in Historical Perspective," American Economic Review 59:2 (May, 1969), 386-400.

                  Rowbotham, Women, Resistance and Revolution, Ch. 8 (pp.200-47).

                  Etienne and Leacock, Introduction (pp. 1-24).

April 18   Comparative and historical perspectives I: Latin America and the Pacific.

                  Readings: Lavrin, Latin American Women: Historical Perspectives, Ch. 5 (pp. 150-72).

                  Etienne and Leacock, Ch.s 6-7, 11-12 (pp. 134-85, 270-322).

April 25	Comparative and historical perspectives II: North America and Australia.

April 25 — Comparative and historical perspectives II: North America and Australia.

Readings: Etienne and Leacock, Chs. 1-4 10(pp. 25-108, 239-69).

May 2 — Comparative and historical perspectives III: Asia - China.

Readings: Li, <u>The Ageless Chinese, A History,</u> pp. 391-400.

Pruitt, <u>Daughter of Han</u>, entire life story (250 pages).

May 9 — Comparative and historical perspectives IV: Africa.

Readings: Hafkin and Bay, articles by Van Allen, Hay, Robertson, and Mullings (pp. 59-134, 239-64).

Etienne and Leacock, Chs. 8-9 (pp. 186-238).

May 16 — Comparative and historical perspectives V: Central Asia.

Reading: Massell, <u>The Surrogate Proletariat,</u> pp. 3-36, 93-182, 213-46, 256-359, 390-411.

May 23 — Relations between the colonizers and the colonized I

Recommended: See the Jewel in the Crown, Passage to India.

Readings: Oliver, <u>Western Women in Colonial Africa</u>, Chs. 3-6, (pp. 76-196).

Inglis, <u>The White Women's Protection Ordinance, Sexual Anxiety and Politics in Papua,</u> Chs. 1-3 (1-88).

May 30 — Relations between the colonizers and colonized II
Readings: Inglis, Chs. 4-6 (pp. 89-143).

Fanon, <u>A Dying Colonialism</u>, Chs. 1, 3 (pp. 35-67, 99-120).

Good, "Settler Colonialism: Economic Development and Class Formation,: <u>Jl of Modern African Studies</u> 14 (1976: 597-620.

Burkett, "In Dubious Sisterhood: Race and Class in Spanish Colonial South America, "<u>Latin America Perspectives</u>, IV: 12-13 (1977): 18-26.

Bernstein, _For their triumphs and for their tears,_ entire (68 pages).

June 6   Contemporary colonialism I

Readings: Mies, _Lacemakers of Narsapur,_ entire (180 pages).

Nash and Fernandez-Kelly, _Women, Men and the International Division of Labor,_ Chs. 1, 3 (pp. 3-38, 70-92).

June 13   Contemporary colonialism II Conclusions

Reading: de Chungara, _Let Me Speak!_ entire (approx. 250 pages).

History 96
Seminar on Women, Patriarchy and Capitalism
Tufts University, Fall Term, 1986
Wednesdays, 1:30 - 4:40

Instructor: J. Penvenne, Miner Hall, Room 4
        Office Hours, Monday 1:30 to 5:30 PM and by appointment.

Introduction:
        Through scholarly readings, novels, films and class discussion
students will consider the nature of patriarchal and lineage controls over
women's time, services and offspring and the extent to which such controls are
undermined, reproduced or reinforced by the penetration of capitalist
relations of production. The course will begin with an overview of
theoretical literature on women, patriarchy and class followed by case studies
from Africa and Latin America. Students will write several short essays on
the readings. By the fourth week of class each student will select a research
topic which will be developed as a term paper throughout the seminar.

Student Evaluation Procedure : Students are expected to attend class, and be
prepared to discuss the materials indicated on the syllabus.
Grading will be as follows: class participation 20%, short essays, 30%, term
paper 50% of the final grade.

Course Readings:
M.J. Hay and Sharon Stichter,eds. African Women South of the Sahara (New York,
        1984)
Hazel Johnson and Henry Bernstein, Third World Lives of Struggle (London,
        1982)
C.B. Davies and A.A. Graves, Ngambika: Studies of Women in African Literature
        (New Jersey, 1986
Carolina Maria de Jesus, Child of the Dark (New York, 1964)
Buchi Emecheta, The Joys of Motherhood (New York, 1979)
June E. Hahner, Women in Latin American History - Their Lives & Views
        (Los Angeles: UCLA Latin American Center Publications, 1980)

Source Book Packet, available at Bookstore.

Week One: 3 September - Introduction to the Perspectives and Literature
        (Assignment 1)

        Reading: Third World Lives, Introduction to all sections, pages
                xi - xiv, 2-5, 92-95, 160 - 163 and conclusion page
                259-268.
                African Women, pages ix to xiv
                Women in Latin America, 1-17.

Week Two: 10 September - Kinship as Ideology - How do women fit in?
                Discussion of Assignment 1 & Distribution of Assignment 2
        Reading: Source Book Packet Readings 1 to 3 or 4 & 5 (as per team)
                African Women, Ch 6

172

eek Three: 17 September - Power Realms: Spirituality and Manipulation of
                        Possibilities
                   Discussion of Assignment 2

eek Four : Classes Suspended - Semester Break Day
        Reading: African Women, 1,5,9.
                 Women in Latin America, 43-68.

eek Five : Women's Role in Production: Agriculture and Pastoralism
                   Comparative Analysis - Africa and Latin America
        Reading: African Women, 2.
                 Third World Lives, 20,23,26.
ERM PAPER TOPICS DUE TODAY!

EEK SIX- 8 Oct. : "Between Patriarchy and Capitalism in Africa"
        Class: Discussion of JOYS OF MOTHERHOOD informed by readings from
                 African Women Ch. 1 & 2.
        Readings for Week 7:
                 CHILD OF THE DARK and Third World Lives [TWL],14.
        Writing for Week 7:
                 Essay on JOYS OF MOTHERHOOD

EEK SEVEN- 15 Oct. : "Women in Rural and Urban Struggles"
        Class: View "Vidas Secas"
                 Discussion of "Vidas Secas," CHILD OF THE DARK, and Miguel
                 Duran - Perspectives on rural to urban migration.
        Hand in: Essay on JOYS OF MOTHERHOOD

        Reading for Week 8: Penvenne Working Paper, Latin American Women,III,
                 Source Book Selections 6,7, or 9.
        Writing for Week 8: PRELIMINARY BIBLIOGRAPHY FOR SEMINAR PAPER
                 Think out critique of Penvenne paper.

EEK EIGHT- 22 Oct. : Dry Run Adversary Presentation Session followed by:
Power Realms and Women in Latin America"
        Class: Penvenne paper presentation and Student critiques
        Discussion: Readings on Latin American Women.
        Hand in: PRELIMINARY BIBLIOGRAPHY FOR SEMINAR PAPER
        Reading for Week 9 :Read as many of the following as possible BUT
                           be prepared to CRITICALLY PRESENT at least
                           one selection.
                           Latin American Women, Selections 2,9,20
                           TWL, Selections 21,25
                           African Women,Ch. 7 & 8.
                           Ngambica, Part One, Choose One.
                           Source Reading 9 & 10

EEK NINE 29 October. "Women and the Ideologies of Creative Expression.
                   Africa and Latin America"
        Class: Discussion of Readings.
        Writing for Week 10: PRELIMINARY OUTLINE OF SEMINAR PAPER DUE
        Reading for Week 10: Students should read as much of the following

BUT be prepared to CRITICALLY PRESENT at least one.
Latin American Women, Selections 14,18,19
TWL,Selections, 20,23,26,29
African Women, 9,10, 11

WEEK TEN- 5 November:"Sisters in Struggle in Africa and Latin America"
Class: Discussion of Readings
Hand in : PRELIMINARY OUTLINE OF SEMINAR PAPER
Reading for Week 11: African Women, Ch. 3 & 4
Source Readings, 8
Latin American Women, 15,16
TWL, Selection 24

WEEK ELEVEN- 12 November: "Constraints and Opportunities for Urban Women"
Class: Discussion of Readings
Film and discussion: "Maids and Madams" Cabot Auditorium

17 November MONDAY,10 AM - Papers due in History Department Office from
Presenters 1 to 3

WEEK TWELVE: 19 November: Paper Presentation Session I
Papers By Presenters 1 to 3 followed by Critiques by Critics 1 to 3.
FILM: "You have Struck a Rock" 4-4:30 Wessel AV

24 November MONDAY,10AM - Papers due in History Department Office from
Presenters 4 to 6

WEEK THIRTEEN- 26 November: Paper Presentation Session II
Papers by Presenters 4 to 6 followed by Critiques by Critics 4 to 6.

1 December MONDAY,10AM - Papers due in History Department Office from
Presenters 7 to 9.

WEEK FOURTEEN- 3 December: Paper Presentation Session III
Papers by Presenters 10 to 12 followed by Critiques by Critics 10 to
12.

FINAL DRAFT OF TERM PAPERS DUE BY 15 DECEMBER

Tufts University
History 96 - World Seminar
Women, Patriarchy and Capitalism
Comparative Perspectives from Africa and Latin America

Assignment One

This is a diagnostic exercise in the basics of historical research. The purpose is to assess your research skills, to develop special skills and become familiar with special literatures which address women's historical experience. You will not be graded on this exercise, except with regard to your effort and participation in class.

1. Choose a topic with regard to women's historical experience in either Africa or Latin America. If you have any problem selecting a topic please see me. Be sure your topic has a specific place and time frame.

Example - Topic Selection:

I am interested in prostitution in Africa. From the index of my text I see that there has been work done on this topic in a number of African cities, and I select Nairobi Kenya. From the bibliography at the end of my text I find that a Ph D thesis has been written on prostitution in Nairobi which took as its time period 1900 - 1952, so I select that as my time frame.

2. Build a bibliography Once you have your topic, build as complete a bibliography on the topic as you can. I am less concerned that you can actually set hands on the material than that you can ascertain that the material exists.

Example - Bibliography

What has been written about Prostitution in Nairobi in the first half of the twentieth century. Look for books, articles, chapters in edited collections.

3. Preliminary assessment of Current Research on Topic Skim all the material in the bibliography that you can get your hands on and note the titles of material you can not. From this rapid overview of the research available, summarize the lines of research. What do scholars know about prostitution in Nairobi from the research to date? What kinds of questions has research addressed? Briefly summarize the themes which emerge from the research.

Tufts University
History 96 - World Seminar
Women, Patriarchy and Capitalism
Comparative Perspectives from Africa and Latin America

Assignment Two

    This assignment is designed to familiarize you with the current lines
of historical research on Women in Africa and Latin America. We want to see
what scholars are asking (and NOT asking) about women in Africa and Latin
America. In part we want to know how this compares to the broad historical
themes for Africa and Latin America which have emerged in our historical
studies to date. That will tell us how "women's history" is cast in
comparison to "history history". How is "women's history" different? For
example, had those of you with background in Latin American history, assumed
before that you were studying the history of men in Latin America? Does the
literature on women consider topics that DO NOT CONCERN MEN?

1. Chose a research team : Africa or Latin America

2. Read the research overviews for your selected area.

3. Summarize very briefly the topical themes which emerge in the overview
essays. (ie. family structure, health, women in development efforts)

4. Chose one theme from those which emerge for your selected area and examine
the research more carefully. Be prepared to tell the class the following
about the theme you have selected:
    What kinds of questions are asked by researchers working on the theme?
    What kinds of research techniques have they used to answer the
questions they have posed for themselves?
    What do you think about the questions asked? Are they relevant? What
kinds of questions would you ask about the topic?
    Are these historical themes?

When we have gone through the above material we will try to pull the themes
together to see how they relate to our concern for patriarchy and capitalism
(both in themselves and in interaction with one another) as socio-economic
dynamics which shape women's behavior and choices in important ways.

Tufts University
History 96 - World Seminar
Women, Patriarchy and Capitalism
Comparative Perspectives from Africa and Latin America

Source Packet

1. Marysa Navarro " Research on Latin American Women : Review Essay", Signs: Journal of Women in Culture and Society [SIGNS], Vol.5, No.1 (Autumn 1979).111-120.

2. Asuncion Lavrin, "Recent Studies on Women in Latin America", Latin American Research Review [LARR], Vol. 19, No. 1 (1984):181-189.

3. June E. Hahner, "Recent Research on Women in Brazil," LARR, Vol. 20, No. 3 (1985): 163-180.

4. Margaret Strobel, "Review Essay: African Women" SIGNS, Vol. 7 (1982): 109 - 131.

5. Davis A. Bullwinkle," Women and their Role in African Society: The Literature of the Seventies," Current Bibliography of African Affairs, Vol. 15, No. 4 (1982-1983): 263-291.

6. Evelyn P. Stevens, "Marianismo: The Other Face of Machismo in Latin America," in Ann Pescatello, ed., Female and Male in Latin America: Essays (Pittsburgh: University of Pittsburgh, 1973): 90 - 101.

7. Elsa M. Chaney," Women in Latin American Politics: The Case of Peru and Chile," in Pescatello, ed., Female and Male, 103-139.

8. Jeanne M. Penvenne, "Here Everyone Walked with Fear: The Mozambique Labor System and the Workers of Lourenco Marques, 1945-1962," in Frederick Cooper, ed. Struggle for the City: Migrant Labor, Capital and the State (Berkeley: Sage Publications, 1983):131-166.

9. Jane S. Jaquette, "Literary Archtypes and Female Role Alternatives: The Women and the Novel in Latin America," in Pescatello, ed., Female and Male, 3 - 27.

10. Ann Pescatello," The Brazileira: Images and Realities in the Writings of Machado de Assis and Jorge Amado,: in Pescatello, ed., Female and Male, 29 - 58.

Winter Quarter, 1988   Instructor: Susan Geiger
M,W, 9:45-11   Office: 494 Ford Hall
Ford 175   Hours: M,W,F, 11:15 -12, or by
                                       appointment
                                     Phone: 624-7502, or 624-6006,
                                       for messages

    WoSt 5401: WOMEN, COLONIALISM AND PROBLEMS OF UNDERDEVELOPMENT
    (upper division undergrad./lower division grad. students)

Required reading:
    Domitila Barrios de Chungara, Let Me Speak!
    Maria Mies, Patriarchy and Accumulation on a World Scale
    Gita Sen, with Caren Grown, Development, Crises, and Alterna-
        tive Visions: Third World Women's Perspectives
    Articles and book chapters, available for purchase at Kinkos,
    306 15th Ave. S.E., 379-0454, and on reserve in Wilson Library.

Course framework, format, expectations, requirements:
    In this course, we will be examining the impact of colonial
domination and economic underdevelopment on women -- primarily,
Third World women. In order to understand how women's lives,
societal roles and "status" have changed as a result of these
factors, we must consider pre-colonial circumstances. We will
also consider the kinds of strategies women have employed to
resist, accomodate to or overcome oppressive conditions.
Finally, we will analyze "women in development" policies and
programs with a view to assessing the nature of western aid
interest in Third World women, and the extent to which aid
policies and programs meet (or do not meet) the needs of women
and reflect (or do not reflect) Third World women's interests.

    In so far as it is possible, the class format will be based on
active class participation, with discussion of readings, the
raising and answering of relevant questions, and the construction
of hypotheses, theories and models for consideration as our
primary goals. As instructor, I will consider it my responsibility
to facilitate discussion, provide relevant information where
appropriate or when it is directly sought, and to raise those
questions I believe to be important. I will also provide assistance
with sources and resources.

    Class participation and discussion are expected and required,
and students are expected to have completed reading assignments
in preparation for the class for which the assignment has been
made. Regular attendance is also expected, and all but minimal
absence should be explained to the instructor.
    Assessment and grades will be based on the following:
    1) Three short (3-5 typed pp.) critical or analytical
responses to "thought questions" derived from the material we are
covering in class and reading - due on Wednesday, January 20;
Monday, February 8; and Monday, February 29. You will be asked
to present one of these critiques to the class. Please make
three copies of your papers: One for you, one for me, one for
the class. (70%)

2) A research proposal (c. 10 typed pp., footnotes and bibliography required) focused on a well-defined aspect of the course content of particular interest to you. Students should seek any necessary discussion of their proposed topic by the fifth week of class, and should be prepared to discuss their research in class during the ninth week. All research proposals are due March 15. (30%)

COURSE OUTLINE

Week I   INTRODUCTION, AND THE ISSUE OF ANALYTICAL FRAMEWORKS
1/4   Tasks and terminology

1/6   Conceptual problems and analytical frameworks
          Reading:
              Susan C. Rogers, "Women's Place: A Critical Review of
              Anthropological Theory," Comparative Studies in
              Society and History, Vol. 20, No. 1, Jan., 1978, pp.
              123-162.
              Jane Guyer, "The Raw, The Cooked, and the Half-Baked: A
              Note on The Division of Labor by Sex," Boston Univ.
              African Studies Center Working Paper #48, 1981.

Week II   THE IMPACT OF COLONIALISM
1/11   Assumptions and understandings
          Reading:
              Susan C. Bourque & Kay B. Warren, "Analyzing Women's
              Subordination: Issues, Distortions, and Definitions,"
              in Bourque & Warren, Women of the Andes, pp. 41-86.
              Eleanor Leacock, "Women's Status in Egalitarian
              Society: Implications for Social Evolution," Current
              Anthropology, Vol. 19, No. 2, June 1978, pp. 247-257.

1/13   Economics and ideology
          Reading:
              Mona Etienne, "Women and Men, Cloth and Colonization,"
              Christine Ward Gailey, "Putting Down Sisters and Wives,"
              Annette Weiner, "Stability in Banana Leaves," Chs. 9,
              12 and 11 in Mona Etienne and Eleanor Leacock (eds.),
              Women and Colonization.

Week III THE SEX/GENDER DIVISION OF LABOR: MYTH AND MEANING
1/18   Holiday, no class

1/20   Discussion of 1st Thought Papers

Week IV   WOMEN'S STRATEGIES
1/25   Revolt and Protest
          Reading:
              Judith Van Allen, "'Aba Riots' or Igbo 'Women's War'?
              Ideology, Stratification, and the Invisibility of
              Women," in Nancy Hafkin & Edna Bay (eds.), Women in
              Africa, pp. 59-85.

          (reading for 1/25, continued on next pg.)

reading for 1/25, continued)
>Caroline Ifeka-Moller, "Female Militancy and Colonial
Revolt," in Shirley Ardener (ed.), Perceiving Women.
pp. 127-157.
Shirley Ardener, "Sexual Insult and Female Militancy,"
in S. Ardener, Perceiving Women, pp. 29-53.

1/27   Towards an analysis of female solidarity
Reading:
Janet Bujra, "Introductory: Female solidarity and the
sexual division of labour," pp. 13 - 45; and
Melissa LLewelyn-Davies, "Two contexts of solidarity
among pastroal Maasai women," pp. 206-237, both in
Patricia Caplan and Janet Bujra (eds.), Women United,
Women Divided.

Week V WOMEN'S STRATEGIES (2):
2/1   Adaptation/Economic innovation
Reading:
Marcia Wright, "Bwanikwa: Consciousness and Protest
among Slave Women in Central Africa, 1886-1911," in
Claire Robertson & Martin Klein,(eds.)Women & Slavery in
Africa, pp. 246-267.
Margaret Jean Hay, "Luo Women and Economic Change
During the Colonial Period," in Hafkin & Bay (eds.)
op.cit., pp. 87-109.

2/3   Women's labor strategies
Reading:
Kate Young, "Modes of appropriation and the sexual
division of labour," in Annette Kuhn & AnnMarie
Wolpe (eds.), Feminism & Materialism, pp. 124-154.
Luise White, "Prostitution, identity, and Class Con-
sciousness in Nairobi during World War II, in SIGNS,
vol. 11, no.2, 1986, pp. 255-273.
Carmen Diana Deere & Magdalena Leon de Leal, "Peasant
Production, Proletarianization, and the Sexual
Division of Labor in the Andes," in SIGNS, vol 7,
no. 2, 1984, pp. 338-360.

Week VI ORIGINS AND STRUCTURES OF UNDERDEVELOPMENT
2/8   Discussion of 2nd Thought Papers
Reading:
Domitila, Let Me Speak! (begin reading)

2/10   Women and theories of underdevelopment
Reading:
Domitila, Let Me Speak! (continue)

Week VII SEX/GENDER DIFFERENTIATION IN UNDERDEVELOPMENT
2/15   The Case of Domitila
Reading:
Domitila, Let Me Speak! (complete)

Week VII, cont.
    2/17   Origins of women's "underdevelopment"
                Reading:
                    Mies, Patriarchy and Accumulation,' pp. 1-111.

Week VIII MANIFESTATIONS OF UNDERDEVELOPMENT
    2/22   Film: "The Global Assembly Line"
                Reading:
                    Mies, pp. 112 174.

    2/24   Women's Organizations: What kind of "development"?
                Reading:
                    Mies, pp. 175-204
                    Margaret Strobel, "Women's Collectivities," in M.
                    Strobel, Muslim Women in Mombasa, 1890-1975, pp.
                    156-217.
                    Patricia Caplan, "The Women's Organizations," chs.
                    6-8, in P. Caplan, Class & Gender in India, pp.
                    105-167.
                    Susan Geiger, "Women in Nationalist Struggle: TANU
                    Activists in Dar es Salaam, INTERNATIONAL JOURNAL
                    OF AFRICAN HISTORICAL STUDIES,20,1,1987, pp. 1-26.

Week IX   "FIGHTING TWO COLONIALISMS"
    2/29   Discussion of 3rd thought papers

    3/2   Defining the crisis
                Reading:
                    Development, Crises, and Alternative Visions:
                    Third World Women's Perspectives, pp. 11-70
                    Jeanne Henn, "Feeding the Cities and Feeding the
                    Peasants: What Role for Africa's Women Farmers?"
                    World Development, Vol. 11, No. 12, 1983, pp.
                    1043-1055.

Week X   TOWARDS WOMEN'S DEVELOPMENT
    3/7   Alternatiive formulations
                Reading:
                    Development, Crises, etc., complete (71-89).
                    Mies, pp. 205-235.

    3/9   Summary and conclusions

                Research Proposals due March 15, by 4 p.m.

Spring, 1986
Ford 175
9:45-11:00 TTh

Instructor: Susan Geiger
Office: 494 Ford Hall
Hours: TTh 11:15-12:30
or by appt.

Grad. TA: Susan Cahn
Office: 476a Ford Hall
Hours:
Phone: 373-2331

WoSt 3333: WOMEN IN LIBERATION STRUGGLE: CHINA, CUBA, MOZAMBIQUE, AND SOUTH AFRICA
(Intermediate Undergraduate)

Required Course Books:
    Ellen Kuzwayo, Call Me Woman
    Ida Pruitt, A Daughter of Han
    Margaret Randall, Women in Cuba: Twenty Years Later
    Judith Stacey, Patriarchy and Socialist Revolution in China

Please purchase the required books (all paperbacks) at Williamson Bookstore. In addition, a number of required readings are available for purchase (ask for Geiger, WoSt 3333) at Kinko's (306-15th Avenue SE, phone: 331-6970). All required readings and many suggested readings will also be on reserve in Wilson Library.

Course Framework, Format, Expectations, and Requirements

In this course, we will be examining the nature of women's participation in movements of revolutionary social change in China, Cuba, and Africa (Mozambique and South Africa). An attempt to compare and contrast the changing lives of women on three continents during a period roughly defined as the 20th century is ambitious to say the least, and will require a clear focus and constant refinement of issues and questions of interest to us. In so far as it is possible, our focus will be on women's lives, pre-, during, and (with the exception of South Africa) post- the period of revolutionary struggle. Moreover, we will be examining the nature of those struggles and their outcome through the lives of women, and from a feminist perspective.

Among the questions we shall be addressing throughout the course are the following:*

1.   What have been the ideological, physical, and socio-economic factors responsible for the oppression of women in the countries under consideration?

2.   Are there tensions between the goals of socialism and women's liberation? If so, how have these tensions been expressed?

3.   Is women's participation in productive labor a necessary condition for gender equality? Is it a sufficient condition?

_____
*Adopted, with modifications, from Elisabeth Croll, Feminism and Socialism in China.

182

4.   How has feminism been <u>defined</u> in China, Cuba, Mozambique, and South Africa?

5.   What has been the role of separate and organized women's movements in the countries considered?

Class participation and discussion building are expected, and required reading should be completed <u>in preparation</u> for the classes/weeks for which it is assigned. Regular attendance is expected and we would appreciate being informed of necessary absences.

Assessment of grades will be based on the following:

1.   A critique of required reading will constitute evidence of your under-standing of, reflections on, and ability to summarize and integrate course content and materials. Students are expected to purchase a separate (prefer-ably loose leaf) notebook for their reading critique. This critique should demonstrate your grasp of the major ideas or issues being raised in each reading, your reactions to what you are reading/learning and any questions you might have about the material itself or larger issues raised. As you read, you should bear in mind the five major course questions being ad-dressed, and note "answers" to them. In a "summary and conclusion" sec-tion following your critique of the required reading for <u>each area</u> (i.e., China, Cuba, Mozambique, and South Africa) we would like you to respond to the questions on the basis of your reading for the area. Please hand in your notebooks on   April 24 (A-L) or May 1 (M-Z) (so that we can see how you are doing/give suggestions, etc.) and on <u>June 9</u> (if you are doing a search paper) or <u>June 12</u> if you are taking the final exam. (Reading critique = 50% of grade).

AND

2.   A search paper (c. 10-12 typed pages; footnotes and bibliography re-quired) focused on a <u>well-defined</u> and <u>researchable</u> question of particular interest to you. Your topic must be approved by the instructor and you must be able to demonstrate that necessary sources to pursue the topic are AVAILABLE. Students must schedule a meeting with the instructor to discuss their proposed topic by the FOURTH WEEK of class, and must have the topic formally approved by the sixth week. Assistance, advice, help, etc. is available if you have not written such a paper before (or even if you have) and need more support. But we cannot know unless you ask, and it is your responsibility to let us know the kinds of assistance you need. <u>Papers are due by 10 a.m. on June 9.</u> (50% of grade)

OR...

3.   A Final Exam, "closed book," in-class essay answers to <u>three</u> of the <u>five</u> course questions, incorporating relevant readings, lectures, and discussion from all the areas. <u>Thursday, June 12, 4-6 p.m.</u> (50% of grade) If you take the final, your reading critique is due on this day.

Course Schedule:

CHINA

WEEK I, APRIL 1 & 3   THE NATURE OF WOMEN'S OPPRESSION IN
CHINA: CONTINUITY AND CHANGE

Required reading:
  Ida Pruitt, Daughter of Han

Suggested reading:
  Kay Ann Johnson, Women, the Family, and Peasant Revolution in China,
    Chs. 1 & 2.
  Elisabeth Croll, Feminism and Socialism in China, pp. 12-116.
  Vera Schwarcz, "Ibsen's Nora: The Promise and the Trap," Bulletin
    of Concerned Asian Scholars, Jan-March, 1975.
  Paul Ropp, "The Seeds of Change: Reflections on the Condition of
    Women in the Early and Mid Ch'ing," SIGNS, 2,1, 1976.

WEEK II, APRIL 8 & 10   CHINESE WOMEN: CRISIS AND REVOLUTION-
ARY STRUGGLE

Required reading:

  Judith Stacey, Patriarchy and Socialist Revolution in China, Chs. 1-
    4.

Suggested reading:
  Kay Ann Johnson, Women, The Family,..., Chs. 2-8.
  Elisabeth Croll, Feminism and Socialism in China, pp. 117-259.
  Delia Davin, Woman-Work, pp. 1-114 & appendices 1 & 2.
  Agnes Smedley, Portraits of Chinese Women in Revolution.
  Margery Wolf and Roxane Witke (eds.), Women in Chinese Society.
  Jane Price, "Women and Leadership in the Chinese Communist Move-
    ment, 1921-1945."
  Life histories selected from When They Were Young (1983).

WEEK III, APRIL 15 & 17   PERSPECTIVES ON WOMEN IN CONTEMPORARY
CHINA

Required reading:
  Judith Stacey, Patriarchy... Chs. 5-Epilog.

Suggested reading:
  Jean C. Robinson, "Women in a Revolutionary Society: The State and
    Family Policy in China," in Irene Diamond (ed.), Family Politics
    and Public Policy. (1983)
  Phyllis Andors, "The Four Modernizations and Chinese Policy on Women"
  H. Yuan Tien, "Age at Marriage in the People's Republic of China,"
    China Quarterly, 93 (March, 1983)
  Judith Stacey, "When Patriarchy Kowtows: The Significance of the
    Chinese Family Revolution for Feminist Theory," in Z. R. Eisen-
    stein (ed.), Capitalistic Patriarchy and the Case for Socialist
    Feminism, pp. 299-348.

four

Selections from Women in China and China Reconstructs.
Kay Ann Johnson, Women, The Family..., Chs. 9-15.
Elisabeth Croll, Chinese Women Since Mao
_____, Women in Rural Development: The Peoples Republic of China.
_____, Feminism and Socialism in China, pp. 260-333.
_____, The Politics of Marriage in Contemporary China (Law Library)
_____, The Women's Movement in China: A Selection of Readings, 1949-73.
Delia Davin, Woman-Work, pp. 115-197 & appendix 3.
Irene Diamond, "Collectivisation, Kinship and the Status of Women in Rural China," Bulletin of Concerned Asian Scholars, Jan.-March, 1975.
Phyllis Andors, "Social Revolution and Women's Emancipation: China During the Great Leap Forward," BCAS, Jan.-March, 1975.
_____, The Unfinished Liberation of Chinese Women, 1949-1980.
_____, "Politics of Chinese Development: The Case of Women, 1960-1966," SIGNS, 2, 1, 1976.
Marilyn Young, Women in China: Studies in Social Change and Feminism, Michigan Reports in Chinese Studies, No. 15, University of Michigan, 1973.
Mary Sheridan, "Young Women Leaders in China," SIGNS, 2, 1, 1976.
Irene Eber, "Images of Women in Recent Chinese Fiction," SIGNS, 2, 1, 1976.
Mariam Frenier, "Aids and Barriers to Feminism in Modern China," IJWS, 1, 3, May/June, 1978, pp. 272-80.
Batya Weinbsum, "Women in Transition to Socialism: Perspectives on the Chinese Case," The Review of Radical Political Economics, 1976.
Yue Daiyun and Carolyn Wakeman, To the Storm: The Odyssey of a Revolutionary Chinese Woman.

>>>>>>>>>>Think about Search Paper Topic<<<<<<<<<<
Make appointment with Susan or Susan to discuss it.

CUBA

WEEK IV, APRIL 22 & 24 *COLONIALISM, IMPERIALISM, CLASS AND COLOR: WOMEN'S OPPRESSION IN PRE-REVOLUTIONARY CUBA.

*Reading Critiques due, A-L.

Required reading:
Lourdes Casal, "Revolution and Conciencia:Women in Cuba" [K]

Suggested reading:
Cuba Review, Vol. IV, No. 2, 1974.
N. R. Calvet, "The Role of Women in Cuba's History," Granma Weekly Review, Jan. 13, 1978.
M. Randall, Cuban Women Now.

185

WEEK V, APRIL 29 & May 1*   CUBAN   WOMEN   IN   REVOLUTIONARY
                                                          STRUGGLE
*Reading Critiques due M-Z.

Required reading:
   M. Randall, Women in Cuba: Twenty Years Later.
   Max Azier, "Women's Development Through Revolutionary Mobilization,"
      IJWS, 2, 1, 1979. [K]
   Marjorie King, "Cuba's Attack on Women's Second Shift 1974-1976"[K]

Suggested reading:
   M. Randall, Cuban Women Now: Afterword 1974.
   Oscar Lewis, et. al., Four Women Living the Revolution: An Oral His-
      tory of Contemporary Cuba.

WEEK VI, MAY 6 & 8   CUBAN WOMEN TODAY

Required reading:
   Lourdes Arguelles & R. Ruby Rich, "Homosexuality, Homophobia, and
      Revolution: Notes Toward an Understanding of the Cuban Lesbian
      and Gay Male Experience," Part I [K]
   Carollee Bengelsdorf & Alice Hageman, "Emerging from Underdevelop-
      ment: Women and Work in Cuba," in Z. R. Eisenstein (ed.), Capi-
      talist Patriarchy and the Case for Socialist Feminism, pp. 271-
      295. [K]
   Norma Chinchilla, "Mobilizing Women: Revolution in the Revolution."[K]
   Muriel Nazzari, "The 'Woman Question' in Cuba: An Analysis of Materi-
      al Constraints on Its Solution," SIGNS, 9, 2, 1983, pp. 246-263.[K]

AFRICA

**WEEK VII, MAY 13 & 15   WOMEN   IN   MOZAMBIQUE: "TRADITIONAL"
                                             AFRICAN SOCIETY AND PORTUGUESE COLONI-
                                             ALISM**

Required reading:
   Allen Isaacman and Barbara Isaacman, "The Role of Women in the
      Liberation of Mosambique" [K]

Suggested reading:
   Sherilynn Young, "Mozambican Women in Transition: Reflections on
      Colonialism, Aspiration for Independence," 1977.

**WEEK VIII, MAY 20 & 22   WOMEN   AND   THE   LIBERATION   STRUGGLE
                                             IN MOZAMBIQUE**

Required reading:
   Stephanie Urdang, "The Last Transition? Women and Development in
      Mozambique" [K]
   Sonia Kruks, "Mozambique: Some Reflections on the Struggle for Wo-
      men's Emancipation" [K]
   Mozambican Women's Conference, Peoples Power, No. 6 [K]
   "The Mozambican Woman in the Revolution," LSM Pamphlet, 1974.[K]

Suggested reading:
Organization of Mozambican Women (O.M.M.) Information Bulletin.
Ruth Minter, "The Intertwining of the Struggles for Women and Social-
ism in Mozambique," 1978.
Barbara Isaacman & June Stephen, Mozambique: Women, the Law,
and Agrarian Reform.

**WEEK IX, MAY 27 & 29   WOMEN AND THE LIBERATION STRUGGLE
IN SOUTH AFRICA**

Required reading:
Ellen Kuzwayo, Call Me Woman
Belinda Bozzoli, "Marxism, Feminism & South African Studies" [K]

Suggested reading:
Hilda Bernstein, For Their Triumph and for Their Tears.
Jacklyn Cock, Maids and Madams: A Study in the Politics of Exploita-
tion, (especially ch. 6, "Changing Patterns" - on Wilson Reserve)
Cheryl Walker, Women and Resistance in South Africa
Suzanne Gordon, A Talent for Tomorrow: Life Stories of South African
Servants.

WEEK X, JUNE 3 & 5   THE STRUGGLE CONTINUES...

Required reading:
"Debate Feminism IN Africa: Feminism AND Africa" [K]

Suggested reading:
Winie Mandela, Part of My Soul Went with Him.
Beata Lipman, We Make Freedom: Women in South Africa.

*******All papers due (with reading critiques) on JUNE 9, 10:00 A.M.*******

*****Final Exam, JUNE 12, 4-6 P.M. (reading critiques due from students
taking final*****

University of California, Los Angeles
Women's Studies M198/Anthropology M198
Winter Quarter, 1988

WOMEN AND SOCIAL MOVEMENTS
INSTRUCTOR: SONDRA HALE

ABSTRACT: Using case studies of different types of social
movements (e.g. nationalist, socialist, liberal/reform), beginning with Russia and China and moving to Cuba, Algeria, Guinea-
Bissau, Mozambique, Nicaragua, Iran and the Palestinians,
questions are raised about women's participation in social
transformations.   Course will assess in which situations women
fare better in terms of gender interests addressed.

COURSE GOALS: The study of comparative social movements has most
often excluded the roles of women.   Only within the last few
years has women's participation in social movements become an
interdisciplinary subject of considerable interest to scholars of
Women's Studies, anthropology, political science, history,
sociology, and to various area studies (e.g. Middle Eastern or
Latin American Studies), as well as to community-based people,
including feminists, and theoreticians of the Left (e.g. Marx-
ists).   UCLA, with its large multicultural student body and its
location in a cosmopolitan area which contains all of the above
constituencies, does not have a course which has women as the
subject of major social movements. The comparative method used
in this course contributes not only to our cross-cultural
knowledge, but also to an understanding of mechanisms, institutions, and strategies for change.   The course will serve the
intellectual interests of the multicultural campus community
through culturally specific regional case studies, while offering
students new theoretical ideas and hypotheses about social
movements, in general, and women in the transformation processes,
in particular.

COURSE STAFFING: Principal instructor, Sondra Hale: Ph.D. in
anthropology; M.A. in African Studies; six years fieldwork in
Middle East/Africa; publications/papers on women and social
movements; experience teaching similar course at two other
institutions (in both Anthropology and Women's Studies Depart-
ments), as well as offering a version at UCLA under "Special
Topics". Guest Lecturers: (1) Norma Chinchilla, Ph.D. Sociolog-
y; foremost expert on women in Central American movements;
publications and fieldwork in area; Women's Studies Program,
California State University, Long Beach, California 90840.
(2) Kathleen Sheldon, Can.Phil., African History; foremost expert
on Mozambican women in the revolution; publications, papers, and
fieldwork on Mozambique; History Department, Bunche Hall, UCLA.

SYLLABUS--WOMEN AND SOCIAL MOVEMENTS

COURSE STATEMENT: This course is an investigation of women's movements and of women's participation in social movements in general. The emphasis will be on revolutionary movements in mainly Third World societies. However, the grounding (introduction) for the course will be a discussion of the Russian and Chinese socialist revolutions, which will be contrasted to later nationalist liberation movements (e.g. Algeria) and to Third World socialist movements (e.g. Cuba, Vietnam, Nicaragua, and Mozambique). Because my own primary research regions are the Middle East and Africa, these areas will be dealt with more frequently in the lectures. There will be a de-emphasis of U.S. and European women's movements. However, these will be touched upon in our discussions of women and war, women in the military, women and the peace movement, women and labor movements and strikes, and women's roles in such crises as food riots.

Our goal is to make a contribution to the growing body of theoretical ideas around women and revolutionary movements. Toward that goal, some of the questions we will raise are: (1) Do women fare better in reform or revolutionary movements? (2) What _kind_ of revolutionary movement benefits women most? (3) How significant is it for women to make their own revolution and in their own name? (4) Do women do this through participation in gender-integrated mass organizations or through their own autonomous organizations? (5) Have women been more successful in smaller, more "spontaneous" revolts? (6) In social movements are there "<u>women's</u>" issues" or are these "<u>gender</u> issues"? (7) Are these usually practical or ideological/strategic? (8) What are the ways in which "<u>culture</u>" (especially "traditional culture") has been used, or can be used, to forward women's claims? And the opposite: How has culture been used to impede women's claims? These questions emerge as the themes of the course, the case-study-oriented lectures focusing on these as we proceed.

LECTURE SCHEDULE: [two sessions reserved for student oral presentations]
I. Introduction: Rationale for Women's Revolutionary Activity--Conditions for Women [two lectures].

II. Types of Movements and Forms of Resistance: Overview and Theoretical Issues [one lecture].

III. Introduction to the First Major Revolutions of the 20th Century and a Typology for Other Revolutions in this Century [one lecture]. A. Russia [two lectures]. B. China [two lectures], with a 60 min. film, "A Small Happiness" (Chinese women after the revolution) [one session].

IV. Third World Revolutions/Movements. A. Introduction/Typology [one lecture]. B. Cuba [one lecture]. C. Colonialism and Women [one lecture]. D. Algeria: A Nationalist Movement [one lecture]. E. Iran and the Palestinians [two lectures]; Contrasting Cultural Nationalisms and the filming of "A Veiled Revolution" (Egypt) [one session]. F. Mozambique--Guest Lecturer, Kathleen Sheldon [one lecture]. G. Central American Struggles-- Namely Nicaragua--Guest Lecturer, Norma Chinchilla [one lecture].

V. Some Theoretical Questions: Using Hale Case Study of the Sudanese Communist Party and Its Relationship to the Sudanese Women's Union [one lecture].

VI. Conclusion

READINGS AND TENTATIVE SCHEDULE:
A. Required:
(1) The first required book is Female Revolt: Women's Movements in World and Historical Perspective by J. Chafetz and A. Dworkin (1986). Its focus is on women's movements, with an emphasis on Euroamerican movements. Students should read the first two chapters (pp. 1-62) and be selective thereafter (i.e. in accordance with selection of case study).
(2) By the third week students should have read Women and Political Conflict: Portraits of Struggle in Times of Crisis, edited by R. Ridd and H. Callaway (1987). For general grounding, read Chap. 1 (pp. 1-24) and Chap. 10 (pp. 214-230).
(3) By the fifth week students are required to read (from a packet of photocopied materials at Kinkos) sections from the best book on the subject, which is out-of-print, S. Rowbotham's Women, Resistance and Revolution (1972). This work may also be on reserve in the WS Library. Read pp. 15-58 and Chaps. on Russia and China.
(4) From the fifth week to the end of the quarter, students are required to read the remaining two required books, the optional reading, and the packet of photocopied materials:
(a) K. Jayawardena's Feminism and Nationalism in the Third World (1986)--the Introduction and then chaps. on Egypt, Iran, India, China, Vietnam, and the brief conclusion (students should read the China study in this book and in Rowbotham during lectures on China); (b) M. Davies', Third World, Second Sex (1983)--read one case study from each of these sections: I, II, III, IV, and V.
(5) Students are expected to use the Seager/Olson atlas, Women in the World to give them facility in discussing the situation/conditions of women in the world and to help you locate the societies.

B. Recommended books are Women in the World--A Survey; Latin American and Caribbean Women's Collective, Slaves of Slaves; S. Rowbotham, et al, Beyond the Fragments; O.Sembene's God's Bits of Wood; K. Johnson, <u>Women, the Family and Peasant Revolution in China</u>; and S. Urdang, <u>Fighting Two Colonialisms</u>. Additionally the following books are useful:

Afshar, Halen, ed. <u>Women, State and Ideology: Studies from Africa and Asia</u> (1987)

Andors, Phyllis, <u>The Unfinished Liberation of Chinese Women</u>

Andreas, Carol, <u>When Women Rebel: The Rise of Popular Feminism in Peru</u> (1985)

Angel, Adriana and Fiona Macintosh, <u>The Tiger's Milk: Women of Nicaragua</u> (1987)

Azari, Farah, <u>Women of Iran: The Conflict with Fundamentalist Islam</u> (1983)

Bassnett, Susan, <u>Feminist Experiences: The Women's Movement ment in Four Cultures</u> (1986)

Bendt, I. and J. Downing, <u>We Shall Return: Women of Palestine</u> (n.d.) [included in the packet]

Bernstein, Hilda, <u>For Their Triumphs and Their Tears: Women in Apartheid South Africa</u> (n.d.) [included in packet]

Chinchilla, Norma, <u>Women in Revolutionary Movements: The Case of Nicaragua</u>. East Lansing, Michigan State University Working Paper, No. 27 (1983)

Clements, Barbara, <u>Bolshevik Feminist: The Life of Aleksandra Kollantai</u> (1979)

Cliff, Tony, <u>Class Struggle and Women's Liberation: 1640-to the Present Day</u> (1984)

Croll, Elizabeth, <u>Feminism and Socialism in China</u> (1978); <u>Chinese Women after Mao</u> (1983)

Dahlerup, Drude, <u>The New Women's Movement: Feminism and Political Power in Europe and the USA</u> (1987)

Davin, Delia, <u>Woman-Work: Women and the Party in Revolutionary China</u> (1976)

De Chungara, D., <u>Let Me Speak</u> [Bolivia]

Duiker, W., "Vietnam: War of Insurgency." In <u>Female Soldiers--Combatants or Noncombatants?</u> N. Goldman, ed. (1981)

Edmondson, L., <u>Feminism in Russia, 1900-1917</u>

Eisen, Arlene, <u>Women and Revolution in Vietnam</u> (1984)

Enloe, Cynthia, "Women--The Reserve Army of Army Labor." <u>Review of Political Economics, Fourth Special Issue on the Political Economy of Women</u>, Vol. 12, No. 2 (1980); and <u>Does Khaki Become You? The Militarization of Women's Lives</u> (1983)

Elshtain, Jean, <u>Women and War</u> (1987)

Farnsworth, B., <u>Alexandra Kollontai and the Russian Revolution</u> (1980)

Freeman, Jo, "A Model for Analyzing the Strategic Options of Social Movement Organizations. In <u>Social Movements of the Sixties and Seventies</u>. J. Freeman, ed. (1983)

Geiger, Susan, "Women in Nationalist Struggle: TANU Activists in Dar es Salaam [Tanzania]. _International Journal of African Historical Studies_, Vol. 20, No. 1 (1987) [in packet]

Gerlach, Luther and V. Hine, _People, Power, Change: Movements of Social Transformation_

Gjerstad, Ole and Chantel Sarrazin, _Sowing the First Harvest: National Reconstruction in Guinea-Bissau_. Oakland: Liberation Support Movement [LSM] (1978)

Gronewold, Sue, "Women in China: A Revolution of Their Own?" _Trends in History: A Review of Current Periodical Literature in History_, Vol. 4, No. 1 (1985)

International Defense and Aid Fund, _To Honour Women's Day: Profiles of Leading Women in the South African and Namibian Liberations Struggles_ (1981)

Kaplan, Temma, "Female Consciousness and Collective Action: The Case of Barcelona, 1910-1918." In _Feminist Theory: A Critique of Ideology_, N. Keohane, et al, eds. (1982)

Kishwar, Madhu and Ruth Vanita, eds., _In Search of Answers: Indian Women's Voices from "Manushi"_ (1984)

Liberation Support Movement [LSM], _The Mozambican Woman in the Revolution_ (1974) [included in packet]

Lapidus, Gail, _Women and Soviet Society_ (1978)

Latin American Perspectives: Special Issue on Women and Class Struggle, Vol. IV, Nos. 1 & 2 (1977)

MacKinnon, Jan and Steve Mackinnon, eds., _Portraits of Chinese Women in Revolution_ (1976)

Massell, Gregory, _The Surrogate Proletariat: Moslem Women and Revolutionary Strategies in Soviet Central Asia, 1919-1929_ (1974)

Mumtaz, Khawar and F. Shaheed, eds. _Women of Pakistan_ (1987)

Molyneux, Maxine, "Women and Revolution in the People's Democratic Republic of Yemen," _Feminist Review_, No. 1 (1979); and "Mobilization without Emancipation? Women's Interests, the State, and Revolution in Nicaragua," _Feminist Studies_, Vol. 11, No. 2 (1985)

Nashat, Guity, eds., _Women and Revolution in Iran_ (1983)

Nekola, C. and P. Rabinowitz, eds., _Writing Red: An Anthology of American Women Writers, 1930-1940_ (1987)

New Movement in Solidarity with the Puerto Rican and Mexican Revolutions, _Have You Seen La Nueva Mujer Revolucionaria Puertorriguena: The Poetry and Lives of Revolutionary Puerto Rican Women_ (n.d.) [in packet]

Omvedt, Gail, "On the Participant Study of Women's Movements: Methodological, Definitional, and Action Considerations." In _The Politics of Anthropology: From Colonialism and Sexism Toward a View from Below_ (1979); and _We Will Smash This Prison: Indian Women in Struggle_ (1980)

Quest: Special Issue on International Feminism, Vol. IV, No. 2 (1978)

Randall, Margaret, Cuban Women Now (1974); Women in Cuba: Twenty Years Later (1981); and Sandino's Daughters [Nicaragua]

Reynolds, Sian, ed., Women, State and Revolution: Essays on Power and Gender in Europe since 1789 (1987)

Rossiter, Margaret, Women in the Resistance (1986)

Sacks, Karen, "Class Struggle in Sembene's `God's Bits of Wood', Signs (Winter, 1979).

Saywell, Shelley, Women in War (1985) [Britain, France, Italy, Poland, Soviet Union, Palestine, Indochina, Vietnam, "Falklands", El Salvador]

Stacey, Judith, "When Patriarchy Kowtows: The Significance of the Chinese Family Revolution for Feminist Theory." In Capitalist Patriarchy and the Case for Socialist Feminism. Z. Eisenstein, ed. (1979); and Patriarchy and Socialist Revolution (1983)

Stites, Richard, The Women's Liberation Movement in Russia: Feminism, Nihilism, and Bolshevism, 1860-1930 (1978); and "Women in Communist Revolutions: Some Comparative Observations," Comparative Communism, Vol. XIV, Nos. 2 & 3 (1981)

Tabara, A. and N. Yeganeh, The Shadow of Islam: The Women's Movement in Iran (1982)

Thompson, Marilyn, Women of El Salvador: The Price of Freedom (1986)

Vogel, Lise, Marxism and the Oppression of Women: Toward a Unitary Theory (1983)

Wilson, Michael and Deborah Rosenfelt, Salt of the Earth [screenplay]

Wolf, Margery, Revolution Postponed: Women in Contemporary China (1985)

The Woman Question: Selections from the Writings of Karl Marx, F. Engels, V.I. Lenin, and Joseph Stalin (1951)

Women and Politics. MERIP Middle East Report, Vol. 16, No. 1 (1986) [case studies by Sondra Hale on Sudan, J. Peteet on Palestinian women, M. Hegland on Iran, and an introduction by Suad Joseph]

Young, Marilyn, eds., Women in China: Studies in Social Change (1973).

STUDENT WORK: (Evaluation/Grading: Students will be given two grades in the course. 40% will be given for a 10-15 page case study of women's participation in a social movement (approved by instructor). An option is an oral presentation of 20-25 minutes on the same topic, with an abstract and reading list submitted. Because of the limited course time, the number of students who are allowed this option will be limited. The remaining 60% of the grade will be for a final essay exam covering all of the material. The exam will consist of two questions (choice out of three). Samples: (1) Contrast two different types of social movements (or movements in two societies which are characterized by contrasting modes of production) in terms of women's participation and the end result for women; (2) Contrast gender interests which are "practical" with those which are "strategic", indicating in which situations these seem more effective for women; (3) Indicate ways in which "traditional" culture has been used to impede or forward women's goals in social movements. In all of these questions and in the paper, students are expected to have a grasp of socioeconomic conditions (material base and culture), historical background, and changing gender ideologies cross-culturally. Participation in class discussions will determine borderline grades.

Kathy Staudt
Balch 26
x3154

WOMEN IN INTERNATIONAL DEVELOPMENT #150

This course examines the effects of "development" on women and on gender. We will connect theory and practice in interdisciplinary reading, discussion, and written work. We critically examine the remark of geographers Seager and Olson, "In the world of women there are few 'developed' nations," and ask: why? what is to be done?

We begin first with a dissection of the term development, followed with generalized "UN-ese" from the 1985 Nairobi conference, summarizing women's experiences. We then read anthropologically rich works from three world regions (Africa (Botswana), Latin America (Peru), and Asia (China)). These contrasting contexts allow us to comparing hunting/gathering with agriculturally-based societies. Given the practice-focus of the course, the comparison of market with socialist economies is crucial as well.

We then pause to reflect on theories of women's subordination and how well those theories address the anthropological studies. Students will write and present a critique of 3-5 pages on a major feminist theorist from among the list on the syllabus. A thorough understanding of the sources of subordination is necessary before embarking on solutions.

In the last half of the course, we will consider women's experience in specific policy and program development issues, including agriculture, health, and employment. Students will acquire expertise on a particular country, take on the role as "insider" or "outsider," and then develop a policy analysis, political mobilization strategy, or development project proposal. Students will present their ideas and drafts in class for feedback. The final paper will be placed on reserve for their colleagues' review in the take-home final examination.

Students will also be expected to keep a journal which will be picked up periodically. The journal should contain reflection on all readings, class discussions, and connections between readings in this and possibly other courses.

The course will be run in seminar style, with student participation expected. The journal and discussion will constitute a fourth of the grade, and the exam, critique, and final proposal each count for a fourth as well.

Required books:

Marjorie Shostak, <u>Nisa: The Life and Words of a !Kung Woman</u>

Susan Bourque & Kay Warren, <u>Women of the Andes: Patriarchy and Social Change in Two Peruvian Towns</u>

Margery Wolf, <u>Revolution Postponed: Women in Contemporary China</u>

Sue Ellen Charlton, <u>Women in Third World Development</u>

Joni Seager & Ann Olson, <u>Women in the World: An International Atlas</u>

Kathleen Staudt, <u>Agricultural Policy Implementation</u>

Reading List

Introduction

Sept. 9   **Joan Didion, "On Keeping a Notebook," from
Slouching Towards Bethlehem

**"The State of the World's Women: 1985," World
Conference to Review and Appraise the Achievements of
the U.N. Decade for Women

"Development" and Gender Differentation

Sept. 11   Charlton, Ch. 1-2
Recommended:

Ester Boserup, Woman's Role in Economic
Development, 1970
Signs, Special Issues, 1977, 1981
Irene Tinker and Michele B. Bramsen, Women
and World Development, 1976
Gita Sen and Lourdes Beneria, "Accumulation,
Reproduction, and Woman's Role in Economic
Development," Signs, 1982
DAWN, Development, Crisis, and Alternative
Visions: Third World Women's Prospectives,
1987
Jane Jaquette, "Women and Modernization Theory: A
Decade of Feminist Criticism," World Politics, 1982
Lynn Iglitzin & Ruth Ross, Women in the World:
The Women's Decade 1975-1985

Measuring Women's "Status(es)"

Sept. 14   Atlas, see selected maps, (#1, 4, 13, 21, 25, 27, 28,
34) and their notes (pp. 101 ff) (In these and other
maps, consider the validity of indicators, authors'
interpretation, missing data, and explanatory notes)

Recommended:

Lourdes Beneria, "Conceptualizing the
Labor Force: The Underestimation of Women's
Economic Activities," in Nici Nelson, ed. African
Women in the Development Process, 1984.
Family Planning Perspectives, "Learning About
Rural Women," (special issue), 1979.

197

Hunting and Gathering Societies: The !Kung Case

Sept. 16 <u>Nisa</u> Introduction, pp. 1-44

Sept. 18 Socialization, <u>Nisa</u>, Chs. 1-4

Sept. 21 Relations Between Men & Women, <u>Nisa</u>, Chs. 5-7, 10-12

Sept. 23 Reproduction, <u>Nisa</u>, Chs. 8-9

Sept. 25 Aging, <u>Nisa</u>, Chs. 13-15
Atlas, note Botswana figures

Recommended:

Martin and Voorhies, <u>Female of the Species,</u>
Eleanor Leacock and Mona Etienne, <u>Women and</u>
<u>Colonization: Anthropological Perspectives</u>

Non-Socialist Agricultural Societies: The Peruvian Case

Sept. 28 Bourque & Warren, Introduction and Chs. 1-3

Sept. 30 Reproduction, Bourque & Warren, Ch. 4

Oct. 2 Labor, Bourque & Warren, Ch. 5

Oct. 5 Class, Bourque & Warren, Ch. 6

Oct. 7 Political Power & the State, Bourque & Warren, Chs. 7-8

Oct. 9 Bourque & Warren, Ch. 9
Atlas, note Peru figures

Urban/Rural Socialism: The Chinese Case

Oct. 12 Prerevolutionary Reality, Wolf, Ch. 1

Oct. 14 Methodology, Wolf, Ch. 2
*Cultural Revolution Propaganda

Oct. 16 Socialization, Wolf, Ch. 5

Oct. 21 Rural & Urban Labor, Wolf, Chs. 3-4

Oct. 23 Marriage, Wolf, Chs. 6-7

Oct. 26 Cross-generational Relations, Wolf, Ch. 8-9

Oct. 28 Reproduction, Wolf, Ch. 10
Movie: Nova: China's Population Program

Oct. 30   Wolf, Ch. 11
           Atlas, note China figures

               Recommended:

                   Hilda Scott, _Does Socialism Liberate Women?_
                   (Eastern Europe)
                   Gail Lapidus, _Women in Soviet Society_

                   _Theoretical Reflections: Toward Political,
                   Economic and/or Ideological Solutions_

Nov. 2   **PAPER DUE** Presentations Begin: From the feminist
           theorists listed below, write a critique and present
           analysis in class. (Consider the following: What is
           the author's main argument and how is it supported?
           How does the author characterize women? Men? Are they
           all alike across cultures and time? What is/are the
           source/s of women's subordination? (Is this plausible?
           What's the evidence?) What are the key problem issues
           for women? How does the author propose to solve the
           problems of women's subordination? (Is it realistic?
           What are its politics?) Evaluate the solution(s) and
           consider whether they raise new problems.

                   *Gerda Lerner, _The Creation of Patriarchy_

                   *Karen Sacks, _Sisters and Wives_

                   *Peggy Sanday, _Female Power and Male Dominance:
                       On the Origins of Sexual Inequality_

                   *Nancy Chodorow, _The Reproduction of Mothering_

                   *Maria Mies, _Patriarchy and Accumulation on a
                       World Scale_

                   *Frederich Engels, _The Origin of the Family,
                       Private Property and the State_

                   *Susan Brownmiller, _Against Our Will: Men, Women
                       and Rape_

                   Ursula LeGuin (science fiction), _The Dispossessed_

                   _Development Policies and Programs:
                   Gender Neutral or Gender Specific_

Nov. 9   Atlas, map 14
           Food and Agriculture, Charlton, Chs. 3-4

               Recommended:

                   Barbara Lewis, _Invisible Farmers: Women and the
                       Crisis in Agriculture, 1981_

Jamie Monson and Marian Kalb, Women as Food Producers in Developing Countries, 1985

Carmen Diana Deere & Magdalena Leon de Leal, Rural Women and State Policy: Feminist Perspectives on Latin American Development, 1987

Nov. 11   Staudt, Agricultural Policy Implementation

*Uncaptured or Unmotivated: Women, Farmers, and the Food Crisis in Africa", Rural Sociology, 1987

Nov. 16   Marriage: Atlas, maps #S 2-5, 12, 16

Nov. 18   Bodies and Health: Charlton, Ch. 5
           Atlas, maps 6-11, 26, 35-37

           Recommended:

           Germaine Greer, Sex and Destiny, 1984
           Ruth Dixon, Rural Women at Work, 1978
           Helen Ware, Women, Demography and Development, 1981

Nov. 20   Employment, Charlton, Ch. 6
           Atlas, maps 15-20

Nov. 23   *Fernandez-Kelly in Sacks and Remy, My Troubles Are
               Going to Have Trouble with Me. (or Fernandez-Kelly, For
               We Are Sold, I and My People: Women and Industry in
               Mexico's Frontier, 1983, Ch. 3)

           *Gay Young, "Women, Development, and Human Rights:
           Issues in Integrated Transnational Production," Journal
           of Applied Behavioral Science, 1984

           Movie: The Global Assembly Line

Nov. 25   Education. Charlton, Ch. 7
           Atlas, maps 22-24, 33
           Be prepared to discuss briefly country of policy,
               political or project analysis

           Recommended:

           Comparative Education Review, 1980 (special issue)
           *Robertson, Robertson & Berger, Women and Class in
               Africa, 1986

           Development Strategies in International Context

Nov. 30   Charlton, Ch. 8
           *Lynn Bolles, "IMF Destabilization: The Impact on
               Working Class Jamaican Women," TransAfrican Forum, 1983

Dec. 2   Agencies and Organizations, Charlton, Ch. 9

Recommended:

Staudt, Women, Foreign Assistance and Advocacy
Administration

Barbara Rogers, The Domestication of Women

Catherine Overholt, et al., Gender Roles in
Development Projects

*SEEDS Cases

*Interamerican Foundation Report on Women's
Projects

*Ingrid Palmer, The Nemow Case

Women's Politics

Dec. 4   Charlton, Ch. 9
Atlas. maps 29-37, 34, 38-39, 40
*Molara Ogundipe-Leslie, (poet), "On the Globality of
Sisterhood," in Women in Nigeria

*(suggested) Maxine Molyneux, "Mobilization
Without Emancipation?   Women's Interests, State, and
Revolution," in Fagen,   Deere & Coraggio, Transition
and Development

*(suggested) Selections in Robertson and Berger, Women
and Class in Africa, 1986, esp. Christine Obbo and
Jane Parpart

Recommended:

Elsa Chaney, SuperMadre, 1979

Carolyn Adams & Kathryn Winston, Mothers at Work,
1979

ISIS, The Latin American Women's Movement

Hilda Bernstein, For Their Truimphs and Their
Tears, Women in Apartheid South Africa,1975

Patricia Caplan and Janet Bujra, Women United,
Women Divided, 1978

Dec. 7   DRAFT PAPERS DUE/PRESENTATIONS BEGIN

Dec. 14   FINAL COPY DUE, TO BE PLACED ON DENISON RESERVE

DEPARTMENT OF AFRO-AMERICAN STUDIES

Course: Afro-American Studies #302   Instructor: Dr. Cheryl Johnson-Odim
Semester: Fall 1986   Office: Humanities Bldg.#4213
Day & Time: T & Th 1-2:15 p.m.   Office Hours: Thurs 11 - 1 p.m. or
                                                      By Appointment

Third World Women in Development: Africa and the Caribbean

In this course we will seek to understand different conceptual views
of development. We will especially examine the experiences of women in
parts of Africa and the Caribbean with development policy and strategies.
Included in this examination will be explorations of feminist and Third
World criticisms of development theory particularly as it relates to the
conditions of women's lives. The ways in which women's work and
education have been helped or hindered by views on technology transfer
and international agency priorities will also be explored. The
'politics' of development and the dialogue between Third World and
Western women regarding development will be examined. Among the
questions we will be asking ourselves in this process are:

1) Is there a universally accepted vision/definition
   of development? If so, what is it? If not, what
   are various visions?

2) How have the critical assessments of women's
   experiences of development policy, both external
   and internal, affected development theories and
   strategies? What are the central themes of these
   critical assessments?

3) What impact, if any, has a growing international
   women's movement had on development issues?

4) How have politics (both international and national)
   impacted 'development debates' and development
   policies? How has culture?

5) What historical issues are important to our understanding of the 'development debates'?

All students are expected to do all the reading as this is a
lecture/discussion course. In the second week of classes students will
be divided into panels of equal number. Each panel will make an oral
presentation on some aspect of the course material in the final week of
classes. Each member of the panel will also hand in a 4-5 page essay on
an aspect of her/his panel's presentation.

Course grades will be determined according to the following:

10% Class participation
40% In-class essay (November 25th)
25% Panel presentations (Week of December 9 and 11)
25% Essay from Panel Presentation (Due December 11)

Required Books

1) Boserup, Ester. Woman's Role in Economic Development. (New York: St. Martin's Press,1970)

2) Women in Development: A Resource Guide. International Women's Information and Communication Service (Philadelphia· New Society Publisher, 1984).

3) Rogers, Barbara. The Domestication of Women: Discrimination in Developing Societies. (New York: St. Martin's Press, 1979)

Readings and Topics by Date

Sept 2
Defining Our Tasks. Introduction to course content, requirements and expectations.

Sept 4
Development Theory: Origins and Transitions.

1) "Towards A New International Development Strategy: The Scheveningen Report" in development dialogue, 1980:1, pp.55-67, KINKO'S.
2) "Re-thinking Women and Development" and "Women and Development Literature" in Women in Development,(Hereafter WID).

Sept 9 & 11
Historical Perspectives

1) Mayo, Marjorie, Underdevelopment and Class. KINKO'S.
2) "Forward" and "Introduction". WID.
3) Chapter 3, "Loss of Status Under European Rule" in Woman's Role in Economic Development.
4) Joseph, Gloria, "Caribbean Women: The Impact of Race, Sex and Class in Linsay, Beverly, Comparative Perspectives of Third World Women (New York, Praeger, 1980). KINKO'S.
5) Cole, Johnetta B., "Women in Cuba: The Revolution Within the Revolution" in Comparative Perspectives. KINKO'S.

Sept 16 & 18
Women's Work/Women's Health

1) Bengelsdorf, Carrollee and Hageman, Alice. "Emerging from Underdevelopment: Women and Work in Cuba". KINKO'S.

2) Beneria, Lourdes, "Conceptualizing the Labor
Force: The Underestimation of Women's Economic
Activities" in Journal of Developmental Studies,
special issue on "African Women in the
Development Process", 1980, pp. 10-23. KINKO'S.

3) "Women and Health" and "Migration and Tourism"
in WID.

4) Chapters 1,2,4,5,6,8,9,10,11 in Woman's Role in
Economic Development.

Sept 23 & 25   Women and Multinationals

1) "By the Sweat of Her Brow: Women and
Multinationals", series of articles in Multinational Monitor, August 1983, KINKO'S.

2) "Women and Multinationals" in WID.

Sept. 30 & Oct 2   Women in the Rural Environment

1) Jaquette, Jane, "Women, Population and Food: An
Overview of the Issues" in Monson, Jamie and
Kalb, Marion, Women as Food Producers in
Developing Countries (Los Angeles, UCLA Press,
1985). KINKO'S.

2) Cloud, Kathleen, "Women's Productivity in
Agricultural Households: How Can We Think About
It? What Do We Know?" in Women As Food
Producers. KINKO'S.

3) Blumberg, Rae Lesser, "Rural Women in Development" in Black, Naomi and Cottrell, Ann Baker
Women and World Change: Equity Issues in
Development (Beverly Hills: Sage Publications,
1981). KINKO'S.

4) "Women and Rural Development" in WID

5) Part Three: "The Effects of Development
Planning on Women and Their Dependents" in
Domestication of Women.

Oct 7 & 9   Women's Education

1) Lindsay, Beverly, "Issues Confronting
Professional African Women: Illustrations from
Kenya" in Comparative Perspectives. KINKO'S.

2) Miller, Kaity and Mendelsohn, Micaela,
"Education and the Participation of Women in
World Development: A Brief Survey (Washington,
D. C.: Women's Equity Action League, 1975).
KINKO'S.

3) "Education and Communication" in WID.
4) Chptr. 7 "The Educated Woman" and Chptr 12 "The Design of Female Education" in Woman's Role in Economic Development.

Oct 14 & 16   **Women, 'Modernization', and Technology**

1) Van Allen, Judith, "Modernization Means More Dependency" in The Center Magazine, May/June 1074. KINKO'S.
2) Boulding, Elise, "Integration into What? Reflections on Development Planning for Women" in Cain, Melinda and Dauber,, Roslyn Women and Technological Change in Developing Countries (Boulder Colo: Westview Press, 1981, KINKO'S.
3) "Women, Technology and the Development Process", ILO Office for Women, in Women and Technological Change, KINKO'S.
4) Dauber, Roslyn, "Applying Policy Analysis to Women and Technology: A Framework for Consideration" In Women and Technological Change. KINKO'S.
5) Seidman, Ann, "Women and the Development of 'under-development': The African Experience" in Women and Technological Change. KINKO'S.

Oct 21 & 23   **The Politics of Development**

1) Staudt, Kathleen, "Women's Political Consciousness in Africa: A Framework for Analysis" in Women as Food Producers. KINKO'S.
2) Lewis, Shelby, "African Women and National Development" in Comparative Perspectives. KINKO'S.
3) "Northern Women and the New International Economic Order", United Nations Development Programme Development Issue Paper for the 1980s Np. 16. KINKO'S.
4) Tinker, Irene, "Policy Strategies for Women in the 1980s" in Africa Report, March/April 1981. KINKO'S.
5) Van Allen, Judith, "African Women, 'Modernization' and National Liberation" in Iglitzin, Lynne B. and Ross, Ruth, Women in the World: A Comparative Study (Santa Barbara: Clio Press, 1976). KINKO'S.

Oct. 28 & 30   **The International Agencies**

1)   "Towards A New International Economic Order:
The Implications for Women", United Nations
Document, April 1978. KINKO'S.
2)   "International Workshop on Technical Cooperation
Among Developing Countries and Women", U.N.
Document, April 1978. KINKO'S.

3)   Meena, Ruth E., "Foreign Aid and the Question of
Women's Liberation" in The African Review, Vol.
11, No. 1, 1984. KINKO'S.
4)   Part Two, "Discrimination in Development
Planning" in Domestication of Women.

Nov 4 and 7   **Feminist Criticisms of Development Theories &**
Policies

1)   Elliott, Carolyn M., "Theories of Development:
An Assessment" in Women and National Develop-
ment, Wellesley Editorial Committee, (Chicago:
University of Chicago Press, 1977) KINKO'S.
2)   Papanek, Hanna, "Development Planning for Women"
in Women and National Dev. KINKO'S
3)   Pala, Achola O., "Definitions of Women and
Development: An African Perspective" in Women
and National Dev. KINKO'S.
4)   Beneria, Lourdes and Sen, Gita, "Class and
Gender Inequalities and Women's Role in
Economic Development--Theoretical and Practical
Implications" in Feminist Studies 8, No. 1,
Spring 1982. KINKO'S.
5)   Beneria, Lourdes and Sen, Gita, "Accumulation
Reproduction, and Women's Role in Economic
Development: Boserup Revisited" in Signs,
Vol. 7, No. 2, 1981. KINKO'S.
6)   Part One: "Problems of Perception" in Domesti-
cation of Women.

Nov 11 and 13   **Third World Women Speak for Themselves**

1)   The Experience of the Association of African
Women for Research and Development (AAWORD),
U.N. Document. KINKO'S.
2)   Tau, Mildred Malineo, "Women: Critical to
African Development" in Africa Report, March/
April 1981. KINKO'S.
3)   The Dakar Declaration on Another Development
With Women, development dialogue,1982:1-2.

4) Savané, Marie-Angélique, "The Dakar Seminar
on 'Another Development with Women'" in dev.
dial, 1982: 1-2. KINKO'S.
5) Arizpe, Lourdes, "Women and Development in Latin
America and the Caribbean" in dev.dial, 1982: 1-
KINKO'S.
6) Ahooja-Patel, Krishna, "Another Development With
Women: in dev dial 1982: 1-2. KINKO'S.

Nov 18 & 20   The Meaning of Development for Women

1) Barrett, Nancy Smith, "Women in Industrial
Society: An International Perspective" in
Chapman, Jane Roberts, Economic Independence for
Women (Beverly Hills: Sage Publications, 1976).
KINKO'S.
(2) Tinker,Irene, "Women in Developing Societies:
Economic Independence is Not Enough" in Economic
Independence. KINKO'S.
(3) McCormack, Thelma, "Development with Equity for
Women" in Women and World Change. KINKO'S
(4) Childers, Erskine, "The Development Approach to
Liberation: Suggestions for Planning " in Tinker
Irene and Bramsen, Michele Bo, Women and World
Development (Washington, D. C.: Overseas
Development Council, 1976) KINKO'S.

Nov 25   In Class Essay
Nov 27   Thanksgiving Holiday

Dec 2 & 4   International Women's Dialogue

1) Awe, Bolanle, "Reflections" in Women and
National Development (hereafter WAND). KINKO'S.
2) Leacock, Eleanor, "Reflections" in WAND.
KINKO'S.
3) Nyoni, Sithembiso Baka, "Women's Rights Are Not
Enough" in Africa Woman No. 26, March/April,
1980. KINKO'S.
4) "U.S. Delegates Support Goals Opposed Here" in
Washington Post, July 20, 1985. KINKO'S.
5) Okeyo, Achola Pala, "Reflections on Development
Myths" in Africa Report, March/April 1981.
KINKO'S.
6) Zollner, Joy, "Women's Rights in Africa and the
United States" in Africa Report, Jan-Feb 1977.
KINKO'S.
7) Steady, Filomina Chioma, "African Women at the

End of the Decade" in _Africa Report_, March/Apr 1985. KINKO'S.

8) Cagatay, Nilufer, Grown, Caren and Santiago, Aida, "Nairobi Women's Conference: Toward A Global Feminism?" in _Feminist Studies_ Vol. XII, No. 2, Summer 1986. KINKO'S.

Dec 9 & 11   Panel Discussions/ Wrap-Up.

History 201N (Introductory Graduate Seminar)   Professor E.A. Alpers
Spring Quarter 1985   Bunche 5351: M 10-1
M 2-5; Geology 4645   825-2347; 825-4601

African Women's History

Introduction

This course is intended to provide an introduction to the geometrically increasing scholarly literature on African women's history. To avoid the need to establish what would inevitably be a huge reserve reading list, the required reading for the course will focus on a series of readily available books which together will raise the full range of theoretical, methodological, and thematic questions that a more topically designed syllabus would hope to achieve. All of these books are available for purchase through the ASUCLA Bookstore.

Each week we will discuss a single volume, whether it is the product of an individual author or an edited collection of essays. In this way you should be able to follow the development of the literature historiographically and to become familiar with the key issues that have emerged from this new scholarship over the past decade.

Organization of Class Meetings

Each week there will be three assigned tasks for different members of the seminar. One person will be responsible for providing an introductory focus for that week's discussion by identifying what he or she understands to be the key issues that are raised by the book. A second person will be responsible for providing a review of reviews of that week's reading. Finally, a third member of the seminar will serve as rapporteur for that week's class discussion.

Each week's discussion leader will be expected to provide the class with a brief, typed outline of the main points of her or his oral presentation. This should be available for distribution at the beginning of that week's class meeting. The reviewer for that week will be responsible for distributing a typed list at the beginning of the class of the reviews that were consulted in preparing his or her oral presentation. Finally, each week's rapporteur will be responsible for distributing a typed copy of her or his notes to all members of the seminar at the following week's meeting.

In addition to providing a structure for the class discussions, this set of shared responsibilities should also result in a useful set of supplementary material for each member of the seminar.

Required Essay

Each student in the seminar is required to write a substantial essay (20-25 pages) on a topic of direct relevance to African women's history. This essay may be either a research paper on a topic of particular interest to you or a critical review essay of the literature on some aspect of our broader subject. Whichever option you choose, it is important for you to begin to do the reading and research for the paper as soon as possible so that you can identify your bibliography and sources, discuss your ideas for the paper, including its possible structure and argumentation, with me before beginning to produce a draft, and complete the assignment before the end of the quarter.

The final sessions of the seminar will be devoted to panels of oral presentations of your papers. So that I can schedule these panels intelligently, I will need to know your topics as soon as possible so that each session has as much coherence as possible. The format of these sessions will be very similar to those of the African Studies Association or any other professional organization and should provide you with a valuable learning experience. I will serve as Chair and Commentator for each of these final sessions. They should also help you in revising the final drafts of your essays.

Schedule of Class Meetings

April 1 - Introduction

April 8 - Nancy J. Hafkin & Edna G. Bay (eds.), Women in Africa (Stanford University Press, 1976).

April 15 - Claire G. Robertson & Martin A. Klein (eds.), Women and Slavery in Africa (University of Wisconsin Press, 1983).

April 22 - Karen Sacks, Sisters and Wives: The Past and Future of Sexual Equality (University of Illinois Press, 1982).

April 29 - Mary F. Smith, Baba of Karo: A Woman of the Muslim Hausa (Yale University Press, 1981).

May 6 - Margaret Jean Hay & Marcia Wright (eds.), African Women and the Law: Historical Perspectives (Boston University, Papers on Africa, Vol. VII, 1982).

May 13 - NO CLASS (I will be out of town at a conference.)

May 20 - Christine Obbo, African Women: Their Struggle for Economic Independence (Zed Press, 1980).

May 27 - Margaret Jean Hay & Sharon Stichter (eds.), African Women South of the Sahara (Longman, 1984).

June 3 - Term Paper Panel

June 6, 6-9 p.m. - Term Paper Panel (Tentative)

June 10, 8-11 a.m. (Exam Code 8) - Term Paper Panel

June 10 - Term Paper Panel (Tentative)

Women in African History

WSS 23U/ASS 246

Spring 1982

TU, TH 11:05-12:35
Dr. Iris Berger

Books

Students are advised to purchase the following books:

Nancy Hafkin and Edna Bay, Women in Africa: Studies in Social and Economic
    Change
Buchi Emecheta, The Slave Girl
Ramatoulie Kinteh, Rebellion
Ousmane Sembene, God's Bits of Wood
Hilda Bernstein, For Their Triumphs and For Their Tears
Additional readings will be either on reserve in the library or will be
    handed out in class.

Requirements

1. Class participation and attendance will be important considerations, and
    may be decisive in the case of boarder line grades. You will be
    expected to have read the material and to be prepared to discuss it on
    the assigned day.

2. Midtern exam -- 30%

3. Final Exam (take-home) -- 40%

4. Paper -- 30%
    A comparative analysis of the three novels read in class that should focus
    on at least two of the themes we have been discussing. The paper should
    compare and contrast the roles and status of women in these novels and
    the attitudes toward women that they reflect. 7-10 pages.

5. During World Cultures Week all students will be required to attend the
    programs on Feb. 16 and 17. The Feb. 18 program is highly recommended
    and may, if necessary, be substituted for the Feb. 16 lecture.

Part I: Family and Rural History: Women in Pre-colonial African Societies

    Jan. 26: Introduction

    Jan. 28: Women in the Political Economy: Farmers and Gatherers
              Paulme, ed., A. Lebeuf. "The Role of Women in the Political
                  Organization of African Societies," pp. 93-120, in D. Paulme,
                  Women of Tropical Africa
              Boserup, "Male and Female Farming Systems," pp. 15-36, in
                  Women's Role in Economic Development

    Feb. ?:   Women in the Political Economy: Pasteralists, Film:
                  "Boran Women" or "Women of the Toubou"

    Feb 4:   Marriage and Family Relationships:
                  Anthropological and Personal Perspectives
              Boserup, "The Economics of Polygamy," pp. 37-52.

211

Ardener, ed., W. James, "Matrifocus on Women," pp. 140-162.
Shostak, Nisa, pp. 169-213.

Feb. 9:   Women in African Legends
          Guest speaker: Pearl Primus (tenative)

Feb. 11: Marriage and Family Relationships: A Novelist's Perspective
          Flora Nwapa, Idu

Feb. 16: World Cultures Week
          Speaker: Perdita Huston

Feb. 17: Film: "You Have Struck a Rock"

Feb. 18: Film on the infant formula controversy

          See readings for week of Feb. 23 and Feb. 25

Part II: Development of Underdevelopment? The Social and Economic History
          of Women Under Colonialism

Feb. 23: The Changing Position of Women: Theoretical Perspectives
          Boserup, "Loss of Status Under European Rule," pp. 53-65.
          C. Elliot, "Theories of Development," pp. 1-8, Signs, (1977)
          A. Pala, "Definition of Women and Development," pp. 9-13, Signs, (1977)
          H/B, L. Mullings, "Women and Economic Change in Africa."

Feb. 25: Women, Slavery and the Slave Trade
          Buchi Emecheta, The Slave Girl

Mar. 2:   Women's Organizations and Anti-Colonial Resistance: The Igbo Revolt
          H/B, K. Okonja, "The Duel-Sex Political System in Operation," in
          S. Ardenen, Perceiving Women, pp. 45-58.

          C. Ifeka-Moller," Female Militancy and Colonial Revolt," H/B,
          J. Van Allen, "'Aba Riots' or Igbo 'Women's War'?,"pp. 58-86.

Mar. 4:   Rural Perspectives on Economic Change: Luo Women (Kenya)
          H/B, M.J. Hay, "Luo Women and Economic Change During the Colonial
          Period," pp. 87-109.

Mar. 16: Marriage and the Family - I
          C. Obbo, African Women, pp. 33-53.
          R. Kinteh, Rebellion

Mar 18:   Marriage and the Family - II
          R. Kinteh, Rebellion

Mar. 23: Midterm Examination

Mar. 25: Women and Migration
          C. Obbo, African Women, pp. 70-85
          M. Mueller, "Women and Men, Power and Powerlessness in Lesotho,"
          pp. 154-166, Signs (1977)

N. Sudarkasa, "Women and Migration in Contemporary
West Africa," (Signs, 1977), pp. 178-189
H. Sibisi, "How African Women Cope with Migrant Labor
in South Africa," (Signs, 1977), pp. 167-177

Mar. 30: Women's Work in Urban Areas: Traders, Entrepreneurs and the
Informal Economy
J. Bujra, "Women 'Entrepreneurs' of Early Nairobi," Canadian Journal
of African Studies (1975), pp. 213-234
H/B, C. Robertson, "Ga Women and Socioeconomic Change, Accra,"
pp. 111-133
Film: "Fear Women"

April 1: Strategies for Urban Survival: A Uganda Case Study
C. Obbo, African Women, pp. 101-142.

April 6: Women's Associations: Changing Forms of Ceremony and Community
H/B, I. Berger, "Rebels or Status-Seekers?", pp. 157-181
F. Mernissi, "Women, Saints and Sanctuaries," (Signs, 1977),
pp. 101-112.

April 13: The Status of Women in Comparative Perspective

Guest Speaker: Fran Mascia-Lees

April 15: Puberty Rites and Cultures of Resistance: The Kikuyu Circumcision
Controversy
Jomo Kenyatta, Facing Mount Kenya, pp. 125-148
Fran Hosken, The Hosken Report

Part III: Nation, Class and Gender: The Politics of Liberation

April 20: Worker's Struggles and Women's Consciousness
and 22: Ousmane Sembene, God's Bits of Wood
PAPER DUE

April 27: Nationalism, Socialism and Women's Liberation: Kenya and Tanzania
K. Santilli, "Kikuyu Women in the Mau Mau Revolt," pp. 143-159,
Ufahamu
A. Wipper, "Equal Rights for Women in Kenya?", pp. 463-476
H/B, J. Brain, "Less Than Second Class," pp. 265-282

May 29: Women's Liberation and National Liberation: Mozambique and
Guinea-Bissau
S. Urdang, Fighting Two Colonialisms
A. Isaacman, A Luta Continua, pp. 32-36
S. Urdang, "Mozambique," pp. 4-5

May 4: An Ongoing Struggle: Women in the Political Economy of South
Africa, Hilda Bernstein, For their Triumphs and For their Tears

May 6: Class and Gender among Women Workers in South Africa.

NOTE: I would now use two new books: J. Hay and S. Stichter, African
Women South of the Sahara and J. Goodwin, Cry Amandla! (on S. Africa).
I also would replace R. Kinteh, Rebellion, with a more complex novel.

HISTORY 5436/WOMEN'S STUDIES 5400
Spring, 1987
HHH Center 30
Time: 1:15 – 3:00

Instructor: Susan Geiger
Office: 494 Ford Hall
Phone: 624-7502 or
624-6006 (messages)
Office hours: Wed. 1:15-3:00
Fri. 9:00-10:00 (or by appointment)

SOCIAL HISTORY OF AFRICAN WOMEN: 1850 TO THE PRESENT

In this seminar, we will address the subject of African women's lives, focusing not only on questions of change over time, but on issues of theory and method of analysis. Recent writings on the subject of African women, written from a variety of perspectives, utilizing diverse sources and data, and testing as well as employing different frameworks of historical analysis will be considered in their own right as well as in terms of the extent to which they challenge existing frameworks, historical generalizations and foci in the study of African peoples.

Expectations and assignments

Seminar participants are expected to complete required readings in preparation for each session, and to participate in seminar discussions. In addition, you are responsible for the following assignments:

1. All students are responsible for a written assessment (at least two typed pages) of either a recently written (since 1980) African History text designed for college use or an SSRC "State of the Arts" essay (published in the African Studies Review). These assessments are due at the second class period, and along with the assigned readings, will constitute the basis for our discussion that week. (See under Week II for details)

2. Undergraduates are responsible for three "thought papers" at least 5 typed pages in length, analyzing the issues raised in the readings for the weeks selected. Each paper is to be submitted within two weeks of the date for which the readings focused on have been assigned. The third paper must be submitted by June 11.

3. Graduated Students are responsible for either four "thought papers" (see above) or two "thought papers" and a research paper, 12-15 typed pages in length, addressing a particular issue of your choice within the general topic area of the seminar. If you intend to do a research paper, please consult with me about it by the fourth week of the quarter. All research papers and the final "thought papers" are due by **June 11**.

Week I   **INTRODUCTION**
3/30   Seminar requirements, format, expectations; approaches and issues in the study of African women's social history: the questions of invisibility and androcentric bias; working definitions.
          *Attend Jean Hay's lecture, April 2, 12:15; 710 Social Sciences

Week II   **AFRICANS, AFRICAN HISTORY AND AFRICAN WOMEN**
4/6   *Required reading for Week II discussion:*
          Strobel (1) and Guyer (2) and at least one of the following:
          Select a "State of the Arts" essay (essays by Lonsdale, Cooper, and Freund are on reserve) or a recent African History text (Wilson Library has many. Be sure the one you select is post 1980). Whether you have selected one of the essays or a text, you are looking for 1) African women (how frequently do they appear or become "visible"? In what context? How would you assess their treatment as "actors" in African history, based on this essay or book?; and 2) for examples of androcentric

214

bias (do the generalizations made about Africans really include women as well as
men? Does "gender-neutral" terminology includewomen as well as men? Do the
particular theoretical formulations or frameworks of analysis employed seem more
or less able to incorporate the lives of African women? How, in general, are
African women conceptualized in the text or essay you read? **YOUR WRITTEN
ASSESSMENT (BE SURE TOPROVIDE A FULL IDENTIFICATION OF WHAT
YOU READ) SHOULD ADDRESS THE QUESTIONS ABOVE, AND THESE ARE
THE ISSUES YOU SHOULD BE PREPARED TO DISCUSS IN THE
SEMINAR SESSION.**
The following texts are only suggestions. A look through the
general African history section of the stacks in Wilson will produce dozens more.
Philp Curtin, et. al., African History (revised edition only) P.L. Wickins, Africa
1880 -1980: An Economic History A.J. Wills, An Introduction to the History of
Central Africa (Fourth Edition)
Bill Freund, The Making of Contemporary Africa:The Development of African Society
Since 1800 (1984)

Week III 4/13	**KINSHIP, PAWNSHIP, AND SLAVERY** *Required reading for Week III discussion:* Robertson and Klein (3), Wright (4 and 5), Strobel (6).
Week IV 4/20	**AFRICAN WOMEN AND THE ANALYSIS OF CHANGING MODES OF PRODUCTION** *Required reading for Week IV discussion:* Afonja (7), Mandala (8), and Chs. 1 and 2 in Hay and Stichter (eds.)
Week V 4/27	**THE IMPACT OF COLONIALISM ON AFRICAN WOMEN'S LABOR** *Required reading for Week V discussion:* Etienne (9), Hay (10), Chauncey (11), Cock (12)
Week VI 5/4	**LAW AND THE CHANGING LEGAL RIGHTS OF AFRICAN WOMEN** *Required reading for Week VI discussion:* Chanock (13), Merry (14), Hay (15), Wells (16)
Week VII 5/11	**PRODUCTION, REPRODUCTION, URBANIZATION AND SEX** *Required reading for Week VII discussion:* Hansen (17), Bryceson (18), White (19, 20), Bujra (21, 22)
Week VIII 5/18	**WOMEN'S ANTI-COLONIAL PROTEST AND PARTICIPATION IN LIBERATION MOVEMENTS** *Required reading for Week VIII discussion:* Van Allen (23), Ifeka-Moller (24), Ardener (25), Johnson (26), and Chs. 9 and 10 in Hay and Stichter (eds.).
Week IX 5/25	**No class - holiday** But please read Ba (27) and attend lecture on Friday by Prof. Shula Marks.
Week X 6/1	**CONTEMPORARY SITUATION OF AFRICAN WOMEN: SEVERAL VIEWS** *Required reading for week X discussion* Dinan (28), Bozolli (29), Berger (30), Robertson (31) andd

215

Ch. 11 in Hay and Stichter (eds.).

REQUIRED READING:

The following articles, papers and chaters constitute <u>required</u> reading for **History 5436.** They are available for purchase at Kinkos, 306 15th Avenue S.E., (Dinkytown Branch). They are listed below according to the manner in which they are numbered at Kinkos, and [mostly] according to the order in which they will be considered in the seminar. These and other sources are also on Reserve under **History 5436** in Wilson Library. Whether you use Kinkos or Wilson, please note that in several cases there is more than one article by a given author, so check the <u>title</u> to be sure you are reading the right one at the right time. Whether you purchase these materials or use Wilson, you are expected to have read them as assigned for each seminar session.

1 Margaret Strobel, "African Women, " Review Essay," <u>SIGNS</u>, 8.1 (1982): 109-131.

2 Jane Guyer, "The Raw, the Cooked, and the Half-Baked: A Note on the Division of Labor By Sex, " Boston University, <u>AFRICAN STUDIES WORKING PAPERS</u>, 48 (1981).

3 Claire Robertson and Martin Klein, "Women's Importance in African Slave Systems," in Robertson and Klein (eds.), <u>WOMEN AND SLAVERY IN AFRICA</u> (1983), 3-25.

4 Marcia Wright, "Women in Peril, "<u>AFRICAN SOCIAL RESEARCH</u>, 20 (December 1975): 800-819.

5 Marcia Wright, "Bwanikwa: Consciousness and Protest Among Slave Women in Central Africa, 1886-1911," in Robertson and Klein, eds., <u>WOMEN AND SLAVERY IN AFRICA,</u>, 246-267.

6 Margaret Strobel, "Slavery and Reproductive Labor in Mombasa," in Robertson and Klein, eds., <u>WOMEN AND SLAVERY IN AFRICA,</u> 111-121.

7 Simi Afonja, "Changing Modes of Production...," <u>SIGNS</u>, 7.2 (1981): 299-313.

8 Elias Mandala, "Capitalism, Kinship and Gender in the Lower Tchiri (Shire) Valley of Malawi, 1860-1960: An Alternative Theoretical Framework, " in <u>AFRICAN ECONOMIC HISTORY</u>, No. 13, 1984: 137-169.

9 Mona Etienne, "Women and Men, Cloth and Colonization, " in Etienne and Leacock (eds.), <u>WOMEN AND COLONIZATION</u>, 214-233.

10 Margaret Jean Hay, "Luo Women and Economic Change During the Colonial Period," in Hafkin and Bay (eds.), <u>WOMEN IN AFRICA</u>, 87-109.

11 George Chauncey, Jr., "The Locus of Reproduction: Women's Labor in the Zambian Copperbelt, 1927-1953, "<u>JOURNAL OF SOUTHERN AFRICAN STUDIES (JSAS)</u>, 7.2 (1981): 135-164.

12 Jacklyn Cock, "Changing Patterns," in <u>MAIDS AND MADAMS: A STUDY IN THE POLITICS OF EXPLOITATION</u>, 173-228.

13 Martin Chanock, "Making Customary Law: Men, Women and Courts in Colonial Northern Rhodesia, " in Margaret Hay and Marcia Wright (eds.), <u>AFRICAN WOMEN AND THE LAW: HISTORICAL PERSPECTIVES</u> (1982), 53-67.

14 Sally Merry, "The Articulation of Legal Spheres, " in Hay and Wright (eds.), AFRICAN WOMEN AND THE LAW, 68-89.

15 Margaret Jean Hay, "Women as Owners, Occupants and Managers of Property in Colonial Western Kenya," in Hay and Wright (eds.), AFRICAN WOMEN AND THE LAW, 110-123.

16 Julia Wells, "Passes and Bypasses: Freedom of Movement for African Women Under the Urban Areas Act," in Hay and Wright (eds.), AFRICAN WOMEN AND THE LAW, 125-150.

17 Karen Hansen, "Negotiating Sex and Gender in Urban Zambia," JSAS, 10.2 (1984): 219-238.

18 Deborah Bryceson, "The Proletarianization of Women in Tanzania," in Review of the African Political Economy, 17 (1980): 4-27.

19 Luise White, "Compradores and Barren Women: Sexuality, Gender, and Close Formation in East Africa, 1890-1920." (Unpubl. ms.)

20 Luise White, "Prostitution, Identity and Class Consciousness in Nairobi," in SIGNS, Vol. II, No. 2, 1986: 255-273.

21 Janet Bujra, "Production, Property, Prostitution, 'Sexual Politics' in Atu, " CAHIERS D'ETUDES AFRICAINES 65, 17.1 (1977): 13-39.

22 Janet Bujra, "Urging Women to Redouble Their Efforts," in WOMEN AND CLASS IN AFRICA, 117-140.

23 Judith Van Allen, " 'Aba Riots' or Igbo 'Women's War'? Ideology, Stratification, and the Invisibility of Women," in Hafkin and Bay (eds.), WOMEN IN AFRICA, 59-85.

24 Caroline Ifeka-Moller, "Female Militancy and Colonial Revolt," in Shirley Ardener (ed.), PERCEIVING WOMEN, 127-157.

25 Shirley Ardener, "Sexual Insult and Female Militancy," in Shirley Ardener (ed.), PERCEIVING WOMEN, 29-53.

26 Cheryl Johnson, "Class + Gender," in WOMEN AND CLASS IN AFRICA, 237-254.

27 Mariama Ba, SO LONG A LETTER, 90 pp.

28 Carmel Dinan, "Pragmatists or Feminists? The Professional 'Single' Women of Accra, Ghana, " CAHIERS D'ETUDIES AFRICAINES 65, 17.1 (1977): 149-176.

29 Belinda Bozzoli, "Marxism, Feminism and South African Studies," JSAS, 9.2 (April 1983): 139-171.

30 Iris Berger, "Sources of class Consciousness: South African Women in Recent Labor Struggles, " in WOMEN AND CLASS IN AFRICA, 216-236.

31 Claire Robertson, "Women's Education and Class formation in Africa, 1950-1980," in WOMEN AND CLASS IN AFRICA, 92-113.

The University of North Carolina - Chapel Hill
History 13H
Prof. David Newbury

Spring 1988

History 13H

WOMEN IN AFRICAN HISTORY

(Freshman Honors Seminar)

Understanding women's roles in food production, in domestic well-being, and in the formation of social alliances is essential to understanding African societies. But more than that, women are important in their own right, and they are affected by the social processes often referred to as "historical change" differently than are men. Yet it is only recently that adequate materials have become available to make the study of such issues possible, and women are still all too frequently omitted from conventional presentations of "history." This course will provide an overview of the structures of women's activities in Africa and consider how they have changed over the past century or so.

We will be examining specific cases of women's activities, but we will be asking general questions of these cases: Why study "women in history" specifically? How do we best understand these issues and how should we undertake such a study? In what ways are women's roles distinct from those of men? What makes them so? How do women respond to this reality? How are these roles changing? Is change and "modernization" always a positive step for women -- and for which women?

The materials are presented under selected themes, though the readings are all inter-related. The course will include readings on women and the domestic economy, women and the global economy, women and slavery, women and resistance, women in religious organizations, women in the urbanization process, and women and liberation movements. No previous study or experience of Africa is required; all you need is an interest in the subject, a desire to understand people living in cultures different from our own, and a willingness to share your assessment of the readings openly with others in class discussions.

The course will be organized as a seminar, giving a central role to class discussions of the readings; occasional lectures will provide background to the readings or relate specific readings to the wider issues involved. Frequent short (3-5 pp.) papers will be assigned. These are not intended as research papers, but rather as brief commentaries on the readings or analyses of the issues presented. In these papers, you may want to address specific issues which arise in the readings or compare the different approaches among various authors addressing similar topics. No supplementary reading will be required for the papers; they will be assessed more on the clarity of the writing -- and of the thinking -- than on original research. Students will occasionally be asked to serve as discussion leaders for a specific day's readings.

218

It is essential that students in the course attend class regularly, keep up with the readings, and be willing to enter freely into class discussions. Class participation will account for about 40% of the term grade; the papers will account for about 60%. There will be no mid-term and no final exam.

All students will be expected to purchase the following books, available (in paperback editions) at the bookstore:

> Buchi Emecheta, The Joys of Motherhood.
> Margaret Jean Hay and Sharon Stichter, African Women.
> Willian Strunk and E. B. White, The Elements of Style.
> William Zinsser, On Writing Well.

All other readings are included in the CoursePak available at Copytron.

Jan. 13   Introduction

DOMESTIC PRODUCTION: WOMEN AS GATHERERS

Jan. 15   Reiter, "Toward an Anthropology of Women."
          Hay and Stichter, African Women (herafter AW), Introduction.
          Zinsser, On Writing Well (hereafter OWW), Chapters 1, 2, 3.
          Strunk and White, Elements of Style (hereafter Elements),
                    Introduction and pp. 18-20.

Jan. 18   holiday: Martin Luther King Day

Jan. 20   Draper, "!Kung Women."
          Zinsser, OWW, Chapters 4, 5.

Jan. 22   Shostak, "Nisa."
          Strunk and White, Elements, Chapter 5.

Jan. 25   paper #1.

WOMEN IN AGRICULTURE

Jan. 27   Boserup, "Male and Female Farming Systems."
          Henn, "Women in the Rural Economy," in AW.

Jan. 29   Hay, "Luo Women and Economic Change."
          Zinsser, OWW, Chapter 6.

Feb. 1   Sacks, "Engels Revisited."
          Strunk and White, Elements, 21-25.

Feb. 3   Hay, "Women as Owners, Occupants, and Managers of Property."
          Zinsser, OWW, Chapter 7.

Feb. 5   Achola Pala Okeyo, "Daughters of the Lakes and Rivers."
          Strunk and White, Elements, 1-14, 28-33.

Feb. 8   paper #2.

WOMEN AND SLAVERY

Feb. 10   Klein, "Women in Slavery in the Western Sudan."

Feb. 12   Mousser, "Women Slavers of Guinea-Conakry."
          Brooks, "The Signares of Saint-Louis and Goree" (on reserve).

Feb. 15   Wright, "Bwanikwa."
          Zinsser, OWW, Chapter 8.
          Strunk and White, Elements, pp. 15-17, 25-28.

Feb. 17   film: "With These Hands."
          paper #3.

WOMEN IN THE GLOBAL ECONOMY

Feb. 19   Guyer, "Women in the Rural Economy," in AW.
          Berger, "South African Women in Recent Labor Struggles."

Feb. 22   Etienne, "Women and Men, Cloth and Colonization."
          Zinsser, OWW, Chapter 9, 10.

Feb. 24   Bujra, "Urging Women to Redouble Their Efforts."

Feb. 26   paper #4.

WOMEN AND RESISTANCE

Feb. 29   Perham, "The Aba Women's Riot."
          van Allen, "Sitting on a Man."

Mar. 2   Mba, "The Women's War in Eastern Nigeria."
          Okonjo, "The Dual-Sex Political System: Igbo Women."

Mar. 4   Bujra, "Female Solidarity and the Sexual Division of Labor."
          O'Barr, "African Women in Politics," in AW.

          Spring Break

Mar. 14   Newbury, "The Tyranny of Cassava."

Mar. 16   des Forges, "The Drum is Greater than the Shout."

Mar. 18   Bernstein, "Women Under Apartheid," and "Migrant Labor and
             Segregation."

Mar. 21   film: "You Have Struck a Rock."
          paper #5.

WOMEN IN RELIGIOUS ORGANIZATIONS

Mar. 23   Lewis, "Affliction and its Apotheosis."
           Zinsser, OWW, Chapter 13.

Mar. 25   Berger, "Rebels or Status Seekers: Women as Spirit Mediums."
           Robins, " Women in the East African Revival Movement."
           Strunk and White, Elements, Chapter 3.

Mar. 28   Jules-Rosette, "Women as Ceremonial Leaders in an African
                   Church."
           Steady, "Protestant Women's Associations in Freetown."
           Zinsser, OWW, Chapter 16.

Mar. 30   Strobel, "Women in Religion and in Secular Ideology," in AW.
           paper #6.

Apr. 1   holiday: Good Friday

WOMEN IN THE URBANIZATION PROCESS

Apr. 4   Robertson, "Women in the Urban Economy," in AW.
           Emecheta, The Joys of Motherhood, Chapters 1-7.
           film: "Asante Market Women."

Apr. 6   Emecheta, The Joys of Motherhood (finish).
           Robertson, "Naa Afuwa."

Apr. 8   Nelson, "Women Must Help Each Other."
           Obbo, "Strategies for Urban Survival."

Apr. 11   White, "Prostitution, Property, and Class Struggle."
           Bujra, "Production, Property, and Prostitution."
           Zinsser, OWW, Chapter 17.

Apr. 13   Wright, "Justice, Women, and the Social Order in Abercorn."
           film: "Maragoli."
           paper #7.

WOMEN AND LIBERATION: POLITICAL AND ECONOMIC

Apr. 15   Urdang, "Women in National Liberation Movements," in AW.
           Urdang, "We are Part of the Same Fight."
           Drew, "Andree Blouin and Pan-African Nationalism."

Apr. 18   Staudt, "Women Farmers and Agricultural Services."
           Brain, "Less than Second-Class: Women in Rural Settlement
                   Schemes."

Apr. 20   Overview.
           Paper #8.

History 262   Dr. Kathleen O'Mara

Women in Africa and the Middle East   S.U.N.Y. - Oneonta
Upper Division   Fall, 1987

This is a topical survey course which examines the roles and positions of
women in various African and Middle Eastern societies in different historical
periods. The analytical concepts of class, gender and mode of production will
be utilized in explaining the differences in women's roles and lived experiences
in different eras and societies.

TEXTS: Fernea, Elizabeth. Women and the Family in the Middle East.
             Austin: University of Texas Press, 1985.
         Hafkin, Nancy & Edna Bay. Women in Africa. Palo Alto: Stanford
             University Press, 1976.
         Hay, Margaret J. & Sharon Stichter(eds.) African Women: South of
             the Sahara. New York: Longman, 1984.
         Mikhail, Mona. Images of Arab Women: Fact and Fiction. Washington:
             Three Continents Press, 1979.

         (A number of short articles and excerpts from other books are also
           required reading. These will be either ditto handouts (H) or
           materials placed on reserve (R) in the library.)

SYLLABUS and READINGS:

I. Women in Traditional Islamic Society.

   The historical development of women's position in muslim society.
   Muslim women's rights and obligations under shari'a (Islamic Law).

   Readings: Fernea, Women & Family in the Middle East, pp. 27-46; 215-228.
              Mikhail, Images of Arab Women, chap. 1.
              Esposito, J.L. Women in Muslim Family Law, chap. 2 (R)
              Mernissi, Fatima, Beyond the Veil, chap. 1 (R)
              el Saadawi, Nawal, The Hidden Face of Eve, chaps. 15/16 (H)

II. A Comparative Look at Muslim Women in the Mid East, Maghreb & Africa.

    An examination of the similarities and differences in women's lives in
    various environments & societies. Women's work in traditional society.

    Readings: Fernea, Women & Family in the Middle East, pp.111-119; 148-158;
               and 255-266.
               Dupire, Marguerite, 'The Position of Women in a Pastoral Society
                  (Fulani WoDaBe)' in Paulme, Women of Tropical Africa, #2 (H)
               Robertson, C.C. & M. Klein(eds.) Women and Slavery in Africa,
                  pp. 3-25; 67-92. (R)

III. Women in Traditional Africa.

     An ethnohistorical look at women's various political and economic roles
     in precolonial African societies.

                                    223

III. cont'd.

Readings: Hay & Stichter, African Women: South of the Sahara, chaps. 1-2
Lebeuf, Annie, 'The Role of Women in the Political Organization
of African Societies,' in D. Paulme, Women in Tropical
Africa. (H)
Mullings, Leith. 'Women & Economic Change in Africa,' in
Hafkin & Bay (eds.) Women in Africa. chap.10.

IV. The Impact of Colonialism on Women in the Maghreb & Sub-Saharan Africa.

The impact of colonial systems on women's socio-political and economic
roles. Women's resistance and adaptation to the colonial political
economy.

Readings: Hay & Stichter, African Women, chaps. 4 & 5.
Gordon, David. Women of Algeria: An Essay on Change, chaps. 2/4(H)
Maher, Vanessa, 'Women and Socioeconomic Change in Morocco,' in
Beck & Keddie, Women in the Muslim World. Chap. 4 (R)
Van Allen, Judith, 'Aba Riots or Igbo Women's War?' in
Hafkin & Bay, Women in Africa. chap. 3.

V. African Women in Cities.

An historical examination of the impact of urbanization on women.
Women & migration in Africa.

Readings: Hay & Stichter, African Women, chap. 3.
Lewis, Barbara. 'The Limitations of Group Action Among Entre-
preneurs: The Market Women of Abidjan, Ivory Coast,' in
Hafkin & Bay, Women in Africa . ch. 6.
Obbo, Christine, African Women: Their Struggle for Economic
Independence. chap.8, 'Occupations of Migrant Women.' (H)
Robertson, Claire. 'Ga Women & Socioeconomic Change in Accra,
Ghana,' in Hafkin & Bay, Women in Africa. chap. 5.
Sibisi, Harriet, 'How African Women Cope with Migrant Labor
in South Africa,' and Niara Sudarkasa, 'Women and Migration
in Contemporary West Africa,' in SIGNS, III, 1 (H)

VI. Origins of the Feminist Movement in the Middle East.

Modernization, reform and nationalism in 19th & 20th century Middle East.
The Salafi movement and the roots of Middle Eastern feminism. The fore-
runners: Qasim Amin, Nazli Fadl, May Ziyada, Malak Hifni Nasif. Huda
Sharawi and the Egyptian Feminist Union.

Readings: Fernea, Women & the Family in the Middle East, pp. 233-53.
Soha AbdelKader, Egyptian Women in a Changing Society, ch.1-3 (R)
Nawal el Saadawi, The Hidden Face of Eve, ch. 18 (H)
Mervat Hatem, 'The Politics of Sexuality & Gender in Segre-
gated Patriarchal Systems :the Case of 19th C. Egypt,'
Feminist Studies, 12, 2, pp. 251-274. (H)
Mona Mikhail, Images of Women, chaps. 2/3.
Huda Sha'rawi, Harem Years: The Memoirs of an Egyptian Femi-
nist, trans. M. Badran. Excerpt. (H)

VII. Women, Religion and Protest.

An examination of African and Arab women's religious participation in unorthodox activities such as spirit possession, spirit mediumship, sufism and saint worship.

Readings: Fernea, Women & the Family in the Middle East, pp. 233-268.
            Berger, Iris, 'Rebels or Status Seekers? Women as Spirit
                Mediums in East Africa,' in Hafkin & Bay, Women in Africa.
            Cloudsley, Anne, Women of Omdurman. chaps. 5 & 6-- 'Zar' and
                'Possession'. (H)
            Cutrufelli, Maria, Women of Africa: Roots of Oppression. chap.5,
                'Women's Participation in Religious Liberation Movements.'(H)
            Mernissi, Fatima, 'Women, Saints and Sanctuaries,' in SIGNS,
                III, 1, pp. 101-112. (H)

VIII. Images of Women in African and Middle Eastern Literature.

A comparative examination of women, their concerns and condition, as they are revealed in contemporary fiction.

Readings: Hay & Stichter, African Women, chap. 7
            Mona Mikhail, Images of Arab Women, chaps.7-8,10-11
            Fernea, Women & the Family in the Middle East, pp. 301-350.

            Students must read three(3) of the following for their paper:

            Achebe, Chinua. Things Fall Apart. (Nigeria)
            Ama A. Aidoo. No Sweetness Here. (Ghana)
            Beti, Mongo. Perpetua & the Habit of Unhappiness.(Cameroon)
            Bruner, Charlotte (ed.) Unwinding Threads: Writing by Women
                in Africa. (the continent)
            Cossery, Albert. Men God Forgot. (Egypt)
            Emecheta, Buchi. The Bride Price. (Nigeria)
            Head, Bessie. A Question of Power. (South Africa)
            Konadu, Asare. A Woman in Her Prime. (Ghana)
            Mahfouz, Naguib. Midaq Alley. or Miramar. (Egypt)
            Modern Arab Short Stories. (Iraq, Syria)
            Nwapa, Flora. Efuru or Idu. (Nigeria)
            Ogot, Grace. The Promised Land. (Kenya)
            Ortzen, Len (ed.) North African Writing.
            Ousmane, Sembene. God's Bits of Wood. or Tribal Scars.(Senegal)
            el Saadawi, Nawal. Two Women in One. (Egypt)
            Salih, Tayib. The Wedding of Zein. (Sudan)
            Vieira, J.L. Luuanda. (Angola)

IX. Women in Revolution.

Women's aspirations and participation in various revolutionary situations, e.g., Algeria, Eritrea, Mozambique, Namibia. Analyses of women's
oppression and 'liberation' within national liberation struggles.

IX. (cont'd)

Readings: Fernea, <u>Women & Family in the Mid East</u>, pp.8-23; 161-208.
Hay & Stichter, <u>African Women</u>, chap. 10
Fernea, <u>Middle Eastern Muslim Women Speak</u>, #16 'Interview
with Djamila Buhrayd' (R)
Gordon, D.C., <u>Women of Algeria</u>, chaps. 5/6 (R)
E.P.L.F. Women and Revolution in Eritrea. (H)
F.R.E.L.I.M.O. The Mozambican Woman in the Revolution. (H)
S.W.A.P.O. Determined to Be Free. (H)
Z.A.N.U. Women's Liberation in the Zimbabwean Revolution. (H)

X. <u>Muslim Women Today: Public Work and Other Problems.</u>

An evaluation of muslim women today using various indices, e.g., legal
rights, education, access to employment, but emphasizing the integration
of women into the labor force in the Mid East & the Maghreb.

Readings: Fernea, <u>Women & Family in the Mid East</u>, pp.56-71; 273-88;
and 293-302.
Makhlouf,Carla, <u>Changing Veils: Women & Modernization in
North Yemen</u>, chap.4 (R)
Minority Rights Group, <u>Arab Women</u>, Report #27. (R)
M.E.R.I.P. Reports, #82 'Egypt's Working Women' and #95
'Women and Work in the Middle East: Egypt,Iran, Jordan.' (R)
Tabari, Azar, 'The Women's Movement in Iran: A Hopeful
Prognosis,' <u>Feminist Studies</u>, 12,2. (H)

XI. <u>African Women Today: Women and Work.</u>

A critical survey of women today in various African countries with an
emphasis on economic change and the impact of development policies.

Readings: Brain, J.L. 'Less than 2nd Class: Women in Rural Settlement
Schemes in Tanzania,' <u>Women in Africa</u>, ch. 11.
Cutrufelli, M.R., 'Function of Women's Labour in Less Developed
Countries,' <u>Women of Africa</u>, chap. 3. (R)
Lewis, Barbara. 'Impact of Development Policies on Women,'
<u>African Women</u>, chap. 11.
Sudarkasa, Niara, <u>Where Women Work: A Study of Yoruba Women in
the Market Place & in the Home</u>, chaps. 3/4. (R)
Cagatay, Grown & Santiago, 'The Nairobi Women's Conference:
'Toward a Global Feminism,' <u>Feminist Studies</u>, 12,2 (H)

<u>COURSE REQUIREMENTS:</u>

There will be two written examinations (brief identification and essay
questions) at mid-semester and at the end of the term. A short paper is
also required, based on the readings in topic 8 on African and Middle
Eastern fiction. Class participation is not only encouraged but expected.

AFRICAN WOMEN

Woman's Studies 620
Winter Quarter, 1985

Instructor: Claire Robertson
Office: 230 Dulles Hall
Phone - Office: 422-2174
Home: (812) 336-3696
Office Hours: TW 3-4 P.M.

Goals

The goal of this course is to present an overview of African women, which includes an appreciation of various cultural differences, history, legal and socioeconomic status, religious and political roles, productive and reproductive roles, and the impact of colonialism and post-independence development. Students are expected to participate fully by taking part in ° discussions, doing one short and one long paper, and keeping a notebook on the readings. A seminar format will be used for the course (no examinations).

Requirements

25% of grade - Class participation. This involves not only attending but also participating in discussion.

25% of grade - Notebook. Keep a notebook in which you write down any comments and questions you may have arising from the readings and make a short outline of the main points in the readings. This will help you to participate in class discussions since all readings are due on the date listed on the syllabus. Doing all readings on time is essential to get full value out of the course and a good grade.

20% of grade - Short paper (4-8 pages in length, typed, double-spaced with 1 inch margins). At the beginning of the class you will be asked to choose a topic from those listed on the syllabus opposite class dates for this paper, which you will present on the date listed and we will discuss it.

30% of grade - Long paper (10-15 pages in length, typed, double-spaced with 1 inch margins). For this paper you are asked to do an overview of the position of women in any sub-Saharan African country which shows an appreciation of at least two of the areas mentioned under goals on this syllabus, and delineates contemporary problems facing them. This paper will be presented by you at the end of the term on a date I will assign according to the paper's topic, in conjunction with other papers on related topics. The outline for it is due on Feb. 14, 1985 in class.

There will be no examinations.

Books

There will be approximately 100 pages of reading a week for this course, most in article form. All required books are on reserve in the Women's Studies collection at the Main Library. The following books are on sale at SBX Bookstore.

Hay and Stichter, African Women South of the Sahara
Martin and O'Meara, Africa
Emecheta, The Joys of Motherhood
Rogers, The Domestication of Women

Schedule

Jan. 8   Organization of course and introduction to Africa

Jan. 10   Women in African society. Introduction
          Reading: Martin & O'Meara, pp. 3-49, 169-207
          Discussion questions:
                  How does polygyny affect the position of African women?
                  What are the most important basic differences you see
                  between African and American social structures regarding
                  women?

Jan. 15   Women's productive and reproductive roles in precolonial times.
          Reading: Hay and Stichter, Ch.1, pp 1-18; Robertson and Klein,
                  "Women's Importance in African Slave Systems," in
                  Robertson and Klein (eds.), Women and Slavery in Africa.
          Discussion questions:
                  What effect did African women's rights to own property
                  independently of men have on their roles historically?
                  How can women's reproductive activities be defined in the
                  precolonial African context?
                  Why were so many slaves female?

Jan. 17   Women in politics in precolonial and colonial times.
          Reading: Hay and Stichter, Ch.9, pp. 140-55; Okonjo article in N.
                  Hafkin and E. Bay, Women in Africa, pp. 45-58.
          Paper topic: Was precolonial politics the province of elite women
                  only? (Sources recommended - Awe article in Schlegel,
                  A. (ed.), Sexual Stratification: a Cross-Cultural View,
                  pp. 144-60; an Aidoo article in F. Steady (ed.), The
                  Black Women Cross-Culturally, pp. 65-77).
          Discussion questions:
                  How did women wield political power in precolonial times?
                  How did colonialism affect the political status of women?

228

Jan. 22   Women and religion
           Reading: Martin and O'Meara, Ch.13, pp. 208-20; Hay and Stichter,
                Ch.6, pp. 87-101.
           Paper topic: What did participation in Christian sects offer
                women? (Sources recommended - Berger chapter in Hafkin
                and Bay (eds.), Women in Africa; Jules-Rosette in B.
                Jules-Rosette, (ed.), The New Religions of Africa;
                Spring in Spring and Hoch-Smith (eds.), Women in Ritual
                and Symbolic Roles.
           Discussion questions:
                Why did women become so involved in spirit-possession cults?
                What kind of roles have women had in African churches?

Jan. 24   Women, society and colonialism
           Reading: Hay and Stichter, Ch.4, pp.53-58; Emecheta, 1/2.
           Paper topic: How did western education affect African women?
                (Note this does not mean only those women who went to
                school.) (Sources recommended: Emecheta whole;
                Robertson in Comparative Education Review 28 (Nov.,
                1984); McSweeney and Freedman, and Yates article in G.P.
                Kelly and C.M. Elliott (eds.), Women's Education in the
                Third World.
           Discussion questions:
                How did colonialism affect women's domestic roles?
                Is marriage the most important institution for African
                women?
                Was it formerly the most important?

Jan. 29   Marriage and contemporary women
           Reading: Emecheta, second half; Quimby, "Islam, Sex Roles and
                Modernization in Bobo-Dioulasso," in B. Jules-Rosette
                (ed.), The New Religions of Africa, pp. 203-18 - on
                reserve; Hay and Stichter, Ch.7, pp. 102-18.
           Discussion questions:
                The Joys of Motherhood, what joys?

Jan. 31   Women, economy and colonialism
           Reading: Hay chapter in Hafkin and Bay, Women in Africa, pp.
                87-110; M. Etienne, "Women and Men, Cloth and
                Colonization," in M. Etienne and E. Leacock (eds.),
                Women and Colonization, pp. 214-38.
           Paper topic: How did colonialism affect the sexual division of
                labor? Did the changes benefit women? (Sources
                recommended: Muntemba in E. Bay (ed.), Women and Work in
                Africa., pp. 83-103; Robertson in Hafkin and Bay, pp.
                111-33).

Schedule - Jan. 31 (cont'd)

        Discussion questions:
           What general changes in women's economic activities were
           caused by colonialism?
           How did colonialism affect women's agricultural and craft
           activities?

Feb. 5   Women in the contemporary rural economy
        Reading: Hay and Stichter, Ch.2, pp. 19-32; Rogers, Ch.7.
        Paper topic: How has urban migration affected rural women's
                economic activities? (Sources recommended: H. Sibisi,
                "How African Women Cope with Migrant Labor in South
                Africa," Signs 3, no. 1 (1977), pp. 167-77; G.
                Hemmings-Gapihan, "International Development and the
                Evolution of Women's Economic Roles" in F. Bay (ed.),
                Women and Work in Africa; also Fortmann article in Bay.
        Discussion questions:
           How have the lives of rural women changed?
           What about their workload and the sexual division of labor?

Feb. 7   Women in the contemporary urban society
        Reading: Hay & Stichter, Chs.3,5, pp. 33-51, 59-86.
        Paper topic: What impact does African urban living have on
                women's fertility? (Sources recommended: B. Lewis,
                "Fertility and Employment" in E. Bay (ed.), Women and
                Work in Africa, pp. 249-76; Rogers - look in index under
                fertility; F. Mernissi, "Obstacles to Family Planning
                Practice in Urban Morocco," Studies in Family Planning
                6, no. 12 (1975).
        Discussion questions:
           Are women's lives easier in town than in the country?
           Why do they move to town?
           What functions do voluntary associations perform for them?
         Film: "Malawi, The Women"

Feb. 12   Is culture sacred? The genital mutilation controversy.
        Reading: R.O. Hayes, "Female genital mutilation, fertility
                control, women's roles and the patrilineage in modern
                Sudan," American Ethnologist 2, no. 4 (1985), pp.
                617-33, - WIN news - both on reserve.
        Paper topic: Who or what is chiefly responsible for perpetuating
                genital mutilation? (Sources recommended: N. El
                Saadawi, The Hidden Face of Eve. Women in the Arab
                World; A. Cloudsley, Women of Omdurman: Life, Love and
                the Cult of Virginity.)

Schedule - Feb. 12 (cont'd)

Discussion questions:
Why does genital mutilation continue?
What problems does it express?
Do African women contribute to their own oppression?

Feb. 14   Women in the anti-colonial struggle I. Countries without white
settlers.
Reading: C. Johnson, "Women in Anti-colonial Activity in
Southwestern Nigeria," African Studies Review 25, nos.
2/3 (June/Sept. 1982), pp. 137-58; J. Van Allen, "Aba
Riots or Igbo Women's War?" in Hafkin and Bay (eds.)
Women in Africa, pp. 59-85 - both on reserve.
Paper topic: How did West African women's resistance to
colonialism differ from East African? (Sources
recommended: today's assigned readings and T. Mutunhu,
"Nehanda of Zimbabwe: The Story of a Woman Liberation
Leader and Fighter," Ufahamu 7, no. 1 (1976), 59-70; K.
Santilli, "Kikuyu Women in the MauMau Revolt," Ufahamu
8, no. 1 (1977), 143-59.
Discussion questions:
In what ways did colonialist oppression most specifically
affect women?
How did they resist?

Long paper outline with brief bibliography due.

Feb. 19   Women in the anti-colonial struggle II. Countries with white
settlers.
Reading: Hay & Stichter, Ch.10, pp. 156-70; I. Mataepe, "Women in
the Struggle for Liberation in South Africa," in D.
Wiley and A. Isaacman (eds.), Southern Africa: Society,
Economy and Liberation, pp. 235-49.
Paper topic: How is the oppression of women in South Africa
related to the capitalist system? (Sources recommended:
Eliz. Schmidt, Decoding Corporate Camouflage; H.
Bernstein, For Their Triumphs and For Their Tears,
Conditions and Resistance of Women in Apartheid South
Africa.)
Discussion questions:
How have women resisted oppression in South Africa?
How far has liberation ideology addressed sexual
inequalities?
Film: "You Have Struck a Rock"

231

Schedule (cont'd)

Feb. 21   Contemporary problems I. Prostitution?
            Reading: L. White, "Women's Domestic Labor in Colonial Kenya:
                 Prostitution in Nairobi, 1909-1950," Boston University
                 African Studies Center Working Paper No. 30 (1980);
                 Hoch-Smith, "Radical Yoruba Female Sexuality. The Witch
                 and the Prostitute," in Spring and Hoch-Smith, Women in
                 Ritual Roles, or, J. Bujra, "Postscript: Prostitution,
                 Class and the State," in Crime, Justice and
                 Underdevelopment, ed. C. Sumner, pp. 145-63.
            Discussion questions:
                 How does African prostitution differ from Euro-American
                 prostitution?
                 What does it indicate about the position of women?

Feb. 26   Contemporary problems II. Persecution of women.
            Reading: F. Wilson, "Reinventing the Past and Circumscribing the
                 Future: Authenticite and the Negative Image of Women's
                 Work in Zaire" in E. Bay (ed.), Women and Work in
                 Africa, pp. 153-70; Robertson, "The Death of Makola and
                 Other Tragedies," Canadian Journal of African Studies
                 17, 3 (1983), pp. 469-95.
            Paper topic: What changes have allowed women to be persecuted
                 (compare with the precolonial/colonial situation)?
                 (Recommended sources: readings for last two sessions and
                 Jan. 17; newspapers on arrest of massive numbers of
                 women in Zimbabwe approximately 8 months ago; C. Clark,
                 "Land and Food, Women and Power in 19c Kikuyu," Africa
                 50 (1980), pp. 357-69.)
            Discussion questions:
                 How does change in the position of African women and their
                 persecution relate to African class formation?
                 Why do women make good victims?
                 What benefits do African governments get out of
                 scapegoating women?

Feb. 28   No class. Put in your time working on your papers and reading
            the rest of Rogers for the next session. Use it well so you can
            discuss your problems with your paper and the issues at the next
            session.

Mar. 5   Contemporary problems III. Women and development.
            Reading: Rogers (all but Ch.7); Hay and Stichter, Ch.11, pp.
                 170-82.
            Discussion questions:
                 How can Americans help Africa most appropriately?
                 What impact does Western sexism have on African economies?
                 How can African women best fight economic oppression?

Mar. 7,   Presentation of papers. Your date will be assigned.
  12, 14.

WS 298/BLST 265 Topics in Women's Studies
WS 498/HIST 498

South African Women

Spring 1987   Peg Strobel
Thursday-Friday 1-3   4075C BSB, 996-2441
339 BSB   Office hours by appt.

In this course we will

1) Examine the forces of race, class and gender in South
Africa as they create different life possibilities for black and
white women and affect the struggles for national liberation and
women's liberation there;
2) Explore the interconnections between individual life
history, the development of consciousness, and historical events;
3) Analyze personal documents as source materials (how they
are written, what they reveal); and
4) Examine the fictional writing of South African women.

The following books are available at the CCC Bookstore and in the
library:

    June Goodwin, Cry Amandla!
    Ellen Kuzwayo, Call Me Woman
    Hilda Bernstein, For Their Triumph and For Their Tears
    Helen Joseph, Side By Side
    Winnie Mandela, Part of My Soul Went With Him

Each week where indicated we will see a film and discuss it on
Thursday; on Friday we will have lecture and discussion of the
reading. I expect you to come prepared for discussion. You are
welcome to invite friends to the Thursday films.

Course requirenments: Three 4-page papers on topics to be handed
out in class, due weeks 4, 9, and Wednesday of finals week.
Graduate students must hand in a longer paper (7 pages) on the
second topic (due week 9) and one 10-15 page paper on a topic
approved by the instructor, due Wednesday of finals week.
Graduate students are expected to do all the assigned readings,
in addition to extra work required for the long paper.

233

Week	Film (Thursday)	Reading

Ap^artheid Today

1: April 2-3		Cry Amandla, 3-91, Appendix A & B
2: April 9-10	South Africa Belongs to Us	Cry Amandla, 95-204
3: April 16-17	Maids and Madams	Bernstein

Oppression and Resistance: 1900-present

4: April 23-24	Country Lovers	Kuzwayo, xi-117
5: April 30-May 1		Kuzwayo, 118-263
6: May 7-8	You Have Struck A Rock	Joseph, 1-130
7: May 14-15	A Chip of Glass Ruby	Joseph, 133-246
8: May 21-22	Mandela	Mandela

Fiction by South African Women

9: May 28-29	City Lovers	Handouts: fiction by Tlali, Head,
10: June 4-5	Good Climate, Friendly Inhabitants	Gordimer, House, maybe Lessing

Films to be shown in WS 298/BLST 265 <u>South African Women</u>, Thursdays, 1-3, 339 BSB. Students other than those in the class are welcome to come.

April 9   <u>South Africa Belongs to Us:</u> Examines the conditions under which rural and urban women live and presents interviews with various leaders of resistance struggles.

April 16   <u>Maids and Madams</u>: Explores the lives and working conditions of domestic servants and their relationships with their madams.

April 23   *<u>Country Lovers:</u> A clandestine affair between a white farmer's son and black servant with whom he was raised leads to tragic consequences.

May 7   <u>You Have Struck A Rock:</u> Women's resistance during the historic anti-pass demonstrations of the 1950s.

May 14   *<u>A Chip of Glass Ruby</u>: A Hindu family confronts the arrest of the mother for helping with political leaflets protesting discriminatory housing.

May 21   <u>Mandela:</u> Documentary of the lives of Winnie and Nelson Mandela.

May 28   *<u>City Lovers:</u> A brief love affair between a foreign visitor and a young "colored" woman leads to arrest for violation of the Immorality Act.

June 4   *<u>Good Climate, Friendly Inhabitants:</u> A white widow has a brief affair with a young man who is a ruthless mercenary.

*Part of a series of works by Nadine Gordimer.

235

History 114
Women in the   Middle East: Past and Present

The aim of this course is to provide an understanding of the role of women in Middle Eastern society. This will be attempted through a historical overview of the development of the role of women in the region. We will draw on a diverse body of sources, both primary and secondary, to reconstruct the past   and to shed light on   developments   that are affecting the role of women in the present.

Course responsibilities:

Students will be required to write one term paper; this will count for 30%. Quizes and class participation will count for 20%. The remaining 50% will be made up of a mid-term and final exam.

All of the reading material for this course has been placed on reserve at the library. Due to the aabsence of satisfactory text book, I will provide you with some of the essential readings in memiographed form from time to time. You are advised to keept up with the readings and to comeplete the assigned reading for every week at the beginning of that week.

Assigned Books:

1. Beck, L., and Keddie,N. , WOMEN IN THE MIDDLE EAST
2. Bizergan,B. and Fernea,E. , MIDDLE EASTERN MUSLIM WOMEN SPEAK
3. Boserup, E. , WOMEN'S ROLE IN ECONOMIC DEVELOPMENT
4. Fernea, E., GUESTS OF THE SHEIK
5. Nashat, G., WOMEN AND REVOLUTION IN IRAN
6. Savory, R., INTRODUCTION TO ISLAMIC CIVILIZATION

Weekly Schedule:

Intorduction and General Background

Sept. 23: Organization Meeting
Sept. 25: Where Is the Middle East, Savory, 1-15
Sept. 26: Historical Overview, Savory, 15-37

Sept. 30: Can We Study "the Invisible Half" of Miuddle Eastern Society?
Oct.   2 : What Determines Women's Role in Society? Boserup, 1-37
Oct.   3 : Women Role in the Middle East, Beck, 1-32

Women in Early Islam

Oct. 7 : Pre-Islamic Women Nashat, 1-16
Oct. 9 : Topic Cont., Bizergan, 3-7; and handout
Oct. 10:Women in Early Islam

Women's Legal Status

Oct. 14: Women in the Qur'an, Nashat, 37-55
Oct. 16: Women in the Shari'a, Selection from the Qur'an
Oct. 17: Women's Rights, Beck, 52-69

Women and the Family

Oct. 21: Childhood and Education, Bizergan, 37-87
Oct. 23: Betrothal and Marriage, Bizergan, 27-36; Fernea, 136-149
Oct. 24: Polygamy: How Has It Worked? Fernea, 161-170

Oct. 28: "I Divorce Thee," One to Three Times
Oct. 30: Women As Saints and Sinners
Oct. 31: Mid-term

Women in the Nineteenth Century

Nov. 4 : The Causes of Change: The Political Factor, Beck, 100-123
Nov. 6 . The Causes of Change: Social and Economic Factors
Nov. 7: A Case Study: Egyptian Women in the 19th and 20th Centuries,
        Beck, 261-2295; Bizergan, 193-201

Women in the Twentieth Century

Nov. 11: Women and Politics, Bizergan, 167-201; Beck, 124-141
Nov. 13: Women in the Workforce,Nashat, 69-87; Interview with Umm Muh.
Nov 14: The Changing Mores, Bizergan, 280-399; Fernea, 256-266

Nov. 18: Village life, Bizergan, 201-230; Fernea, 65-82
Nov. 20: Tribal Women, Beck, 351-431
Nov. 21: Rural Women in Transition, Nashat, 141-195, and 217-261

Nov. 25: Women and Revolution: Algerian Women, Bizergan, 251-261
Nov. 27: Women' Role in the Iranian Revolution, Nashat, 87-195 and 97-109
Nov. 28: Thanksgiving Holiday, No Class

Dec. 2-4: Final Examination Week

1

Department of History
Georgetown University

WOMEN IN EUROPE AND THE MIDDLE EAST
upper level course, Fall, 1985

144-587-01   Professor Tucker
M., 6:00-7:40   Office hours: ICC 622
ICC 214   M. 1-2; W. 11-12
                                        and by appt. x8056

     This colloquium surveys the major developments in women's
history in western Europe and the Middle East. While emphasizing
the modern period, from 1750 to the present, we also examine the
classical and medieval roots of women's present reality. Using a
comparative approach, we consider woman's participation in
productive activities, her place in the family, and the history
of woman's role in political institutions and "public" life. We
are also concerned with the evolution of ideas about and social
perceptions of her proper roles.

     Each weekly session includes a student presentation, a
presentation by the instuctor, and general discussion. All
students are expected to have done the assigned reading and
participate in discussion. In addition, students will be
responsible for presenting a critique of the week's readings on
assigned days. There is no examination, but a long (15-20 pages
for undergraduates and 20-25 pages for graduate students) paper
is due on December 2. The paper may examine any aspect of women's
history in western Europe or the Middle East, but the topic must
be approved by the instuctor by October 14. The paper should be
typewritten and adhere to proper academic form. Grades will be
based on the paper (50%) and class room performance (50%).

                            READINGS

     The following texts are available for purchase at the
bookstore. These texts, and all other assigned readings, are also
on reserve at Lauinger Library.
Beck, Lois and Nikki Keddie, Women in the Muslim World.
Branca, Patricia, Women in Europe since 1750.
Carroll, Berenice, Liberating Women's History.
Fernea, E.W., Women and the Family in the Middle East.
Fernea, E.W. and B. Bezirgan, Middle Eastern Muslim Women Speak.

                 CLASS SCHEDULE AND READINGS

I. Sept. 9: Introduction to the course

II. Sept. 16: Issues of Women's History

Frederick Engels, The Origins of the Family, Private Property
and the State, Leacock, ed., chapt.2, "The Family",
pp.94-146.
Karen Sacks, "Engels Revisited: Women, the Organization of
Production, and Private Property, in Rayna Reiter (ed.),
Toward an Anthropology of Women, pp.211-234.
Ann D. Gordon, Mari Jo Buhle, and Nancy Schrom Dye, "The
Problem of Women's History," in Berenice Carroll,
Liberating Women's History, pp.75-92.
Ann J. Lane, "Women in Society: A Critique of Frederick
Engels," In Carroll, Liberating, pp.4-25.

III. Sept. 23: Roots of Western Women: The Classical Past

Sarah B. Pomeroy, Goddesses. Whores, Wives, and Slaves. Women
in Classical Antiquity, chapts. 3,4,8,9; pp.32-78, 149-
204.
Sarah B. Pomeroy, "A Classical Scholar's Perspective on
Matriarchy," in Carroll, Liberating, pp.217-223.

IV. Sept. 30: Roots of Western Women: Medieval and Early Modern
Europe

Kathleen Casey, "The Cheshire Cat: Reconstructing the
Experience of Medieval Women," in Carroll, Liberating,
pp.224-249.
Allison Heisch, "Queen Elizabeth I and the Persistance of
Patriarchy," Feminist Review, 4 (1980), 45-56.
Shelia Rowbotham, Hidden From History, intro. and chapts. 1-
4; pp.x-xxxiii, 1-22.
Shelia Rowbotham, Women, Resistance, and Revolution, chapt.1;
pp.15-35.

V. Oct. 7: Roots of Middle Eastern Women: Classical and Medieval

Fatima Mernissi, Beyond the Veil, part I; pp.1-41.
Nawal El-Saadawi, The Hidden Face of Eve, parts 2 and 3;
pp.91-168.
E.W. Fernea and B. Bezirgan, Middle Eastern Muslim Women
Speak, part 1, 1,2,3,4; pp.3-67.

VI. Oct. 14: Women and Production: Western Europe

Shelia Rowbotham, Hidden from History, chapt.5; pp.23-30.
Patricia Branca, Women in Europe since 1750, chapts. 1,2;
pp.9-71.
Jane Humphries, "Protective Legislation, the Capitalist
State, and Working Class Men: The Case of the 1842 Mines

Regulation Act," _Feminist Review_, 7 (1981), 1-34.
Renate Bridenthal and Claudia Koonz, "Beyond Kinder, Kuche,
Kirche: Weimar Women in Politics and Work," in Carroll,
Liberating, pp. 301-329.

VII. Oct.21: Women and Production: The Middle East

Ulku Bates, "Women as Patrons of Architecture in Turkey," in
Beck and Keddie, _Women in the Muslim World_, pp.245-260.
MERIP Reports, #95, "Women and Work in the Middle East,"
entire.
Marjorie Hall and Bakhita Amin Ismail, _Sisters under the Sun_,
chapts. 2-4; pp.39-101.
Andrea B. Rugh, "Women and Work: Strategies and Choices in a
Lower-Class Quarter of Cairo," in E.W. Fernea, _Women and
the Family in the Middle East_, pp. 273-288.

VIII. Oct. 28: Women, Ideology, and the Family: Europe

Branca, _Women in Europe_, chapt.3, pp.72-151.
Hilda Smith, "Gynecology and Ideology in Seventeenth Century
England," in Carroll, _Liberating_, pp.97-114.
Ellen Ross, "Fierce Questions and Taunts, Married Life in
Working-Class London, 1870-1914," _Feminist Studies_,
VIII,3 (Fall, 1982), 375-602.

IX. Nov. 4: Women, Ideology, and the Family: the Middle East

Paul Vieille, "Iranian Women in Family Alliance and Sexual
Politics," in Beck and Keddie, _Women_, pp.451-472.
John Esposito, _Women in Muslim Family Law_, chapt. 2; pp.13-
42.
Elizabeth Cooper, _The Women of Egypt_, chapts. 7,8,9; pp.180-
223.
Leila Ahmed, "Western Ethnocentricism and Perceptions of the
Harem," _Feminist Studies_, VIII,3 (Fall, 1982), 521-534.
Halim Barakat, "The Arab Family and the Challenge of Social
Transformation," in Fernea, _Women and the Family_, pp.27-
48.

Nov. 11: Women and Politics: Europe

Branca, _Women in Europe_, chapts.4,5; pp.152-216.
Rowbotham, _Hidden_, chapts. 6-23; pp.31-166.
Amy Hackett, "Feminism and Liberalism in Wilhelmine Germany,"
in Carroll, _Liberating_, pp.127-136.

Nov. 18: Women and Politics: the Middle East

El Saadawi, <u>The Hidden Face</u>, chapts. 18-20; pp.169-194.
Thomas Phillip, "Feminism and Nationalist Politics in Egypt,"
    in Beck and Keddie, <u>Women</u>, pp.277-294.
Mangol Bayat, "Women and Revolution n Iran," in Beck and
    Keddie, <u>Women</u>, pp.159-171.
"Halide Edib Adivar" and "Huda Sh'arawi", in Fernea and
    Bezirgan, <u>Middle Eastern</u>, pp.167-200.
Hall and Ismail, <u>Sisters</u>, chapt.5; pp.102-121.

Nov. 25: <u>Women and Change in the Middle East Today: Issues</u>

    All of the articles listed below are to be found in E.W.
Fernea, <u>Women and the Family in the Middle East</u>:
    Fatima Akeb and Malika Abdelaziz, "Algerian Women discuss the
        Need for Change," pp.8-23.
    Safia Mohsen, "New Images, Old Reflections: Working Middle-
        Class Women in Egypt," pp.56-71.
    Nahid Toubia, "The Social and Political Implications of
        Female Circumcision: the Case of the Sudan," pp.148-159.
    Maroun Baghdadi and Nayla de Freige, "The Kalashnikov
        Generation," pp. 169-182.
    Rosemary Sayigh, "Encounters with Palestinian Women under
        Occupation," pp.191-208.
    Valerie J. Hoffman, "An Islamic Activist: Zaynab al-Ghazali,"
        pp.233-254.
    Shireen Mahdavi, " The position of Women in Shi'a Iran: Views
        of the <u>Ulama</u>," pp.255-268.

Dec.2: <u>Women's History Reconsidered</u>

    Gerda Lerner, "Placing Women in History: A 1975 Perspective,"
        in Carroll, <u>Liberating</u>, pp. 357-367.
    Juliet Mitchell, "Four Structures in a Complex Unity," in
        Carroll, <u>Liberating</u>, pp.385-399.
    Rosemary Sayigh, "Roles and Functions of Arab Women," <u>Arab
        Studies Quarterly</u>, III,3 (1981).
    Judith Tucker, "Problems in the Historiography of Women in
        the Middle East," <u>International Journal of Middle East
        Studies</u>, July 1983.

Department of History
Georgetown University

WOMEN IN THE MIDDLE EAST
(Upper level undergraduate and graduate colloquium)

144-588-01   Prof. Tucker
W. 11:15-1:05   ICC 622
                                     Office hours:
                                     M. 11-12, W. 1:30-2:30
                                     and by appointment

The colloquium surveys the major developments in women's
history in the Middle East from the rise of Islam to the present
with particular emphasis on the nineteenth and twentieth
centuries. We cover women's economic activities, their relation
to political institutions and movements, social and familial
life, and cultural contributions. We are concerned with women's
reciprocal relationship with society: with the ways in which
women have been viewed and treated as well as the ways in which
they have shaped history the history of the region. We try,
whenever possible, to hear the woman's voice through the reading
of first-hand accounts. Throughout, we address the problem of,
and changes in, the gender-based organization of society.

The colloquium revolves around student discussion. It is
essential that all students come to class prepared to discuss the
assigned reading. Such preparation and participation is a
requirement of the course and counts for 25% of the final grade.
There is no examination, but two written assignments are
required:

1) Bibliographical essay
Each student should choose one of the following topics and
prepare a bibliographical essay in which you discuss the major
books and articles relevant to the topic in essay form, focusing
on the approaches used, the major themes in analysis, the debates
or disagreements, etc., among the authors who have contributed to
the question. Your own evaluation of the work should be included.
Please discuss a preliminary bibliography with the instructor
before submitting the final essay, typed and 10 to 12 pages in
length, on October 28. Students will be asked to give brief oral
presentations of their findings at appropriate class sessions.
The essay should cover one of the following areas:

1) Economic activities, the 19th century
2) Economic activities, the 20th century
3) Political structures and participation, the 19th century
4) Political structures and participation, the 20th century
5) Family and society, the 19th century
6) Family and society, the 20th century
7) Religion, the 19th century
8) Religion, the 20th century

Essay constitutes 25% of grade.

2)Final Paper
A research paper of 20-25 pages on a relevant topic of your choice is due on December 9. The paper may examine in depth any aspect of women's history in the Middle East, but should be typewritten and adhere to proper academic form for a research paper. Paper constitutes 50% of grade.

BOOKS

The following books are available for sale at the bookstore:
Lois Beck and Nikki Keddie, Women in the Muslim World.
Berenice Carroll, Liberating Women's History.
Elizabeth Fernea, Women and the Family in the Middle East.
E. W. Fernea and B. Bezirgan, Middle Eastern Muslim Women Speak.
Fatima Mernissi, Beyond the Veil.
Nawal El-Saadawi, Woman at Point Zero.
These books, and all other assigned readings, are also on reserve at Lauinger Library.

READINGS AND CLASS SCHEDULE

Sept. 9: Approaches to Women's History

Reading: Frederick Engels, The Origins of the Family, Private Property, and the State, Leacock ed., chapt.2, "The Family", pp.94-146.
Karen Sacks, "Engels Revisited: Women, and Organization of Production, and Private Property," in Rayna Reiter, ed., Toward an Anthropology of Women, pp.211-234.
Ann J. Lane, "Women in Society: A Critique of Frederick Engels," in Berenice Carroll, Liberating Women's History, pp.4-25.
Ann D. Gordon, Mary Jo Buhle, and Nancy Schrom Dye, "The Problem of Women's History," in Carroll, Liberating, pp.4-25.
Gerda Lerner, "Placing Women in History: A 1975 Perspective," in Carroll, Liberating, pp.357-367.

Sept. 16: Approaches to Women's History, the Middle East

Reading: Rosemary Sayigh, "Roles and Functions of Arab Women," Arab Studies Quarterly, III,3 (1981).
Judith Tucker, "Problems in the Historiography of Women in the Middle East," International Journal of Middle East Studies (IJMES), 15 (1983), 321-336.
Lois Beck and Nikki Keddie, Women in the Muslim World, introduction, pp.1-34.
Mervat Hatem, "Class and Patriarchy as Competing Paradigms," Comparative Studies in Society and History,

forthcoming (ms. on reserve in Library).

Sept. 23: Early Islam

Reading: Charis Waddy, Women in Muslim History, chapts. 1-2, pp.10-56.
E.W. Fernea and B. Bezirgan, Middle Eastern Muslim Women Speak, Part I. sections 2,3, pp.7-36.
Fatima Mernissi, Beyond the Veil, Part I, pp.1-41.

Sept. 30: The Classical Period

Reading: Waddy, Women, chapts.6-9, pp.69-108.
S.D. Goitein, Mediterranean Society, vol.III, pp.312-359.
Basim Musallam, Sex and Society in Islam, chapts. 1,2,6, pp.10-38, 105-121.
Fernea and Bezirgan, Middle Eastern, Part I, sections 4,5, pp.37-76.

Oct. 7: The Ottoman Period

Reading: Fanny Davis, The Ottoman Lady, chapts. 1,3,10,13, pp.1-32, 45-60, 171-186, 217-244.
Gabriel Baer, "Women and Waqf: An Analysis of the Istanbul Tahrir of 1546," Asian and African Studies, XVII, 1-3, 9-28
Ulku Bates, "Women as Patrons of Architecture in Turkey," in Beck and Keddie, Muslim Women, pp.245-260.
R.C. Jennings, "Women in the Early 17th century Ottoman Judicial Records: The Sharia Court of Anatolian Kayseri," Journal of the Economic and Social History of the Orient (JESHO), 28, 1975.

Nineteenth and Twentieth Century Themes

Oct. 14: Women and Production, the 19th Century

Reading: Margot Badran, "Women and Production in the Middle East and North Africa," Trend in History, II,3, 1982.
Judith Tucker, Women in 19th Century Egypt, chapts. 1,2, pp.16-101.
Abraham Marcus, "Men, Women, and Property: Dealers in Real Estate in 18th Century Aleppo," JESHO, XXVI,2,1983, 137-163.

Oct. 21: Women and Production, the 20th Century

Reading: MERIP Reports, #95, "Women and Work in the Middle East,"
3-23.
Susan Schaefer Davis, "Working Women in a Moroccan
Village," in Beck and Keddie, Women, pp. 416-433.
Andrea Rugh, "Women and Work, Strategies and Choices in
a Lower-Class Quarter of Cairo," in Fernea, Women and
the Family in the Middle East, pp.273-288.
Fernea and Bezirgan, Middle Eastern, Part III, section
14, pp.219-230, Part IV, section 21, pp.359-371.

Oct. 28: Women and Politics, the 19th Century

Reading: Judith Tucker, Women, chapts. 3,4, pp.102-163.
Thomas Phillip, "Feminism and Nationalist Politics in
Egypt," in Beck and Keddie, Women, pp.277-294.
Juan Ricardo Cole, "Feminism, Class and Islam in Turn-
of-the-Century Egypt," IJMES, XIII,1981, 384-407.
Shireen Mahdevi, "Women and Ideas in Qajar Iran," Asian
and African Studies, XIX, 1985, 187-197.

Nov. 4: Women and Politics, the 20th Century

Reading: Earl Sullivan, Women in Egyptian Public Life, Intro.,
chapts. 1,2,4,6, pp.1-78, 103-124, 151-170.
Nora Benallegue, "Algerian Women in the Struggle for
Independence and Reconstruction," International Social
Science Journal, XXXV,4, 1983, 703-717.
Suad Joseph, "Women and the Neighborhood Street in Borj
Hammoud, Lebanon," in Beck and Keddie, Women, pp.541-
557.
Rosemary Sayigh,"Encounters with Palestinian Women under
Occupation," in E.W. Fernea, Women and the Family,
pp.191-208.

Nov.11: Society and Culture, the 19th Century

Reading: Afaf Lutfi al-Sayyid Marsot, "The Revolutionary
Gentlewoman in Egypt," in Beck and Keddie, Women,
pp.261-276.
Leila Ahmed, "Western Ethnocentricism and Perceptions of
the Harem," Feminist Studies, VIII,3 (Fall, 1982), 521-
524.
Byron D. Cannon, "Nineteenth Century Arabic Writings
on Women and Society," IJMES, XVII, 4, 436-484.
Erel Sönmez, "Turkish Women in the Literature of
the XIXth Century," Hacettepe Bulletin of Social Science
and the Humanities, 1, 17-42, and 2, 123-157.

Nov. 18: Society and Culture, the 20th Century

Reading: Emrys L. Peters, "The Status of Women in Four Middle
East Communities," in Beck and Keddie, <u>Women</u>, pp.311-
350.
Nermin Abadan-Unat, "Social Change and Turkish Women,"
in Abadan-Unat, ed., <u>Women in Turkish Society</u>, pp.5-36.
Mustafa O. Attir, "Ideology, Value Changes, and Women's
Social Position in Libyan Society," in Fernea, <u>Women and</u>
<u>the Family</u>, pp.121-133.
Fatima Aheb and Malika Abdelaziz, "Algerian Women
Discuss the Need for Change," in Fernea, <u>Women and the</u>
<u>Family</u>, pp.8-23.
Aminah al-Sa^{c}id, "The Arab Woman and the Challenge of
Society," in Fernea and Bezirgan, <u>Middle Eastern</u>, Part
IV, section 22, pp.373-390.

Nov. 25: Women and Religion

Reading: Valerie J. Hoffman, "An Islamic Activist: Zaynab al-
Ghazali," in Fernea, <u>Women and the Family</u>, pp.233-254.
Valerie J. Hoffman-Ladd, "Polemics on the Modesty and
Segregation of Women in Contempoary Egypt," IJMES,
XIX), 1987, 23-50.
Shireen Mahdavi, "The Position of Women in Shi^{c}a Islam:
Views of the <u>Ulama</u>," in Fernea, <u>Women and the Family</u>,
pp.255-268.
Fatna A. Sabbah, <u>Women in the Muslim Unconscious</u>,
chapts.1-3, 9-13, pp.3-22, 63-118.

Dec. 2: Social and Psychological Costs

Reading: Nawal El-Saadawi, <u>Woman at Point Zero</u>, entire.

Dec. 9: Conclusion: PAPERS DUE

WOMEN IN ASIA: INDIA, CHINA, JAPAN   Autumn Quarter, 1984-85
Barbara N. Ramusack   History 15-075-531
Office Hours: MWF 11:00-11:50 a.m. and by appointment
Office: 353B McMicken. Office telephones: 475-6887 and 475-2144

Required texts: Cyril Birch (trans.), Stories from a Ming Collection.
                 Karen Brazell (trans.), Confessions of Lady Nijo
                 R. K. Narayan (trans.), The Ramayana
                 Jonathan D. Spence, The Death of Woman Wang.

*indicates that material is on reserve in the Central Library
#indicates that material will be distributed in class.

Sept. 19   Introduction. Studying Women in Cross-Cultural Perspective.

Sept. 21   WOMEN AS DAUGHTERS, WIVES AND MOTHERS - Social Roles and Legal Rights
             India: The Historical Context. Begin to read The Ramayana.

Sept. 24   India: Women as Wives - Marriage, Divorce, Widowhood
             The Ideal: Discussion of The Ramayana
                        Extracts from the Qur'an#
                        (Optional) Extracts from the Laws of Manu#
             Reality: David G. Mandelbaum, Society in India, I, chap. 5*.

Sept. 26   India: Women as Mothers

Sept. 28   China: The Historical Context.
             Begin to read The Death of Woman Wang.

Oct. 1   China: Women as Wives - Marriage, Divorce, Widowhood.
             The Ideal: Extracts from the Analects#
                        Pan Chao, "Lessons for Women," in Nancy Lee Swann*
                        Pan Chao, Foremost Woman Scholar of China, chap. 7
             Reality: Spence, The Death of Woman Wang.

Oct. 3   China: Women as Mothers

Oct. 5   Japan: The Historical Context
             Begin to read The Confessions of Lady Nijo.

Oct. 8   Japan: Women as Wives - Marriage, Divorce, Widowhood
             The Ideal: Kaibara Ekken, Onna Daigaku (The Women and Wisdom of Japan)*
             Reality: (Optional) Richard K. Beardsley, John W. Hall and Robert E. Ward,
                      Village Japan, chaps. 9 and 11.

Oct. 10   Japan: Women as Mothers

Oct. 12   Film: "Dadi's Family." Two to three page commentary on the film is due
             on October 17.

Oct. 15   WOMEN'S SEXUALITY: AS LOVERS AND AS COURTESANS
             India: Read from Van Buitenen, Tales of Ancient India, "The Tale of
             Two Bawds" and "The Red Lotus of Chastity." (Optional) "The Man Who
             Impersonated Vishnu."*

Oct. 17   China: Read from Birch, Stories from a Ming Collection, "The Pearl
             Sewn Shirt."

247

Oct. 19   Japan: Discussion of <u>Confessions of Lady Nijo</u>, books 1-3.

Oct. 22   WOMEN IN POLITICS
          India. Review the <u>Ramayana</u>.

Oct. 24   China. (Optional) Priscilla Ching Chung, "Power and Prestige: Palace
          Women in the Northern Sung," in Guisso and Johannesson, eds.,
          <u>Women in China</u>*; or skim her <u>Palace Women in the Northern Sung</u>.

Oct. 26   Japan. Review <u>Confessions of Lady Nijo</u>.

Oct. 29   WOMEN IN RELIGION: AS DIVINITIES AND AS DEVOTEES
          India: Heinrich R. Zimmer, <u>Myths and Symbols in Indian Art and
          Civilization</u>, chap. 5, "The Goddess."*

Oct. 31   Film: "Wedding of the Goddess," Two to three page commentary on
          film is due on November 5th.

Nov. 2   MID-QUARTER EXAMINATION. WILL COVER MATERIAL THROUGH "WOMEN IN POLITICS."

Nov. 5   China. Edward Schafer, <u>The Divine Woman</u>, chap. 1*. (Optional) Kathryn
          Tsai, "The Chinese Buddhist Monastic Order for Women: The First Two
          Centuries," in Guisso and Johannesson, eds., <u>Women in China</u>*.

Nov. 7   Japan. <u>The Confessions of Lady Nijo</u>, books 4 and 5.

Nov. 9   WOMEN IN LITERATURE: AS DOERS AND AS PORTRAYED
          India: Review the <u>Ramayana</u>. Poetry of Mirabai*. (Optional) Kalidasa,
          "Sakuntala and the Ring of Recollection," in Barbara Stoler Miller,
          ed., <u>Theater of Memory</u>*.

Nov. 12   VETERAN'S DAY. A HOLIDAY.

Nov. 14   China: Read from <u>Stories from a Ming Collection</u>, "The Lady Who Was a
          Beggar" and "The Fairy's Rescue." Adopt a poet who lived before
          1800 from <u>The Orchid Boat: Women Poets of China</u>, translated and
          edited by Kenneth Rexroth and Ling Chung*.

Nov. 16   Japan: Review <u>Confessions of Lady Nijo</u>. Adopt a poet from the classic
          or Tokugawa periods in <u>The Burning Heart: Women Poets of Japan</u>,
          trans. and ed. by Kenneth Rexroth and Ikuko Atsumi*. (Optional)
          Murasaki Shikibu, <u>Tale of Genji</u>.

Nov. 19   WOMEN IN THE VISUAL ARTS
          India

Nov. 21   China and Japan

Nov. 23   THANKSGIVING HOLIDAY

Nov. 26   Individual Presentations.

Nov. 28   Individual Presentations

Nov. 30   Review Session

This course will focus on the roles and activities of women in India, China and Japan prior to 1800. It will be a combination of lectures and discussions. The reading assignments are heaviest during the first four weeks of the course, and during the latter half of the course we will use the required texts as reference material and examine them from different perspectives. Class participation is encouraged and reading assignments should be done according to the schedule. There will be a mid-quarter and a final examination and the latter will be a take home examination. There will be an individual oral presentation of no more than fifteen minutes on a topic of the student's choice. Graduate students are expected to do the optional reading including one book in the Tale of Genji.

Grade composition.	Class participation	10%
	Two papers on films, @5%	10%
	Mid-quarter examination	25%
	Individual presentation	15%
	Final Examination	40%
	TOTAL	100%

WOMEN IN PREMODERN ASIA: INDIA, CHINA AND JAPAN   1984-85
AN INTRODUCTORY BIBLIOGRAPHY - Barbara N. Ramusack

HISTORY TEXTS FOR GENERAL BACKGROUND
John K. Fairbank, Edwin O. Reischauer, and Albert M. Craig. EAST ASIA: TRADITION
     AND TRANSFORMATION
Stanley A. Wolpert. A NEW HISTORY OF INDIA
Romila Thapar. A HISTORY OF INDIA. Volume I.

BIBLIOGRAPHIES
Carol Sakala. WOMEN OF SOUTH ASIA: A GUIDE TO RESOURCES.

WOMEN AS DAUGHTERS, WIVES AND MOTHERS - Social Roles and Legal Rights
India
THE MAHABHARATA. Translated by J. A. B. Van Buitenen.
Doranne Jacobson and Susan S. Wadley. WOMEN IN INDIA: TWO PERSPECTIVES.
Shakambari Jayal. THE STATUS OF WOMEN IN THE EPICS.
Professor Indra. THE STATUS OF WOMEN IN ANCIENT INDIA.
THE LAWS OF MANU.
THE QUR'AN.

China
Albert O'Hara. THE POSITION OF WOMEN IN EARLY CHINA.
Nancy Lee Swann. PAN CHAO: FOREMOST WOMAN SCHOLAR OF CHINA.
Florence Ayscough. CHINESE WOMEN: YESTERDAY AND TODAY.
Jonathan D. Spence. THE DEATH OF WOMAN WANG.
Ann Waltner, "Widows and Remarriage in Ming and Ch'ing China," in Guisso and
     Johanesson, eds., WOMEN IN CHINA.

Japan
Kaibara Ekken, ONNA DAIGAKU (The Women and Wisdom of Japan).
William McCullough, "Heian Marriage Patterns," in HARVARD JOURNAL OF ASIATIC STUDIES,
     XXVII (1967), pp. 103-167.

WOMEN'S SEXUALITY: AS LOVERS AND AS COURTESANS
India
KAMASUTRA OF VATSYAYANA. Translated by Richard F. Burton.
TALES OF ANCIENT INDIA. Translated by J. A. B. Van Buitenen.
Mirza Ruswa. THE COURTESAN OF LUCKNOW.

China
Robert Van Gulick. SEXUAL LIFE IN ANCIENT CHINA.
Howard Levy. CHINESE FOOTBINDING: THE HISTORY OF A CURIOUS EROTIC CUSTOM.

Japan
Murasaki Shikuku. TALE OF GENJI. In either Waley or Seidensticker translation.
CONFESSIONS OF LADY NIJO. Translated by Karen Brazell.
[Also see section on "Women in Literature" below]

WOMEN IN POLITICS
India
Rekha Misra. WOMEN IN MUGHAL INDIA: 1526-1748 A.D.

China
Richard Guisso. THE EMPRESS WU TSE T'IAN.
C. P. Fitzgerald. EMPRESS WU.
Priscilla Ching Chung. PALACE WOMEN IN THE NORTHERN SUNG.

Japan
THE CONFESSIONS OF LADY NIJO. Translated by Karen Brazell.
Murasaki Shikuku. TALE OF GENJI.
Conrad D. Totman. POLITICS IN THE TOKUGAWA BAKUFU. Chapter V.

WOMEN IN RELIGION: AS DIVINITIES AND AS DEVOTEES
India
N. N. Bhattacharyya. INDIAN MOTHER GODDESS.
Thomas B. Coburn. DEVI MAHATMYA: THE CRYSTALLIZATION OF THE GODDESS TRADITION.
I. B. Horner. WOMEN UNDER PRIMITIVE BUDDHISM: LAYWOMEN AND ALMSWOMEN.
Gerald James Larson, Pratapaditya Pal, and Rebecca P. Gowen. IN HER IMAGE:
        THE GREAT GODDESS IN INDIAN ASIA AND THE MADONNA IN CHRISTIAN CULTURE.
Curt Maury. FOLK ORIGINS OF INDIAN ART.
James J. Preston (ed.). MOTHER WORSHIP: THEME AND VARIATIONS (BL325/.M6M67).

China
Diana Paul. WOMEN IN BUDDHISM.
Edward Schaefer. THE DIVINE WOMAN.
Kathryn Tsai. "The Chinese Buddhist Monastic Order for Women: The First Two
        Centuries," in WOMEN IN CHINA, edited by Guisso and Johannesson.

Japan

WOMEN IN LITERATURE
India
THE MAHABHARATA.
THE RAMAYANA.
Mira Bai. MIRABAI VERSIONS. Translated by Robert Bly.
Kalidasa. "Sakuntala and the Ring of Recollection," in THE THEATER OF MEMORY:
        THE PLAYS OF KALIDASA, edited by Barbara Stoler Miller.
Sudrasha. "Little Clay Cart," in TWO PLAYS OF ANCIENT INDIA. Translated by
        J. A. B. Van Buitenen.

China
STORIES FROM A MING COLLECTION. Translated by Cyril Birch.
THE ORCHID BOAT: WOMEN POETS OF CHINA. Translated and edited by Kenneth Rexroth
        and Ling Chung (PL2658/.E3R43/1972).
Wang Shih-chen. CHIN P'ING MEI (The Golden Lotus). Translated by Clement Egerton.
Hans H. Frankel. THE FLOWERING PLUM AND THE PALACE LADY. "Lonely Women," chap. 6.

251

WOMEN IN LITERATURE continued
Japan
Murasaki Shikubu. TALE OF GENJI. Translated by both Arthur Waley and Edward G.
    Seidensticker.
CONFESSIONS OF LADY NIJO. Translated by Karen Brazell.
Sei Shonagon. THE PILLOW BOOK OF SEI SHONAGON. Translated by Ivan Morris.
Kenreimon. THE POETIC MEMORIES OF LADY DAIBU. Translated by Phillip Tudor
    Harries.
Sugawara Taskasue no musume. AS I CROSSED A BRIDGE OF DREAMS: RECOLLECTIONS
    OF A WOMAN IN ELEVENTH-CENTURY JAPAN. Translated by Ivan Morris.
THE BURNING HEART: THE WOMEN POETS OF JAPAN. Translated and edited by Kenneth
    Rexroth and Ikuko Atsumi (PL782/.E3B84).
Ihara Saikaku. THE LIFE OF AN AMOROUS WOMAN AND OTHER STORIES. Translated and
    edited by Ivan Morris.

SELECTED BIBLIOGRAPHY ON WOMEN IN CHINA - Prepared by Barbara N. Ramusack

I. BIBLIOGRAPHIES
    Bibliography of Asian Studies. Annual issues.
    Cheng, Lucie, Charlotte Furth and Hon-ming Yip. Women in China:
        Bibliography of Available English Language Material. 1984.

II. THEORETICAL PERSPECTIVES ON WOMEN IN CHINA
    Kristeva, Julia. "On the Women of China," translated by Ellen Conroy
        Kennedy, Signs, 1, 1, (1975), 57-82.
    Record, Jane Cassels and Wilson Record. "Totalist and Pluralist Views of
        Women's Liberation: Some Reflections on the Chinese and American
        Settings," Social Problems, 23, 4 (April 1976), 402-414.
    Stacey, Judith. "A Feminist View of Research on Chinese Women," Signs,
        (Winter 1976).
    _____. "When Patriarchy Kowtows: The Significance of the Chinese
        Family Revolution for Feminist Theory," Feminist Studies, 2, 2/3
        (1975).

III. COLLECTIVE VOLUMES
    Guisso, Richard W. and Stanley Johannesen (eds). "Women in China,"
        Historical Reflections, 8, 3 (Fall 1981). Also published as a book
        by Philo Press.
    Wolf, Margery and Roxane Witke (eds.). Women in Chinese Society. 1975.
    Young, Marilyn B. (ed.). Women in China. 1973.

IV. CHINESE WOMEN - SOCIAL ROLES AND LEGAL STATUS
    A. Traditional Period.
    Ayscough, Florence. Chinese Women: Yesterday and Today.
    Cao Xue-qin. The Story of the Stone. (ca. 1754) Volume I. Translated
        by David Hawkes.
    Freedman, Maurice. Chinese Lineage and Society. 1966.
    Levy, Howard. Chinese Footbinding: The History of a Curious Erotic
        Custom. 1966.
    O'Hara, Albert. The Position of Women in Early China-According to the
        Lieh Nu Chuan, "The Biographies of Eminent Chinese Women". 1971.
    Ropp, Paul S. "Seeds of Change: Reflection on the Condition of Women
        in the Early and Mid-Ching," Signs, 2, 1 (1976), 5-23.
    Spence, Jonathan D. The Death of Woman Wang. 1979.
    Swann, Nancy Lee. Pan Chao: Foremost Woman Scholar of China.
    Van Gulik, Robert. Sexual Life in Ancient China. 1974.

B. Modern Period.
Gronewold, Sue. Beautiful Merchandise: Prostitution in China, 1860-1936.
    1982.
Han Suyin. The Crippled Tree. A Mortal Flower. Birdless Summer.
Lang, Olga. Chinese Family and Society. 1946.
Levy, Marion J. The Family Revolution in Modern China. 1949.
Pa Chin. The Family. 1931.
Pruitt, Ida. Madame Yin of Peking. 1979.
Walker, Kathy Lemmons. "The Party and Peasant Women," in Chinese
    Communists and Rural Society, 1927-34 by Philip C. C. Huang,
    Lynda Schaefer Bell and Kathy Lemmons Walker. 1978.
Wolf, Arthur and Chieh-shan Huang. Marriage and Adoption in China,
    1845-1945. 1980.
Wolf, Margery. Women and the Family in Rural Taiwan. 1972.

C. Post-1949 Period.
"Courtship, Love and Marriage in Contemporary China." Special Issue
    of Pacific Affairs (Summer 1984).
Croll, Elizabeth. The Politics of Marriage in the People's Republic
    of China. 1981.
Kingston, Maxine Hong. Woman-Warrior: Memoirs of a Girlhood among
    Ghosts. 1976.
Kristeva, Julia. About Chinese Women. 1977.
Parish, William L. and Martin F. Whyte. Village and Family Life in
    Contemporary China. 1978.
Sidel, Ruth. Women and Child Care in China: A Firsthand Report.
    Revised Edition. 1982.
Yang, C. K. Chinese Communist Society: The Family and the Village. 1959.
Yang, Jiang. Six Chapters from My Life "Downunder." 1984.

V. WOMEN AND RELIGION

Paul, Diana Y. Women in Buddhism: Images of the Feminine in the
    Mahayana Tradition.
Sangren, P. Steven. "Female Gender in Chinese Religious Symbols:
    Kuan Yin, Ma Tsu, and the 'Eternal Mother'," Signs (Autumn 1983).
Schaefer, Edward. The Divine Woman.
Tsai, Kathryn. "The Chinese Buddhist Monastic Order for Women: The
    First Two Centuries." in Women and China edited by Guisso and
    Johannesen.

VI. WOMEN IN POLITICS

A. Traditional Period.
Chung, Priscilla Ching. Palace Women in the Northern Sung 960-1126.
Fitzgerald, C. P. Empress Wu.
Guisso, Richard. The Empress Wu Tse-t'ian.

B. Modern Period.
Belden, Jack. "Goldflower's Story" in China Shakes the World. 1949.
Chen, Yuan-tsung. The Dragon's Village: An Autobiographical Novel
    of Revolutionary China. 1980.
Maloney, Joan M. "Women in the Chinese Communist Revolution: The
    Question of Political Equality," in Women, War and Revolution,
    edited by Carol R. Berkin and Clara M. Lovett. 1980.
Price, Jane. "Women and Leadership in the Chinese Communist Movement,
    1921-45," Bulletin of Concerned Asian Scholars, 7, 1 (Jan-Mar
    1975), 19-24.
Rankin, Mary Bakus. Early Chinese Revolutionaries: Radical Intellectuals
    in Shanghai and Chekiang 1902-1911. 1971. (See Ch'iu Chin.)
Sheridan, Mary. "Young Women Leaders in China," Signs, 2, 1 (1976), 59-88.
Smedley, Agnes. Portraits of Chinese Women in Revolution. 1976.
Snow, Edgar. Red Star Over China. 1938.
Snow, Helen Foster. Women in Modern China. 1967.
Terrill, Ross. The White-Boned Demon: A Biography of Madame Mao Zedong.
    1984.
Witke, Roxane. Comrade Chiang Ch'ing. 1972.

VII. WOMEN AND LABOR.
Gallin, Rita S. "The Entry of Chinese Women into the Rural Labor
    Force: A Case Study from Taiwan," Signs, 9, 3 (Spring 1984).
Kung, Lydia, "Factory Work and Women in Taiwan: Changes in Self-
    Image and Status," Signs, 2, 1 (1976), 35-58.
Pruitt, Ida. A Daughter of Han: The Autobiography of a Chinese Working
    Woman. 1945.
Salaff, Janet and Mary Sheridan (eds.). Lives: Chinese Working Women.
    1984.

VIII. WOMEN AND LITERATURE: AS DOERS AND AS PORTRAYED.
A. Traditional Period.
Rexroth, Kenneth (trans. and ed.) The Orchid Boat. 1972.

B. Modern Period.
Eber, Irene. "Images of Women in Recent Chinese Fiction: Do Women
    Hold Up Half the Sky?" Signs, 2, 1 (1976), 24-34.
Feuerwerker, Yi-tsi Mei. Ding Ling's Fiction: Ideology and Narrative
    in Modern Chinese Literature. 198 .
_____. "Ting Ling's 'When I Was in Sha Chuan (Cloud Village)',"
    Signs, 2, 1 (1976), 255-279.
Hsu, Vivian Ling. Born of the Same Roots: Stories of Modern Chinese
    Women. 1982.
Shimer, Dorothy B. Rice Bowl Women: Writings by and about the Women
    of China and Japan. 1982.

IX.   WOMEN'S RIGHTS MOVEMENT
      A. Republican Period.
      "Women and Feminism in Republican China." Special Issue of Republican
          China, (November 1984).

      B. Post-1949 Period.
      Andors, Phyllis. "Politics of Chinese Development: The Case of Women,
          1960-1966," Signs, 2, 1 (1976), 89-119.
      _____. Unfinished Liberation of Chinese Women, 1929-80. 1983.
      Broyelle, Claudie. Women's Liberation in China. Translated by Michele
          Cohen and Gary Herman. 1977.
      Croll, Elizabeth. Feminism and Socialism in China. 1978.
      Davin, Delia. Woman-Work: Women and the Party in Revolutionary China.
          1976.
      Hemmel, Vibeke and Pia Sindbjerg. Women in Rural China. 1984.
      Johnson, Kay Ann. Women, the Family and Peasant Revolution in China.
          1983.
      Stacey, Judith. Patriarchy and Socialist Revolution in China. 1983.
      Weinbaum, Batya. "Women in Transition to Socialism: Perspectives on
          the Chinese Case," Review of Radical Political Economics, 8, 1
          (Spring 1976).
      Wolf, Margery. Revolution Postponed: Women in Contemporary China. 1984.

X.   WESTERN WOMEN IN CHINA
      Drucker, Alison R. "The Influence of Western Women on the Anti-Footbinding
          Movement 1840-1911," in Women in China edited by Guisso and Johannesen,
          pp. 179-199.
      _____. "The Role of the YWCA in the Development of the Chinese
          Women's Movement, 1890-1927," Social Service Review, 53, 3
          (September 1979), 421-440.
      _____. "Western Women and the Origins of the Women's Movement in
          Transitional China, 1840-1927," Towson State Journal of International
          Affairs, 11, 1 (Fall 1976), 17-24.
      Hunter, Jane. Gospel of Gentility: American Women Missionaries in
          Turn-of-the-Century China. 198 .
      Lubkeman, Lynn. "Radicalism, Feminism, and the Chinese Revolution:
          Agnes Smedley and Anna Louise Strong in China, 1927-1949," Ph.D.
          dissertation in progress, University of Wisconsin-Madison.
      Strong, Tracy B. and Helene Keyssar. Right in Her Soul: The Life of
          Anna Louise Strong. 198 .

Asian Women
History, W/ST, A/ST 406
Spring,1988

Sharon Sievers
FO 2-226/220
 498-4839/4431
TTH 1-2; TH 5-6 and
by appointment

Required texts: Cook and Hayashi,Working Women in Japan; Fuentes,
Women in the Global Factory; Johnson, Women,Family and Peasant
Revolution in China; Kendall, View from the Inner Room; Sievers,
Flowers in Salt; Spence,Death of the Woman Wang.
AND a Kinko's packet for this course, available at the store on
Palo Verde& Atherton, at the SE corner of campus.

The following optional books are available in the bookst ore; you may
want to choose one of these for your opinion paper, or you may simply
want to add one to your library out of interest. They represent
recent, wide-ranging work on women in Asia.
 Croll,Chinese Women Since Mao; Danley, In the Shade of Spring
Leaves; Feuerwerker, Ding Ling's Fiction; Hsieh, Autobiography of a
Chinese Girl; Kendall, Shamans, Housewives and Other Restless Spirits
Kessen, Childhood in China; Lebra, Japanese Women, Constraint and
Fulfillment; Lippit and Selden, Stories by Contemporary Japanese
Women Writers; Paul, Images of Women in Buddhism; Stacey, Patriarchy
and Socialist Revolution in China; Tanaka, To Live and To Write;
Wakeman, To the Storm; Wiswell and Smith, The Women of Suye Mura.

There will be two exams in the course, one of which may be the final.
You will also be asked to write a brief opinion paper on a book of
(not required) of your choice. You may also participate in a panel in
place of the paper, or for extra credit. Since much of the
responsibility for reading in this course will be shared, you should
not miss class except for very good reasons. More than two
unexplained absences will have a sinking effect on your semester
grade.

             DISCUSSION AND READING SCHEDULE*

     January 28.
          Overview
          Buddhist and Confucian Views of Women

Reading: Handouts and Diana Paul's Women in Buddhism (optional).

* (K)=Kinko's Packet, (R)=Reserve Book Room stacks, and (R/PC)=
Reserve Book Room, desk in this syllabus.
     Required texts are listed by last name of author only.

February 4.
Women in Folk Tradition
Religion/Sexuality/Politics

Reading: Kendall, 81-113; Ackroyd, The Catalpa Bow, (R) 1-30.

February 11.
Women in Folk Tradition cont'd.

Reading: Ahern, "The Power and Pollution of Chinese Women" (K); Kendall, 113-139; Ng, "Ideology and Sexuality: Rape Laws in Qing China" (K).

February 18.
Women in Lineage and Kinship Systems

Reading: Kendall, 1-61; Freedman, "Rites and Duties, or Chinese Marriage" (K).

February 25.
Neo-Confucianism and Women

Reading: Mann, "Widows in the Kinship, Class and Community Structures of Qing China" (K); Ackroyd, "Women in Feudal Japan" (R)

March 3.
Women in 19th Century Asia

Reading: Spence, Death of the Woman Wang; Sievers, Chapters 1&2.

¥¥¥¥¥¥¥ EXAM §§§§§§§§

March 10.
The Beginnings of Feminist Consciousness

Reading: Rankin, "The Emergence of Women at the End of the Ch'ing" (K (K); Sievers, Chapters 3&5. On socialism: Sievers, Chapters 6&7.

March 17.
Early Industrialization and Women

Reading: Honig, Chapter 7. "Working Lives" (K); Sievers, Chapter 4; Cheng, "Free, Indentured, Enslaved: Chinese Prostitutes in Nineteenth-Century America" (K); Hanawa, The Several Worlds of Issei Women (R/PC) or Glenn, "The Dialectics of Wage Work: Japanese-American Women and Domestic Service, 1905-1940" (R/PC). Topley; "Marriage Resistance in Rural Kwantung" (K).

March 24.
Women Writers. Early Period

Reading: Sievers, Chapter 8; Tamura Toshiko, "A Woman Writer" and "Glory" (K); Arishima, A Certain Woman, pp.29-69(K)

March 24. Cont'd.

<u>Women Writers</u>. 20s & 30's.

Reading: Feuerwerker,"Chinese Writers in the Twenties and Thirties" (K); Lippit, "Literature,Ideology and Women's Happiness" (K); deBary, <u>Nobuko</u> (R); Tamura, "Miyamoto Yuriko" (K); Akiyama, <u>Ting Ling</u>(K).

March 31. HOLIDAY (wow!)

April 7.
<u>Women, Nationalism and Revolution</u>

Reading: Eisen, "The French Legacy" & "People's War Is Women's War" (K); Lal, "Indian Women Novelists" (K); Croll, "The 'Feminine Mystique'?" (K);"Sandakan No. 8 Brothel" (K).

April 14.
<u>Women, the Family and Revolution</u>

Reading: Johnson, <u>Women, the Family, and Peasant Revolution in China</u> (entire); Stacey, "Introduction" & "The Limitations of Family Reform and the Successful Family Revolution" (K).

April 21.
<u>Contemporary Asia</u>
Women and Population Policy

Reading: Goodman and Goodman, "Sexual Racism in Population Policy" (K); Miller, "Female Infanticide in British India" (K); Wasserstrom, "Resistance to the One-Child Family" (K).

April 28.
<u>Contemporary Asia</u>
Women and Work

Reading:Fuentes, <u>Women in the Global Factory</u>; Cook & Hayashi,<u>Working Women in Japan</u>; Bernstein, <u>Haruko's World</u>, Chapter 6 (K);Salaff, Singapore Women, Work ,and the Family" (K); <u>Off Our Backs</u>, "Prostitution in Southeast Asia" (K).

May 5.
<u>Contemporary Asia</u>
<u>Literature and Film</u>

Reading: Vernon, "Between Osan and Koharu" (K).

Silvia M. Arrom
Office: BH 730
335-1745 or 333-8107
Office hours: Tues.-Thurs. 4-5

Graduate level
History H765/
Women's Studies W701
Indiana University
Spring 1985

Latin American Women: Historical Perspectives

Course description

    This seminar, designed for the non-specialist, provides a broad overview of Latin American Women's history from the 16th to the 20th centuries. The course focuses on the principal questions in the field, its historiography, and methodological problems involved in research. Weekly reading assignments and one research paper.

Texts

Purchase is optional.

Asunción Lavrin, ed.	Latin American Women: Historical Perspectives, 1978). Hardcover.
June Nash and Helen Safa, eds.	Sex and Class in Latin America (1976). Paper.
Ann Pescatello, ed.	Female and Male in Latin America. Essays (1978) Paper.
Wellesley Editorial Committee	Women and National Development. The Complexities of Change (1978). Paper.
Susan Bourque and Kay Warren	Women of the Andes (1981). Paper.
Mona Etienne and Eleanor Leacock	Women and Colonization: Anthropological Perspectives (1980). Paper.
Luis Martín	Daughters of the Conquistadores(1983). Paper.

Syllabus

Jan. 7   Introduction

       1. Concepts and Controversy
       2. Historiography

Jan. 14 The Position of Women: Oppression or Power?

       1. Norms vs. behavior
       2. Machismo vs. Marianismo
       3. The state of feminist movements

Freyre, Gilberto	"Woman and Man," chap. 4 in The Mansions and Shanties (Alfred A. Knopf, 1963).
Youssef, Nadia	"Cultural Ideals, Feminine Behavior, and Family Control," Comparative Studies in Society and

History, 15, 3 (June 1973).

Kinzer, Nora S. "Priests, Machos, and Babies: Or Latin American Women and the Manichean Heresy," Journal of Marriage and the Family, 35, 3 (May 1973), 300-312.

Stevens, Evelyn P. "Marianismo: The Other Face of Machismo in Latin America in Pescatello, ed. Female and Male, pp. 89-101.
"The Prospects for a Women's Liberation Movement in Latin America," Journal of Marriage and the Family, 35, 2 (May 1973), 313-321.

Jacquette, Jane "Literary Archetypes and Female Role Alternatives: The Women and the Novel in Latin America," in Pescatello, ed. Female and Male, pp. 16-27.

Jan. 21 Conquest of Indian America

Mörner, Magnus "The Conquest of Women," in Lewis Hanke, ed., History of Latin American Civilization. Sources and Interpretations (2nd. ed., Little, Brown and Company, 1973), Vol. I, pp. 137-141.

Schurz, William L. "The Woman," chap. 8 in This New World. The Civilization of Latin America (E.P. Dutton & Co., Inc. 1954).

Lockhart, James "Spanish Women and the Second Generation," chap. 9 in Spanish Peru 1532-1560. A Colonial Society (University of Wisconsin Press, 1968) or in Hanke reader, vol. I, pp. 419-430.

Burkett, Elinor C. "Indian Women and White Society: The Case of Sixteenth-Century Peru," in Lavrin, ed. Latin American Women, pp. 101-120.

Nash, June "Aztec Women: The Transition from Status to Class in Empire & Colony," in Etienne & Leacock, Women & Colonization, 134-48.

Silverblatt, Irene "Andean Women under Spanish Rub," in Stienne & Leacock, Women & Colonization, 149-85.

Clendinnen, Inga "Yucatec Maya Women and the Spanish Conquest: Role and Ritual in Historical Reconstruction." Journal of Social History. (Spring 1982): 427-442.

Jan. 28 The Established Colony

Martín, Luis Daughters of the Conquistadores: Women of the Viceroyalty of Peru (Albuquerque, 1983): 1-170, 299-315.

Lavrin, Asunción "In Search of the Colonial Women in Mexico," in Lavrin, Latin American Women, pp. 40-47.

Russell Wood, AJR. "Female and Family in the Economy and Society of Colonial Brazil," in Lavrin, ed., Latin American Women, pp. 60-65, 88-95.

Couturier, Edith.   "Women in a Noble Family: The Mexican Counts
                     of Regla, 1750-1830," in Lavrin, ed., Latin
                     American Women, pp. 129-149.
_____.   "Micaela Angela Carrillo: Widow and Pulque
                     Dealer," in Gary Nash & David Sweet, Struggle &
                     Survival in Colonial America (Berkeley, Ca.,
                     1981): 362-74.
Couturier & Lavrin, "Dowries and Wills: A View of Women's Socio-
                     Economic Role in Colonial Guadalajara and
                     Puebla," HAHR, 59 (May 1979), 280-304.
Tutino, John.   "Power, Class, and Family: Men and Women in
                     the Mexican Elite, 1750-1810," The Americas,
                     39, 3 (Jan. 1983), 359-81.
Socolow, Susan.   "Women and Crime: Buenos Aires, 1757-97,"
                     Journal of Latin American Studies, 12 (May
                     1980), 39-54.
Arrom, Silvia.   The Women of Mexico City, 1790-1857
                     (Stanford University Press, 1985).
                     Chapter 2, "Legal Status."

Feb. 4   Women and Religion

          1. Convents
          2. Virgin Cults
          3. Saints and Healers

Lavrin, Asunción   "Women and Convents: Their Economic and Social
                     Role in Colonial Mexico," in Berenice Carroll,
                     ed., Liberating Women's History. Theoretical
                     and Critical Essays (University of Illinois
                     Press, 1976), pp. 250-277.
                     "Values and Meaning of Monastic Life for Nuns
                     in Colonial Mexico," Catholic Historical
                     Review, 58, 3 (Oct. 1972), 367-387.
Soeiro, Susan A.   "The Social and Economic Role of the Convent:
                     Women and Nuns in Colonial Bahia, 1677-1800,"
                     Hispanic American Historical Review, 54, 2 (May
                     1974), 209-232.
Phelan, John L.   "The Sinners and the Saint," chap. 8 in The
                     Kingdom of Quito in the Seventeenth Century
                     (University of Wisconsin Press, 1967)
Rodríguez, Richard   "Teresa Urrea: Her Life as it Affected the
  and Gloria   Mexican-United States Frontier," El Grito, 5, 4
                     (Summer 1972).
Leonard, Irving   "Sor Juana Inés de la Cruz: 'The Supreme Poet
  or   of Her Time in Castilian,'" in Hanke reader,
                     vol. I, pp. 377-386.
Henderson, James   "Sor Juana Inés de la Cruz, 1651-1695," in Ten
  and Linda R.   Notable Women of Latin America (Nelson-Hall,
                     1978), pp. 73-96.
Wolf, Eric   "The Virgin of Guadalupe: A Mexican National
                     Symbol," Journal of American Folklore, 71
                     (1958), 34-39.

Martín, Luis.   Daughters of the Conquistadores, pp. 171-299.

Feb. 11   Late Colonial Period/Nineteenth Century

1. Changing Norms

Arrom, Silvia   The Women of Mexico City, chapters 1, end of 2,
                      4, 5.
Mendelson, Johanna   "The Feminine Press: The View of Women in the
                      Colonial Journals of Spanish America, 1790-
                      1810," in Lavrin, ed. Latin American Women,
                      198-215.
Calderón, Frances   Life in Mexico. The Letters of Fanny Calderón
                      de la Barca with New Material from the Author's
                      Private Journals, ed. by Howard and Marion
                      Fisher (Doubleday & Co. 1966), pp. 85-97, 125-
                      173, 193-212, 252-267, 283-292, 518-533.
Cherpak, Evelyn   "Participation of Women in the Independence
                      Movement in Gran Colombia, 1780-1830," in
                      Lavrin, Latin American Women, pp. 219-234.
Guy, Donna.   "Women, Peonage, and Industrialization:
                      Argentina, 1810-1914," LARR, 16, 3 (1981): 65-
                      85.

Feb. 18   Marriage and the Family

Balmori, Voss, and   Notable Family Networks in Latin
Wortman.   America. (Chicago, 1984).
Arrom, Silvia M.   "Marriage Patterns in Mexico City, 1811,"
                      Journal of Family History, 3, 4 (Winter 1978),
                      376-391.
Ramos, Donald   "Marriage and Family in Colonial Vila Rica,"
                      Hispanic American Historical Review, 55, 2 (May
                      1975), 200-225.
Lomnitz, Larissa   "Kinship Structure and the Role of Women in the
and Marisol   Urban Upper Class of Mexico," SIGNS, 5, 1
Pérez   (Autumn 1979), 164-168.
Lombardi, John V.   "Marriage," chap. 4 in People and Places in
                      Colonial Venezuela (Indiana University Press,
                      1976).
Johnson, Ann H.   "The Impact of Market Agriculture on Family and
                      Household Structure in Nineteenth-century Chile,"
                      Hispanic American Historical Review, 58, 4 (Nov.
                      (1978), 625-648.
Martínez-Alier,   "Elopement and Seduction in Nineteenth-Century
Verena   Cuba," Past and Present, 55 (May 1972), 91-129.
Lewin, Linda   "Some Historical Implications of Kinship
                      Organization for Family-Based Politics in the
                      Brazilian Northeast," Comparative Studies in
                      Society and History, 21, 2 (April 1979), 262-
                      292.
Kuznesof,Elizabeth   "The Role of the Female-Headed Household in
                      Brazilian Modernization," Journal of Social

263

History, 13, 4 (1980): 589-613.

Feb. 25 Population, Fertility, and Birth Control

Sánchez-Albornoz,   "The Collapse of the Indigenous Population," in
  Nicolás   his book The Population of Latin America. A
                       History (University of California Press, 1974),
                       pp. 37-66.
Arrom, Silvia   The Women of Mexico City, chap. 3.
Socolow, Susan   "Marriage, Birth, and Inheritance: The
                       Merchants of 18th Century Buenos Aires," HAHR,
                       60, 3 (Aug. 1980): 387-406.
D'Antonio,   "The Problem of Population Growth in Latin
  William   America," in Frederick Pike, ed., Latin
                       American History: Select Problems (Harcourt,
                       Brace & World, Inc., 1969), pp. 440-482.
Elu de Leñero,   "Women's Work and Fertility," in Nash and Safa,
                       Maria eds., Sex and Class, pp. 46-68.
Mass, Bonnie   "Puerto Rico: A Case Study of Population
                       Control," Latin American Perspectives, 4, 4
                       (Fall 1977), 66-81.
Kinzer, Nora S.   "Priests, Machos, and Babies . . . " Review
                       from Week II.
McCoy, Terry, ed.   The Dynamics of Population Policy in Latin
                       America. (Cambridge, Mass., 1974), essays by
                       Stycos and Consuegra.

Mar. 4   Modernization

1. Development Theory
2. Women's Work
3. Urbanization

Nash, June   "A Critique of Social Science Roles in Latin
                       America," in Nash and Safa, eds., Sex and
                       Class, pp. 1-24.
Jelin, Elizabeth   "Migration and Labor Force Participation of
                       Latin American Women: the Domestic Servants in
                       the Cities," in Wellesley Conf., Women and
                       National Development, pp. 129-141.
Safa, Helen I.   "The Changing Class Composition of the Female
                       Labor Force in Latin America," Latin American
                       Perspectives, 4, 4 (Fall 1977), 126-136.
Arizpe, Lourdes   "Women in the Informal Labor Sector: the Case
                       of Mexico City," in Wellesley Conf., Women and
                       Nat. Devpt., pp. 25-37.
Smith, Margo   "Domestic Service as a Channel of Upward
                       Mobility for the Lower-Class Women: the Lima
                       Case," in Pescatello, ed., Female and Male, pp.
                       191-207.
Mintz, Sidney   "Men, Women, and Trade," in Comparative Studies
                       in Society and History (1971). 247-269.

Chinchilla, Norma	"Industrialization, Monopoly Capitalism, and Women's Work in Guatemala," in Wellesley Conf., Women and Nat. Devpt., pp. 38-56.
Hahner, June	"Women and Work in Brazil, 1850-1920," in Dauril Alden and Warren Dean, eds., Essays Concerning the Socio-Economic History of Brazil (University of Florida Press, 1977), pp. 87-117.
NACLA or	"Hit and Run: U.S. Runaway Shops on the or Mexican Border," Latin America and Empire Report, 9, 5 (July-Aug. 1975), 6-23.
Safa, Helen	"Runaway Shops and Female Employment: The Search for cheap Labor" SIGNS, 7, 2 (Winter 1981).

SPRING VACATION

March 18 Women & Agrarian Transformation

Bourque & Warren.	Women of the Andes (1981).
Deere, Carmen	"Changing Social Relations of Production and Diana. Peruvian Women's Work," Latin American Perspectives, 4, 1-2 (1977): 48-69.
Rubbo, Anna.	"The Spread of Capitalism in Rural Columbia: Effects on Poor Women," in Rayna Reiter, ed., Toward an Anthropology of Women (1975): 333-57.
León de Leal, Magdalena and Carmen Diana Deere.	"Rural Women and the Development of Capitalism in Colombian Agriculture," SIGNS, 5, 1 (Autumn 1979).
Arizpe, Lourdes & Josephina Aranda.	"The Comparative Advantages of Women's Disadvantages: Women Workers in the Strawberry Export Agribusiness in Mexico," Signs, 7, 2 (Winter 1981).
Rothstein, Frances.	"Two Different Worlds: Gender and Industrialization in Rural Mexico," in New Directions in Political Economy, ed. Madeleine Leons & Frances Rothstein (Westport, Ct., 1979).
Young, Kate.	"Modes of Appropriation and the Sexual Division of Labor: a case study from Oaxaca, Mexico," in Feminism and Materialism: Women and Modes of Production, ed. Annette Kuhn & Ann Marie Wolpe (London, 1978).

Mar. 25 Women's Organized Political Activity

Jane Jacquette,	"Female Political Participation in Latin America," in Nash and Safa, eds., Sex and Class, pp. 221-244.

Elsa Chaney,	Supermadre: Women in Politics in Latin America (Austin, 1979).
Anna Macías,	Against All Odds: The Feminist Movement in Mexico to 1940 (Westport, 1982).
Hahner, June	"The U.S. Suffrage Movement and Latin America," in Hahner, ed., Women in Latin American History, pp. 65-82.
Hahner, June	"The Nineteenth-century Feminist Press and Women's Rights in Brazil," in Lavrin, ed., Latin American Women, pp. 254-285.
Navarro, Marysa	"The Case of Eva Peron," in Wellesley Conf., Women and National Development, pp. 229-240.
Pico Vidal, Isabel	"The History of Women's Struggle for Equality in Puerto Rico," in Nash and Safa, eds., Sex and Class, pp. 202-213.

Apr. 1   Revolution and Counterrevolution

Chile   "Chile: The Feminine Version of the Coup
Mattelart, Michelle d'etat," in Nash and Safa, eds., Sex and Class,
                pp. 279-301.

Mexico
Fisher, Lillian	"The Influence of the Present Mexican Revolution Upon the Status of Mexican Women," Hispanic American Historical Review, 22 (Feb. 1942), 211-228.
Macías, Ann	"The Mexican Revolution Was No Revolution Women," in Hanke reader, Vol. II, pp. 591-601.

Cuba
Fox, Geoffrey	"Honor, Shame, and Women's Liberation in Cuba," in Pescatello, ed., Female and Male, pp. 273-290.
Purcell, Susan K.	"Modernizing Women for a Modern Society: The Cuban Case," in Pescatello, ed., Female and Male, pp. 257-271.
King, Margorie	"Cuba's Attack on Women's Second Shift, 1974-1976," Latin American Perspectives, 4, 1-2 (Winter-Spring 1977), 106-119.
Carrolle Bengelsdorf and Alice Hageman.	"Emerging from Underdevelopment: Women and Work in Cuba," in Zillah Eisenstein, Capitalist Patriarchy and the Case for Socialist Feminism (New York, 1979): 271-95.
Nazzari, Muriel.	"The 'Woman Question' in Cuba: An Analysis of Material Constraints on its Solution," SIGNS, 9, 2 (Winter 1983): 246-63.

Apr. 8   Personal Testimonies

Read Jane H. Kelley, Yaqui Women. Contemporary Life Histories, pp.

266

3-30 (University of Nebraska Press, 1978; Hardcover).

Plus one:

Barrios de Chungara, Domitila (ed. Viezzer) Let Me Speak! Testimony of Domitila, A Woman of the Bolivian Mines (Monthly Review Press, 1979; paperback).

de Jesus, Carolina M. Child of the Dark. The Diary of Carolina Maria de Jesus (New American Library, 1962; paperback).

Lewis, Oscar et.al. Four Women. Living the Revolution. An Oral History of Contemporary Cuba (University of Illinois Press, 1977; hardcover) or Five Families. Mexican Case Studies in the Culture of Poverty (New American Library, 1959; paper).

Apr. 15 Overview

Apr. 22 Research Paper Due.

BIBLIOGRAPHY:

Knaster, Meri Women in Spanish America: An Annotated Bibliography from Pre-Conquest to Contemporary Times (Boston, G. K. Hall & Co.: 1977). A comprehensive bibliography covering the literature through 1974. Includes references to other bibliographies. An indispensible reference source.

Knaster, Meri "Women in Latin America: The State of Research, 1975," Latin American Research Review, 11, 1 (1976), 3-74. Updates her earlier bibliography.

Lavrin, Asunción "Some Final Considerations on Trends and Issues in Latin American Women's History," in Lavrin, ed., Latin American Women, pp. 302-332. Suggests research topics and sources. "Women in Latin American History," The History Teacher, 14, 3 (May 1981): 387-400.

Soeiro, Susan "Recent Work on Latin American Women. A Review Essay," Journal of Inter-American Studies and World Affairs, 17, 4 (Nov. 1975), 497-516.

Journal Issues Devoted to Latin American Women and the Family:

Journal of Marriage and the Family, 35, 2 (May 1973).
Journal of Interamerican Studies and World Affairs, 17, 4 (Nov. 1975).
Revista/Review Interamericana, 4, 2 (Summer 1974).
Latin American Perspectives, 4, 1-2 (Winter-Spring 1977) and 4, 4 (Fall 1977).
Journal of Family History, 3, 4 (Winter 1978).
America Indígena, 38, 2 (April-June 1978).

SIGNS, 3, 1 (Autumn 1977), 5, 1 (Autumn 1979), 7 (Winter 1981), and 8 (Winter 1982).

Boletin del Archivo General de la Nación (Mexico City) 3rd series, 3, 9 (July-Sept. 1979).

FEM [A Mexican feminist magazine] 3, 11 (Nov.-Dec. 1979).